The March of Spare Time

The March of Spare Time

The Problem and Promise of Leisure in the Great Depression

SUSAN CURRELL

PENN

University of Pennsylvania Press

Philadelphia

Published by
University of Pennsylvania Press
Philadelphia, Pennsylvania 19104–4011

Library of Congress Cataloging-in-Publication Data

Currell, Susan.
    The march of spare time : the problem and promise of leisure
in the Great Depression / Susan Currell.
        p. cm.
    Includes bibliographical references and index.
    ISBN 0-8122-3859-1 (cloth : alk. paper)
    1. Leisure—United States—History—20th century.
2. Depressions—1929—United States. 3. United States—Social
conditions—1933–1945. I. Title.

GV53.C79 2005
790.1′0973′09043—dc22
                                              2004057246

Contents

Introduction
The Re-creation of Leisure

Leisure, well used, constitutes one of the greatest forces for human progress; misused in cheap commercial amusement it is the greatest menace to civilization.

—*Frank Hobart Cheley*, Investing Leisure Time

In 1929, no one knew how long the Depression would last, but once it had happened many saw the Crash as the inevitable result of deeply entrenched economic and social problems. Although the start of the Depression did not signify the extent of the catastrophe that was emerging, social leaders and politicians had long been concerned with the problems associated with rapid industrialization and modernity. Anticipating "social stresses," President Herbert Hoover had assembled a group of leading academics and social scientists in the autumn of 1929. Their goal was to provide a two-volume report on the condition of modern America. Compiled by leading social scientists of the day, the report covered every aspect of American society, including the condition of industry, population, marriage, public welfare, education, the arts, entertainment, and recreation. The findings were to stress the problems facing America in the modern age.

By the time *Recent Social Trends in the United States* was published in 1933, the Depression had deepened and the problems it examined seemed more serious than ever. In his foreword, President Hoover stated, "Since the task assigned to the Committee was to inquire into changing trends, the result is emphasis on elements of instability rather than stability in our social structure" and that it "should serve to help all of us to see where social stresses are occurring and where major efforts should be undertaken to deal with them constructively." An "X ray" of social scientific research and thought for the early part of the decade, *Recent Social Trends* described not only problems but solutions to the growing crisis. After four years of debate and hardship, a "cure" for the Depression was yet to be found, and the findings of the President's Research Committee offered pertinent advice for dealing with the emerging problems of modern American society.[1]

One aspect of the crisis highlighted by *Recent Social Trends* was the "problem of leisure." Despite economic hardship, leisure time had continued to grow, and an increasing share of the national income was spent on recreation.[2] In his chapter on recreation and leisure time, sociologist Jesse Steiner outlined the growth and changes in leisure pursuits and mass communications that were revolutionizing the way Americans spent their nonworking hours. Alongside the growth of sports, vacations, and automobiling, he listed how commercial amusements such as movie theaters, radio, dance halls, road houses, burlesque, and spectator sports "continued to attract large crowds in spite of the Depression."[3] To Steiner, the two most important trends in modern recreation were the growth of commercial amusements and the rapid expansion of public and private facilities for active recreational activities.

As the importance of leisure had grown and working hours had decreased, Steiner noted, a new democracy of leisure emerged whereby the mass rank and file now insisted upon the right to participate in diversions that had formerly belonged to the "favored few." The new democracy, however, had its negative side in the form of the more "unwholesome," wasteful, exploitative, and morally questionable leisure practices that had emerged. In other words, the laissez-faire development of recreation and leisure had led to a huge area of national life over which there were no checks or controls.

Steiner concluded his chapter, therefore, by recommending a new government role that would create more "wholesome" leisure for the American public: "There can be no doubt of the right of government to prevent the sale of unwholesome recreation just as it has the right to prevent the sale of unwholesome food."[4] The best way to attack these undesirable amusements was in the provision of more "wholesome" recreation facilities by professionals and experts in the field. Much of the following debate over leisure in the thirties derived its impetus from this dichotomy between good and bad uses of leisure. Cultural battles ensued that were in many ways attempts to define what was "undesirable" and what was "wholesome." In this way leisure became both a problem and the solution to social and cultural recovery during the Depression.

Though few have commented on the structural relation of leisure to economic revival, or its relevance in the decade to getting Americans back to work, many at the time saw leisure as pivotal to the social and political recovery of the nation. The use of leisure could be the catalyst that would revive, and also correct, modernity. Like many social scientists of the era, Steiner recommended that leisure be taken seriously by the government and argued that control over mass leisure needed to be secured through a combination of studies, legislation, and the provision of new facilities. So, although the function of the New Deal government was to get America working again, many of the social programs that took place throughout the decade focused intently on providing the "right" leisure and correcting the "wrong" leisure that had emerged.

This book began as an attempt to understand how, during a period of mass unemployment, leisure came to feature as a central problem of culture. That the Depression should change notions of leisure in society should perhaps come as no surprise, yet the extent to which this happened has never been fully examined. Why did leisure—both proper and improper—become such an intense object of interest, concern, and surveillance by national policy makers, experts, and intellectuals alike in the 1930s?

Although the leisure question had been a concern of some religious and reformist groups prior to the 1930s, it took on a new cultural significance with the onset of the Depression.[5] From the arrival of massive unemployment in the 1930s, the meaning of leisure to American society changed dramatically from that of the 1920s and resulted in thousands of books and articles published in the mass media about a new "problem of leisure." The debate, however, revealed wider concerns about America during this time, and leisure became a battleground for widespread ambivalence about technology, social change, economic change, and new social habits, as well as a domain in which older ideas about individuality and democracy could be mediated or challenged. Judging from the amount of literature produced on leisure—including some bestsellers of the period—the "problem of leisure" was a central cultural issue of Depression America.

Many professionals across the political spectrum—from reformers, social scientists, and doctors to educators, novelists, and artists—saw improper leisure as a principal product of and a major contributor to society's ills, while at the same time viewing proper leisure as a powerful tool for curing those same ills. Although a problem, the new leisure also presented the nation with startling opportunities to reinvent itself. As I shall show, out of all the deeply entrenched problems that faced America in the early thirties, only leisure seemed to offer a panacea for curing the rest. These debates over leisure emerge as narratives of crisis that can be fruitfully dissected to reveal the class, race, and gender discourses contained within them. For experts and intellectuals alike, the stakes surrounding leisure were high indeed.

Recent Social Trends pointed out that advances in technology had increased leisure hours available to all, and yet humans had not evolved leisure that served to balance the social organism. The Depression, despite all expectations, curtailed but did not halt all popular amusements, and in many ways the decade witnessed a huge increase in mass entertainment, despite undeniable poverty and unemployment. In 1931, Harold Rugg, professor of education at Columbia University and author of *An Introduction to Problems of American Culture*, listed as "problematic" those recreations of modern American culture that entailed alterations in traditional customs: automobile driving, movie going, radio listening, jazz dancing, and spectacle sports, along with other "fads and fancies" of the eras.[6] This expansion, critics claimed, had led to leisure that was too technological, too commercial, and too passive. During the thirties, this list of problems and complaints became ubiquitous in discussions of problematic leisure. Instead of "killing off" the poor-quality, low-grade leisure that many thought had characterized the twenties, the Depression appeared to be making things worse.

As early as 1932, Prohibition ended and gambling laws were repealed, effecting huge changes in the way in which people, publicly and privately, had fun. Radio listening and ownership underwent phenomenal growth, boosted by technological enhancements, cheaper sets, and hire-purchase schemes. After a short slump at the start of the Depression, cinema attendance also underwent a boom, boosted by innovations such as sound, the double-bill, and various promotional schemes. Automobiling was also listed among the top leisure activities, for although fewer new cars were bought, more miles were covered during the Depression than ever before. Innovations in printing and publishing saw mass-market reading expand—so that, by 1936, Margaret Mitchell's *Gone with the Wind* had outsold any novel that had preceded it. Comic books and photo magazines such as *Life* were phenomena of the thirties, which contributed heavily to this new mass market. Crazes and fads of the thirties also portrayed a nation feverish for mass leisure: miniature golf, card playing, board games, puzzles, pinball, jukeboxes, gambling, and dancing all increased.[7]

Fears that the quality of the music and entertainment offered would decline as a result of their mass appeal and cheap production added to widespread fears over declining educational standards. Rugg explained that this "unexpected leisure" of the common man had taken America by surprise "due in large part to the failure of education to keep pace with economic and social changes. Universal schooling had taught the masses to read and write and reckon but not to think about social life or to be sensitive to the art of self-cultivation."[8] *Recent Social Trends* agreed that self-cultivation was impaired by the the commercialization of leisure, the mechanization of leisure, and the consequent new social conventions emerging from the new leisure. Like Rugg, Steiner believed that, if used unwisely, leisure would undermine the progress of civilization and democracy.

At the height of the Depression, then, the sheer quantity of leisure hours served to exacerbate these fears, and social scientists embarked on an extensive examination of all facets of this new leisured society. Whereas earlier in the century many would have argued for more, and harder, work to pull the country out of the Depression, by the 1930s this was no longer a cultural truism. Leisure and consumption were now seen as having equal importance within the planned, healthy, balanced, and controlled economy. *Recent Social Trends* illustrated this distinct shift in thinking, wherein useful and productive work was the result of the productive use of leisure, the skills learned in leisure would produce a mentally and physically fit workforce, and leisure could revitalize a sick and ailing economy.

The way leisure could transform the social environment thus played into popular rhetoric concerning the causes of the Depression, and the metaphor of the sick body transformed into a healthy one underlay much social and economic thinking. In many ways, the New Deal was a promise to cure the sickness. In his first fireside address to the nation, Franklin D. Roosevelt described the Depression in terms of an illness, cured by "the killing of the bacteria in the system rather than . . . the treatment of external symptoms."[9] For the diseased patient, new and radical medicines were to be tested for which there had been no precedent. Early on, Roosevelt saw the need to offer guidance and counseling to the nation via the radio in order to help citizens accept the new direction in social and economic policy. For a nation whose economy was based on the studied acceptance of a capitalist work ethic, an adjustment to the new values and aims of the New Deal would be no small thing.

How was this adjustment to be made? To many, the coming of the New Deal was seen as a great opportunity to counteract the decline of American civilization and culture that the Depression so clearly illustrated. During the 1920s, social scientists had feared for a future that relied heavily on random acts of stock market "gambling" that enabled no forward planning. To counteract the irrational and unforeseen trajectories of American development, the use of planners and professionals was highly recommended. Economist and technocrat Stuart Chase offered such a "blueprint of a possible new society where economic activity is controlled by the technician, with a sixteen hour work week."[10] The result of rationalization and control would always necessitate a shorter working week, with resultant leisure, for which adequate planning should be made. Total reorganization and streamlining of society meant a rationally planned economy run by experts rather than amateurs, an economy

that balanced work with leisure. The use of leisure thereby became central to the adjustment to modernity.

By the mid-1930s this new emphasis on leisure as a part of an organized, planned society had created a demand for trained professionals
and experts who could lead or guide the masses in a time of massive
unemployment and psychological stress. The role of the educator and
instructor was to find a way for society to be readjusted to the modern
world. With fewer people working fewer hours "and even more striking
prospects for the future," it could only remain that "guidance in the right
use of leisure" on a national scale had become imperative.[11] Worried
that the unemployed worker would be led astray in his or her increased
leisure hours, the social scientist asked: "The question is, shall the guidance and opportunity be provided by such agencies as the school, the
public library, and the recreation commission, or by cheap magazine
stands and cabarets?"[12] Those who were untrained in their leisure use
were potential victims of commercial operators, sociologists George
Lundberg, Mirra Komarovsky, and Mary McInerney claimed in their
pioneering 1934 work *Leisure: A Suburban Study:* "On every side he is
surrounded by artful operators who have studied his weak points, often
with the aid of psychology, and beset him with the offer of ready-made
pleasures to be purchased at a price. . . . Even those of us who are
immune from the attractions of the cinema, the race-course and the
public house are not masters of our leisure time, at least to the extent
we should like to be."[13]

Often concurring with such views, scientific surveys and journalistic
examinations of leisure multiplied. Charities and quasi-governmental
bodies undertook numerous surveys and studies of leisure-time activities, and magazine articles proliferated on the features of this "new"
leisure and how it could best be utilized. While new social organizations
were often demanded as a result of these studies, there also emerged a
new psychological approach to national welfare that argued for recreation that would help mend the Depression-battered psyche and aid
adjustment to the new social and leisured order. In many ways, the continuation of democracy was seen as reliant on a "proper" adjustment and
accommodation to changing social structures. National and economic
breakdown was paralleled with personal breakdown under the strain
of modern living and economic insecurity—leisure provided the most
effective and nondivisive path out of this personal and national trauma.

Many claimed that mental impairment was increasingly undermining
the fabric of society because, as Lundberg and his colleagues explained,
the mechanical leisure of the masses failed to function as a "nervous
release," leaving one in ten in society eligible for psychopathic institutions.[14] Leisure, then, was described in terms of a pathological illness

that the social scientist could "cure." And the cure could be found within the disease: the proper use of leisure. One commentator for the National Committee for Mental Hygiene emphasized that of all factors that could help create the mentally healthful environment, "none is more important than those which have to do with the development of recreation and other resources of the community that serve the leisure-time needs of our people."[15]

The Depression created what one observer called "a vacuum caused by the diminution of work" that needed to be "wholesomely filled."[16] Another educationalist claimed that "unemployment has revealed to us in a startling way that when leisure is forced on masses of people through the closing down of their jobs, the vast majority of them are utterly at a loss what to do with themselves and merely stagnate as human beings," making them "empty barrels" to be trained and educated for the new use of leisure.[17] Sociologists believed that, without government intervention to change the climate of public outlook, the Depression would never end: what the people needed was something to keep them busy and happy while the government set to work.

This new function of leisure as a tool of government was illustrated by social scientists such as Louis Walker. In his book *Distributed Leisure: An Approach to the Problem of Overproduction and Underemployment*, Walker claimed that the time had come for the government to create a "division of leisure" as well as labor. This new department would focus entirely on the problem of the organization and distribution of leisure.[18] Leisure, he claimed, should be distributed efficiently, packaged and sold to Americans as much as other necessities. Leisure, it appeared, had come of age in America.

The importance assigned to leisure by the New Deal government became visible shortly after the National Industrial Recovery Act was passed. In December 1933, fearing that permanent limits to working hours would unleash even more unregulated leisure hours, the President's Emergency Reemployment Campaign set up a Committee on the Use of Leisure Time to examine the problem. The committee held hearings where professional experts gave evidence on the impact of leisure on crime, education, health, and morals. Available to the experts were many recent publications that outlined the leisure problem, such as Jesse Steiner's *Americans at Play: Recent Trends in Recreation and Leisure-Time*, published that same year. Steiner's book, however, was just one of many written during the period that examined and analyzed this new and unusual "problem of leisure." The growing output of works on leisure at this time would have provided useful reading to committee experts: Paul Frankl's *Machine-Made Leisure*, C. C. Furnas's *America's Tomorrow: An Informal Excursion into the Era of the Two-Hour Working Day*, Henry Forman's

Our Movie-Made Children, Harold Rugg's *The Great Technology: Social Chaos and the Public Mind* and his *Introduction to the Problems of American Culture,* Cecil Burns's *Leisure in the Modern World,* George Cutten's *Challenge of Leisure,* or Jay Nash's *Spectatoritis.*

These books emphasized that this was a "problem of leisure" unlike any that had come before; the "old" leisure was merely a break from work, but the "new" leisure could be harnessed to replace it. In fact, Lundberg, Komarovsky, and McInerney claimed that "the ideal to be sought is undoubtedly the gradual obliteration of the psychological barrier which today distinguishes work from leisure."[19] Leisure reform went further than physical improvement and offered a psychologically driven, collective way of dealing with modernity itself. In order to sustain the rhetoric of progress in the face of apparent industrial breakdown, leisure had to be reinvented as a modern concept through which individuals and society could "succeed" and prosper outside of a work environment.

The New Deal government responded to the leisure crisis as it was articulated in the popular and social science publications by funding the first-ever federal recreation policy. This unprecedented act illustrated a commitment to leisure on a national scale that made provision of training for leisure a part of welfare government. Yet this new policy was influenced by factors outside of the United States. Before implementing their policy, the New Deal bureaucrats looked closely at European leisure policies for models of state planning. While American leisure in the thirties was undoubtedly influenced by these experiments in dictatorial leisure and welfare capitalism, reformers set about making American leisure something that symbolized the founding democratic precepts of the nation. Unlike other nationalist programs, by 1940, American leisure effectively symbolized the freedom and choice associated with American democracy.

At the same time, the fundamental tensions surrounding leisure brought about by the intersection of corporate, state, and individual interests gave shape to the leisure debates of the 1930s. While the almost universal appeal of the leisure programs at the time made them one of the least controversial programs of the New Deal government—giving employment and recreation to Americans at a time of undoubted hardship for many—an examination of wider responses to mass leisure shows more deeply embedded class and gender conflicts.

These wider conflicts were most visible in the cultural sphere. Clues to this emerge in the films, fiction, photographs, and entertainments of the era. Although recreation programs and utopian visions of the future often offered models of cooperative living and social mindedness, along with a dream based on the leisured future, beneath the surface consensus a battle raged over the meaning of leisure that defined the era. Artists, writers, and intellectuals interacted and contributed to this debate as much as social scientists, and I have included their works in my study to illustrate how the cultural scene interacted with concerns and debates over leisure during this time.

One example of the way the problem of leisure emerged on the cultural scene was in the treatment and writing of literature. Although the many surveys of leisure undertaken in the 1930s listed reading as one of the top occupations for spare time, the apparent threat of "spectatoritis" and the challenge to traditional culture from commercial amusements appeared to be undermining the social fabric. Works Progress Administration programs and community leisure activities began promoting reading for cultivation above other amusements and activities, yet fears remained that the "passive" amusements offered by commercial entertainment would create a nation enamored of the visual. This was not just a concern of sociologists, however; writers and artists were equally concerned about this shift toward "low-brow" or commercial entertainment, fearing that their audiences would decline and that their voices would not be heard above the clamor of more universally accessible radio and cinema shows.

Literary engagement with the problem of leisure thus emerged, which initially overlapped with the widely disseminated theories of leisure professionals. Many writers and artists subscribed to the view that modern alienated leisure pursuits were the flip side of routinized, degraded, and alienated labor. Popular leisure had little that could recommend it to the radical writer, and a future of leisure appeared as a dystopian vision where all forms of capitalist control inhered and workers lost any valor and dignity bestowed upon them by productive labor. Despite this, many artists began to question the discourse of leisure reform as a form of unacceptable social control over popular culture. Their concerns, voiced in the literature they produced, indicated a more complex engagement with the leisure debate and modern leisure practices, one that exposed wider fears over limits to freedom of expression, capitalist as well as collectivist. This ambivalence emerged in literary and rhetorical responses to the Depression as well as in the wider perception of the function and role of the writer and writing.

By the mid-thirties, concerns over leisure were ubiquitous. The trickle of books and articles turned into a torrent, and the debate about American leisure raged in all areas of the popular and academic media until the end of the decade.[20] Yet closer inspection of these many different texts shows that the discourse of leisure was also a deeply gendered one. Noting that leisure increasingly involved new social relations between the sexes, Steiner's report revealed what would become a common concern to sociologists of leisure. The concern with an erosion of gender barriers in leisure-time activities was paralleled with concern over bound-ary crossing along class and race lines, all of which served to fuel anxieties over modern leisure practices. The idea that "technological unemploy-ment"—a common metaphor for the new leisure—had emasculated the American male reappeared in fears over passivity, vitality, and culture. Books, articles, fiction, and surveys indicated that men were both victims and possible controllers of leisure.

These anxieties over masculinity were mirrored by concerns that women had become ascendant through the transition to a leisure culture. The rise of consumer culture and leisure in the thirties appeared to be turning America into a matriarchy, where women, as consumers, con-trolled the nation's purse strings. Representations from Hollywood films to cartoons confirmed this perception of the new matriarchy of leisured consumers. These were linked to concerns over women's misuse of lei-sure time, questioning the desirability of female autonomy, fueled and fed by the new-style "back-to-the-hearth" movement that characterized the period. Many feared that, without control over irrational female be-havior, the planned future would be in jeopardy.

Anxiety over women's leisure became most heightened in relation to changing leisure practices that were key features of the decade. This book is a study of the cultural products of concerns surrounding leisure use, not a social history of leisure. Nothing in the literature demonstrates whether recreation reform or commercial recreation was either bene-ficial or detrimental to society. Despite this, moral judgments concern-ing women's activities in movie houses and dance halls had a significant impact on the way sociological and legal experts reacted, and gendered presumptions about women's use of leisure led to increased activity on the part of reformers to induce women into traditional domestic roles through control of leisure practices.

By the mid-thirties, social scientists started to reclaim America's uto-pian vision within descriptions of the new society that would emerge from better organization and planning for leisure. These blueprints frequently focused on population planning alongside guidance in leisure as a way of improving the mental and physical qualities of the population, without appearing to resort to overt methods of social control. So, while reform-ers, sociologists, and politicians attempted to reinvigorate American democracy by new social uses of leisure, the result of this campaign led to increasing hegemony over leisure despite their progressive impulses.

This is shown most forcefully in the interaction of leisure reform with a new type of social welfare eugenics that emerged in the thirties. Reformers hoped to counteract the deficiencies of an "unwise" use of leisure through recreation leadership programs that aimed to promote "healthy heterosexuality" through leisure. Although women continued to "decreate" in ways that bypassed reform goals, the new emphasis on leisure that would lead to proper "mate selection" meant that the principles of eugenics filtered into recreation and leisure management policy at this time. By offering welfare and support to the weakest members of society, many feared that the New Deal government would create a further imbalance to the social organism. Not only would the program be costly to the taxpayers, but the weak would be healthy enough to reproduce more welfare recipients. Many contemporary reformers thereby favored eugenic principles of improving the race, principles supported by a program of health, education, and leisure reform to improve physical and mental fitness for all. Although it is impossible to chart how effective this new policy was in reality, there is much to suggest that it underpinned ideological changes in social thinking on gender and the family well into the 1950s.

At a time of industrial and economic chaos, then, the rhetoric of the leisure debate was about more than dissatisfaction with free-time activities. What I show in this examination of the ideas and discourses concerning leisure in the thirties is how discussions about leisure were very often a subterfuge for dominant opinions to be expressed on class and gender roles and, further how the ensuing discourse formed the basis of laws enacted to control leisure pursuits. The decade between 1929 and 1939 bore witness to momentous social and political upheavals. Perceptions of the way leisure functioned to define the past, present, and future of American culture provide an interesting paradigm for understanding wider issues at stake during the period. From the onset of depression and the widespread belief that leisure was a permanent feature of American life, debates raged over the correct way to use it. Ideas of social betterment through leisure came about at a time when the work ethic seemed most threatened. Some saw leisure as a way of rebuilding society outside of the capitalist mainstream and others as a reformulation, or rebuilding, of the capitalist ethos.

From being symptomatic of the degeneration of American culture, by 1939, in contrast to totalitarian leisure in Europe, leisure had become a symbol of democracy and hope for the future. As a way of reinvesting individuality with social meaning, leisure became reinvigorated with social and political significance. With the outbreak of World War II, increased productivity and full employment put concerns with leisure into the background while workers entered the real battle with fascism. What remained, however, was a commitment to the notion of a self and society defined not only by work but also through leisure.

Chapter 1
The Problem and Promise

Leisure is here. Modern life is being revolutionized by its rapid extension. People have always had some spare time but leisure for everybody is a condition which we are now approaching.

—Martin H. Neumayer, *"The New Leisure and Social Objectives"*

How best to use growing leisure hours is an individual problem in which organized society has a large stake.

—*President's Research Committee on Social Trends,* Recent Social Trends

While European nations had been experiencing revolution, waves of economic depression, and the formation of new state structures, America in the 1920s had appeared somewhat immune to such traumatic events. Commercial, corporate, and municipal recreation had all expanded in an unprecedented way, and the necessity of amusing the unemployed or controlling leisure time appeared to have little urgency outside the progressive reform movement. All of this changed when the Depression struck America. This chapter examines popular and social scientific views of the problem of leisure in the years leading up to the New Deal in order to illustrate the contours and significance of leisure in national thinking during the first half of the decade. As widespread discussions about the function of leisure and the modern state proliferated, pressure increased for a government response, which eventually led to an unprecedented federal policy to promote the "better" use of leisure throughout the nation.

Background to Leisure

Concerns surrounding leisure during the Depression originated from a long history of recreation reform where responses to leisure and unemployment were an inheritance of past trials and hopes concerning national recreation. At the same time, the issue of leisure in the 1930s also diverged from previous debates. In order to illustrate this relationship, it is useful to briefly outline what had happened to American leisure in the decades before the Crash in 1929.

Rapid industrialization in Europe and America during the eighteenth and early nineteenth centuries created a climate that changed work and play patterns for all classes. The emergence of a "leisure class" who lived off the fruits of industrial labor necessitated a redefinition of leisure as an alternative to productive labor. Not just an indulgence, leisure needed to be "productive" and utilitarian in order to counteract the potential physical and mental decline facing the newly leisured business classes. Self-culture and physical fitness became goals of a bourgeois industrial culture, where those who did little manual labor could use their time to achieve physical and moral ideals. In America between 1820 and 1840, several universities and schools opened gymnasiums, influenced by their German counterparts, and competitive sports and games started to appear as an important part of college life.[1] Changes in work patterns and class behaviors from the 1840s led to a nascent "fitness" culture in which displays of bodily perfection and health became a sign of an ascendant class and a signal of success and high breeding.[2] Focused almost solely on the bodies of nonlaboring men and women, or children, the "leisure ethic" appeared at first to apply only to ascendant classes who, in a world increasingly perceived as a Darwinist struggle for physical and social survival, needed to maintain their health and well-being for the improvement of the race and personal success.[3]

At the same time, mass commercial entertainment was growing at a rate parallel to the urbanization of American cities. From having no amusement or baseball parks in 1870, by the early twentieth century, every town and city housed mass commercial amusements. By 1909, more than 20 million people had visited Coney Island during one season. New amusements and modes of mass transportation ensured access for the working classes, who were enjoying increased wages and lower working hours.[4] While few workers could afford a vacation in 1900, by 1930 a vacation "habit" had developed that not even the Great Depression could erase.[5] The development of new styles of amusements and the appearance of large crowds of working men and women in urban amusements led to concerns that moral order and control over the ill-educated masses was diminishing. Critics of "the new amusements" in the 1890s, for example, promoted the notion that women were "out of control" and needed supervision for leisure.[6] Play or recreation reform movements emerged alongside other progressive health and welfare movements that attempted to provide alternative noncommercial play for children that would educate them for civic duty and future leadership. Unlike earlier moral and religious commentators in the late nineteenth century, recreation reformers attempted to utilize rather than repress leisure in order to teach "universal moral character" so that the chaos and anarchy so visible in the urban landscape need not be so feared.[7]

The playground movement emerged out of religious fears that urbanization created moral laxity, yet saw "civic uplift" as the way to inspire control and regulation, rather than more coercive and authoritarian methods of social control. In creating an ideal of good citizenship and a sense of civic duty, reformers hoped to regain control over a populace that was increasingly unswayed by moral and religious pressures to conform. One founding sociologist, Edward Ross, author of *Social Control* (1901), openly wrote that the creation of this new type of citizenship would involve creating a fiction of "illusions and fallacies," which would be woven into the passive "average mind" through moral instruction by an "ethical elite." The goal "was not to force a mere grudging conformity on mass man, but gently entice him to spontaneous and even joyous inward affirmation of the larger social will."[8] As a more effective means of social control, sociologists and progressives were influenced by this idea of benevolent instruction, as opposed to outworn methods of control that no longer worked or that might have resulted in revolutionary conflict.

The rise of the City Beautiful and playground movements in the late nineteenth century were thus a response to rapid urban growth that built on and extended earlier theories of play, incorporating ideas of urban planning and environmental control as part of individual self-improvement through recreation. The creation of large municipal parks—beginning with the purchase of Central Park in New York in 1853—furthered the movement for genteel and "rational" recreation that separated the bourgeois urban dweller from the burgeoning urban chaos of the industrializing city. Yet the municipal park also offered urban dwellers and the working classes a model of rational recreation to which to aspire. The play movement appeared in this context as an attempt to reform working-class leisure in conformity with the bourgeois ideals of self-control, health, and productivity. Controlling the self became extended to the wider community, where individualist approaches to health and well-being were gradually replaced by a broader sense of civic consciousness.

By controlling the leisure environment of the city, reformers hoped to control the behavior of the city's inhabitants.[9] The playground movement thus emerged as a city-based social reform movement that aimed to prevent crime and improve the social conditions of the working classes, and it confidently believed that a "new urban citizenry—moral, industrious, and socially responsible—would emerge" from urban social control via the playground.[10] Like leisure reform of the 1930s, city-based social reform movements tended to appear or become exaggerated during economic crises and waves of immigration, and they exhibited bourgeois

anxieties that society no longer obeyed the rules set by elite and educated members.

Social workers played a large part in the development and organization
of the play movement, where the growth of slums and tenements, the
massive growth in immigration (23 million Europeans between 1880 and
1919), industrialization, and cheap commercial amusements "helped to
create a condition which made the provision of wholesome recreation a
necessity." [11] The founding moment of the playground movement in
America, claimed George D. Butler in 1940, was the opening of the first
sand garden (a sand pile placed in the yard of the children's mission)
in Boston in 1885, where fifteen children for three days a week in July
and August "dug in the sand, sang songs, and marched about under the
guidance of a woman who lived in the neighborhood." Supervision and
training for supervision were, from the onset, given high priority for the
success of the movement. Sand gardens and playgrounds with gymnas-
tic equipment began to proliferate, along with the appearance of trained
supervisors and experts. In 1892, a "model" playground was opened at
Hull House in Chicago, based on similar playgrounds for poor children
in the East End of London.[12] Municipal funding began to support the
play areas and playground committees were formed, along with the professionalization of social workers who specialized in play reform.

By the early 1900s, the playground movement was starting to acquire
professional status, employing many trained leaders and social workers
to raise standards of citizenship and performing social regulation through
leisure. Professional publications and magazines started to appear with
increasing regularity, circulating ideas from the founders of the movement that helped to entrench recreation movement goals within a widen-
ing community of readers. The movement became nationwide in 1906
with the establishment of the Playground Association of America (later
to become the National Recreation Association) and *The Playground,* a
monthly magazine. Founding members were progressive reformers such
as Jane Addams, Henry S. Curtis, Jacob Riis, and Luther Gulick, whose
goal was to promote playground reform in all parts of the United States.
College courses were established to train recreation leaders, culminat-
ing in the establishment of the National Recreation School in 1926, and
recreation leaders were organized into the Society of Recreation Workers
during the 1930s.

Through *The Playground* and national conferences, the Playground Association of America promoted the theory of urban social control through
the management of children in playgrounds. Progressives believed that
the playground could socialize young children at a crucial stage in their
development by providing adult supervision of play and guided leadership
of young boys by older boys. Adult supervision was crucial to the success

of the schemes, and many cities responded to the findings of the movement by hiring trained playground managers. The attempt to control urban leisure only started at the playground, however, as enthusiasts promoted the idea of greater intervention in all forms of popular leisure. Reformers argued that eventually "municipal authorities should operate all dance halls" in addition to all movie theatres and reach out "beyond the training of the youth and include to a considerable extent the care and morals and amusements of adults as well."[13] One playground director and sociologist claimed in 1922 that one long-term goal of the movement was to extend the supervision of children to include adults, resulting in "control of the remaining 80 per cent of the population during the sixty-four hours per week in which even the laboring element is at leisure."[14]

Welfare Capitalism

While recreation programs in the thirties were partly a continuation of these social concerns and observations that had their roots in nineteenth-century progressive reforms, interest in the industrial and social potential of leisure reform took its lead equally from the kind of welfare capitalism commonly practiced by corporations in the 1920s. Large corporations—with the Ford Company as the most well known—took it upon themselves to provide recreation for their workers in the form of musical entertainment, picnics, films, and team sports. Promoting the corporate spirit through work-related leisure activities was an important way in which industrialists attempted to manage the nonworking time of their workers.

Corporate recreation responded to the growing power of trade unions, who also provided their workers with recreation that would provide welfare and fellow-feeling for other workers. Having campaigned for fewer hours in America since the 1820s, unions and craft guilds cohered demonstrations around reducing the maximum hours of work that could be legally demanded of a worker, and more free time was the natural result of workers' protests.[15] Leisure was thereby a right demanded of fair labor policy and fundamental to the work of trade unions. After World War I, increased industrial action in factories led to lower working hours, concessions for vacations, and better pay for some. Not only were trade unions pursuing a "quest for leisure," they were demanding it as a right. As a result, throughout the 1920s, manufacturers began to see that providing leisure facilities and recreation for workers would act as a way of encouraging worker loyalty as well as promoting industrial peace. As a way of controlling industrial action and union organizing, in addition to keeping the newly leisured worker occupied in a "productive" manner, welfare capitalists started to organize the out-of-work activities of their workers. Working-class leisure thus became of even greater interest to the business classes in the twenties, during which companies provided sports facilities, athletic events, baseball games, motion pictures, company dances, singing, and bowling.[16]

Corporate welfare had much in common with the recreation reform movement: both attempted to create an alternative to the commercial leisure pursuits available to workers in the hope that worker behavior and productivity could be improved. Both relied on gender roles modeled on the ideal Victorian family.[17] By the 1920s, large companies often offered a range of recreational opportunities and facilities such as athletic tracks, swimming pools, tennis courts, baseball fields, and children's playgrounds. Companies organized outings, picnics, and dances and provided indoor facilities such as gyms, pool halls, theaters, and bowling alleys. Corporate recreation policies in the first quarter of the century did more than rescue workers from misused leisure, however; they functioned as a form of company advertisement and as a way of proving the fitness of the corporation in the arena of the marketplace.[18] Companies also used recreation to boost nationalism by organizing groups that would practice military drills in uniforms or patriotic pageants, for example.[19] Employers recognized that industrial "peace" was reliant on the provision and control of such facilities, for when workers watched a movie every lunch hour, employers noted that it kept "them from getting together in little groups and talking about their troubles."[20]

In opposition to corporate welfare and the rise of commercial leisure, unions began to organize worker recreation that worked to strengthen class consciousness and solidarity. The International Ladies' Garment Workers' Union (ILGWU) was one of the first to create union education and recreation programs, and in 1917 offered members gyms, dancing, sports, and summer vacation camps.[21] Despite this, union welfare could barely compete with corporate provision until it received federal support in the 1930s. Immigrant groups also supported leisure activities along ethnic lines, with planned rituals, celebrations, feasts, and entertainment that did not always receive official sanction.[22] Recreation reformers, however, worked to break the habits of traditional ethnic affiliations and Americanize immigrants with recreation and welfare that would serve to modernize new citizens and promote loyalty to America.[23]

As historian Lynn Dumenil has written, "Corporate-sponsored leisure was part of the process by which companies tried to mould workers' values, to direct them toward productive leisure that would make them loyal and efficient workers."[24] In the case of Henry Ford, his company promoted leisure that would induce sobriety and Christian values in order to maintain stable and productive machine workers. Setting up a "sociological department," Ford examined the nonworking time of his employees and permitted only those who lived according to his established policies to earn the celebrated five dollars per day.[25] Thus the activities of workers both in and out of work were directly connected to their wages and to the profit of the company. Ford's corporate empire consisted of towns, factories, hospitals, and schools dedicated to the purpose of maintaining the smooth running and profitability of his business. Owning rubber plantations and hydroelectric dams, steel, iron, coal, and forestry works ensured the uninterrupted supply of raw materials, while private railroads and shipyards ensured effective transportation of those materials. Ford's lesser-known activities indicated a further accumulation of control over input, namely, over workers' lives: private welfare programs, hospitals, schools, and colleges ensured a supply of healthy, trained, productive bodies for his factories. Along with this, his activities in radio programming, publishing, and historical presentation illustrate the extent to which corporate welfare aimed to preserve "outside of work, a certain psycho-physical equilibrium which prevents the physiological collapse of the worker."[26]

The growth of corporate-sponsored leisure grew side by side with the expansion of commercially run leisure activities organized for profit rather than uplift. Together these offered both blue- and white-collar workers unprecedented access to cheap amusements. During the 1920s, expenditures on public recreation increased by 300 percent, with the most notable increases in the use of cars for leisure, movie attendance, and professional spectator sports.[27] Over the period from 1919 to 1929 the average working week was cut from 46.3 hours to 44.2, indicating that workers were gradually gaining more leisure time, although for most, the five-day week was still relatively rare and the ten-hour day was common.[28] Nevertheless, with the onset of the Depression, company leisure programs (which had peaked in the mid-twenties anyway) were cut, and the cut in workers' hours was experienced as a form of hardship rather than as a benefit for the working classes.

The New Problem of Depression Leisure

So, by 1929, the dreams of the playground movement for "uplifting" urban leisure for all ages remained unrealized. Laissez-faire economics still dominated the provision of mass urban leisure, and regulation was left to the influence of reform bodies in municipal governments.[29] With the onset of the Depression, even the schemes that had been sponsored were cut, and the play movement was apparently curtailed. Mass unemployment and economic hardship appeared on a scale that few could have anticipated.

After the 1929 stock market crash, a new problem of leisure appeared. It was not just a result of unemployment, however; studies claimed that machines had shortened the working day and had made work easier, so that "leisure time is increasing and is destined to increase more."[30] Many economists argued that "occupational obsolescence" or "technological unemployment"—the replacement of human labor by machines— were permanent features of modern culture, and that public support was necessary to enable workers to adjust to their newly "leisured" condition.[31] "Out of the depression has come unemployment, and born of the union of unemployment and scientific invention has come leisure. . . so leisure and how we spend it becomes of paramount importance to us educationally and morally, individually and as a nation," claimed one sociologist.[32]

While accurate estimates of the amount of available leisure time could rarely be computed, new surveys proliferated that attempted to provide answers. Discussing the problem of scientific data in "The New Leisure and Social Objectives," sociologist Martin Neumayer declared that, while statistics and measurements of leisure were often unreliable, several pieces of significant data were discernable:

The working period has been reduced from seventy to less than fifty hours per week during the past century, which has trebled the spare time of workers; unemployment increased from less than 2,000,000 to from 10,000,000 to 15,000,000 during the present economic depression; vacations and holidays have increased in number and in extent; time is saved by labor-saving devices, rapid means of communication and transportation, and the prevalence of ready-made commodities; child labor has decreased and children stay in school longer than was true a few decades ago; early retirement and the increase of the aged population with fewer opportunities to work have given many free time.[33]

While urban reform movements and corporate welfare certainly influenced debates over the social planning for leisure throughout the thirties, the appearance of so much "extra" time, whether it was from unemployment, a cut in hours, or the efficiency of new technology, meant that leisure now became an urgent matter for national debate.[34] No longer a question of what to do after work or a matter of children's sandboxes, debates over leisure took center stage. The sudden proliferation in articles and books on the subject of leisure saw the problems that America now faced as something that affected the entire nation, all classes and all areas of life. These saw the changes as a permanent transformation to which the nation needed help, physically and psychologically, adjusting. This required much more social organization and planning than the creation of a few humble playgrounds and necessitated the reeducation of the entire nation: the "leisure problem" of the thirties was a problem of modernity, machine technology, mass production, and mass consumption—the problems and their solutions appeared to affect every aspect of American life.

The issue of technological unemployment, as a way of understanding the Depression, became the subject of widespread discussion and debate. Overproduction and unemployment became dominant concerns in the early years of the Depression, and demands were made to regain control over the economy through proper scientific planning, which included more control and planning for leisure.[35] All writing on the "leisure problem" of the thirties held in common this theme that the machine had taken work from men, leaving them with time for leisure and recreation, which they had previously not had. The relationship of man with machines, the image implied, had become a Faustian epic, where man now paid for the material luxuries he had coveted in the 1920s with a surplus of time. The need for leisure facilities that would bring the nation out of the morass appeared more imperative than ever before.

What exactly was wrong with leisure in the early 1930s, and what appeared so wrong with more people having more of it? Why were social scientists talking about leisure when surrounded by poverty and unemployment? Economic and social blueprints for a better society insisted that unless people were trained to use leisure time properly, efficiently, and intelligently, there would be no improvement in society despite technical advances and a return to full employment. Stuart Chase, for example, denigrated standardized, secondhand mechanical play, where even jazz dancing is "but play in a Ford factory":

What the age of machinery has given us in time, it would fain take away again by degrading the opportunities which that time affords; by standardizing our recreations on a quantity production basis, by making us watchers rather than doers, by exploiting our leisure for profit, by surfeiting us with endless mechanical things to monkey with—from gasoline cigar lighters to million dollar cruising yachts, by forcing the pace of competition in play until it turns into work, and above all by brutalizing in recreation millions of human beings who are already brutalized by the psychological imperatives of their daily labor.[36]

To Chase, the ideal definition of recreation was "creating again in play the balance that has been lost in work," although much of the current scene he describes in his book *Men and Machines* describes "decreation": "compounding the lost balance through unrewarding forms of play." "Play is the flywheel of life," he continued, "and America, with the most stupendous recreational equipment ever dreamed of, does not know how to play. It can only step on throttles, insert coins in metal slots, scan headlines, crowd through clicking turnstiles, rush headlong down roller coasters—seeking a balance which these things can seldom give."[37]

Chase argued that recreation needed to employ muscle and to be as natural or simple as possible in order to counterbalance machine-dominated work.

Leisure should therefore reconstruct the body and mind and provide an antidote to machine living, bringing balance back to the national "organism." Chase suggested "we ought frequently take to the woods," rather than seek a balance for industrial living in industrial leisure. Chase listed "road-houses, night clubs, confectionery palaces, soft drink emporiums . . . jazz-palaces, speakeasies," and various sports and racing as examples of unnatural and mechanical pursuits.[38] Similarly in *Play: Recreation in a Balanced Life,* recreation reformer Austen Riggs described how increased leisure, as a "by-product" of the machine, was counteracted by a general "speeding-up process" in all aspects of life.[39] Many concurred with this view. In his sociological study, Martin Neumayer described how the machine affects leisure in two ways—by increasing its amount and by influencing its use: "Overspecialization, standardization, increased speed and the stress and strain of modern life, technological unemployment, and the reduction of people to secondhand participants in their hours of play and recreation are some of the negative effects of the machine."[40]

Recreation reformer Frank Kingdon similarly stated how progress—meaning the "continual mastery of our environment, the ability to control our world more and more effectively"—"carries along with it the threat of degeneration."[41] With technological progress came increasing leisure, which, if not used properly, contained within it an innate threat. Sociologist Arthur Pack predicted with assurance the coming of a two-hour day—leisure properly used, he claimed, would "balance the machine," and "unless the manifest advantages of leisure outweigh the ills of a machine age, civilization as we now understand it is inevitably doomed."[42] Many argued that degeneration of society through the misuse of leisure could be prevented by scientific planning on a national, as well as a personal, scale.

As a result, anthropologically driven views of modern leisure patterns started to increase, where social scientists focused their economic and sociological analyses on white suburban communities as test cases for solving the problems of depression society. Pioneering this closer examination of the problem of leisure during 1932 and 1933, sociologist George Lundberg and his research assistants Mirra Komarovsky and Mary McInerney set about examining the leisure of the suburban community of Westchester County, New York. Published in 1934, *Leisure: A Suburban Study* was a foundational text for the recreation movement during the 1930s. Komarovsky, a graduate student at Columbia, had also studied with anthropologists Ruth Benedict and Franz Boas and sociologist William Ogburn. Ogburn's theory of "cultural lag" (the gap between technology and human advance) influenced her sociological narrative during the research and writing of *Leisure,* as well as her later work on male unemployment with sociologist Paul Lazersfeld. The research was funded by Columbia University, the American Association for Adult Education, and Westchester County Recreation Commission and had Robert Lynd on the advisory committee. In their preface, the authors claimed that their methods could be summed up in a recent statement by historian Charles Beard: "Science can discover the facts that condition realization and furnish instrumentalities for carrying plan and purpose into effect. Science without dreams is sterile. Dreams without research and science are empty."[43] Scientific planning for leisure based on these types of study offered a panacea for social change through leisure that went beyond the dreams of earlier reformers.

Lundberg's study of Westchester in New York proceeded "on the assumption that what people do with their leisure is a matter of practical social concern as well as of scientific interest."[44] While work and occupations "have been studied with some fullness by economists and efficiency experts," he stated, "the uses of leisure time, being presumably subject to the relatively 'free' choice of individuals, and therefore supposedly largely unstandardized, have never been subjected to detailed study from the standpoint of the individual or special group." Lundberg added scientific currency to his survey by asking 2,460 individuals to keep diaries, thereby recording the activities of 4,460 days—all with "possible value of data to educators, social workers, and other community leaders." This new way of surveying and quantifying leisure became part of the utopian ideal for the perfectly planned future, yet the dreams were those of the professional middle class, whose ideas about the better future were undergirded by presumptions to control their social "inferiors."

Lundberg's diaries showed that over 90 percent of leisure was divided between eating, visiting, reading, public entertainment, sports, radio, and motoring. Although little from these diaries indicated that the "problem" had reached the crisis levels sociologists claimed, Lundberg then insisted that such quantitative evaluation of time provided little useful evidence about the quality of leisure occupations. Although social workers had no control over the amount of time available for leisure, they could ensure guidance so that the hour spent listening to the radio, for example, was spent listening to a symphony rather than jazz. Lundberg used an accretion of upper- and middle-class values—what he called the "time-tested value scale of the race"—to judge that reading dime novels, movie going, motoring, and listening to jazz were uses of leisure that did little to contribute to the higher achievements of mankind, whereas serious study, working at handicrafts, or listening to a symphony would forward "the race" toward a higher form of civilization.[45]

Like Chase, Lundberg and colleagues also found that leisure had become too much like work: automated and standardized by mass production. According to this, two problems resulted from the new technology: the monotony of work made workers crave "unnatural" or destructive experiences, and leisure itself now relied on the machine.[46] The sociologists worried that the monotony of modern labor "results in a craving for explosive stimulation."[47] Where traditional folk leisure and community leisure activities were replaced by commercial products, individual control over leisure time was also thought to be diminishing as humans became automatons of leisure: "automobiles, motion pictures and the radio have disrupted traditional leisure pursuits and the individual's control over his spare time."[48]

At the same time, however, it was feared that leisure had become too passive, leading to physical, educational, and psychological problems. Jay B. Nash, author of the 1932 book *Spectatoritis,* pathologized the problem of leisure into an illness and applied Freud's theories on repression and mental illness to the realm of mass culture. Concerns over the sheer quantity of people, from all classes, attending the cinema had triggered speculation over the possible effects that this would have on the mind and actions of individuals en masse. The leisure of the masses had become a cause and symbol of the widespread mental illness apparently affecting Depression society. Nash asked the question on the tip of many professional tongues: "Can America be trusted with leisure?" Repeating his question in more personal form, Nash asked, "Can you be trusted with your leisure?"—asking if the reader would naturally take up some favorite hobby, or "would you drop back to your old reflexes and sleep—sleep in bed, before the radio, before the moving picture camera, or other places." Nash labeled this "disease" of inactivity and inertia as "spectatoritis," claiming that "given leisure, man will turn into a listener, a watcher" and that the effect of this will be increased inertia: "Spectatoritis is the cause of a particular kind of fatigue which must be given special consideration. The spectator is subject to a tenseness; he is subjected to a stimulus to start acting; he becomes adrenalized but, as a spectator, it is impossible for him to act. Hence all of these starts to activity must be inhibited; incomplete combustion results."[49]

In a similar way, theologist and educator Lawrence Jacks feared for a society with so much unused released energy, which has come about "through the transference of toil from man to the machine." Attempting to quantify the total amount of unused energy available, he claimed that "we should think of [economic depression] not alone in terms of the number of human beings that are left unemployed, but rather in terms of the amount of human energy that is released." In fact, he claimed, looking at unemployment figures made little difference to the amount of hours that the machine had released in terms of human energy—to Jacks, the amount of human energy released would be the same whether a result of unemployment or more machinery. Thus it was spare or misused human energy, rather than unemployment, that had become the problem. Without guidance, the direction of leisure in the modern world was a "search for ready-made pleasures, excitements, stimulants, thrills, high-power sensations externally administered and purchasable on the market."[50]

This problem of passivity and inertia was seen as an integral part of commercial leisure, which was associated with low-class and low-quality amusements: "It will not be easy" to change these passive habits, counseled Owen Geer, "we shall find them already set against certain forms of recreation. They have been fed on jazz; they may not know good music when they hear it . . . they have been accustomed to getting their amusements in 'canned' form served out to them by commercial agencies."[51] In fact, as Joel Dinerstein shows, swing and jazz dance culture emerged from popular responses to machine-age modernity that celebrated the way humans could respond to and surpass assembly-line culture. Yet these responses to popular leisure saw such energized and physically demanding dances of the swing age as "passive" waste products of modernity and "disparaged jazz for its fast rhythms, mechanically repetitive beat, and sensual dances."[52] Because of their industrial rhythm, such commercial activities appeared to prevent individual control over time and movement. This lack of control related directly to the introduction of technology, Neumayer complained, for commercialized leisure is so mechanized that the "tools of recreation are provided, many of which are ready-made, allowing little room for initiative and creativeness."[53] Neumayer concluded that the "commercialization of leisure is largely responsible for the abuses and misuses of it." "We are," he claims, no longer "the masters of our time." To Harold Rugg, the "recreations of the common man also reflect the restless spirit of our age." That restlessness was the cause of the industrial revolution, which "swung us into a speedier age," creating mechanical leisure that was responsible for loss of control and individuality.[54]

Other sociologists argued that too many leisure activities involved watching or listening: "Home and neighborhood games and sports are supplanted by billiard 'parlors' and public dance halls. Huge stadia offer vicarious satisfaction for the urges which conditions no longer permit us to fulfill directly. Instead of singing around the piano, we turn on the radio."[55] Accordingly, leisure had become "mass mediated," unoriginal, unauthentic, and unable to satisfy the primitive urges for original and direct experience. To recreation reformers, the cultural and physical degeneracy of America as a nation was a result of this machine-made lifestyle.

This strain and speeding up of everyday life made the Depression, to many of these commentators, a psychological and neurological problem as much as an economic one. The answer, according to Lundberg and associates, was not an increase in the wealth or income of the masses, for, despite mass unemployment, society's problems were psychological: "Man's physical needs are inextricably interdigitated with his psychological wants. The insatiability of the latter in a society where conspicuous and competitive consumption is the basis of prestige is self-evident and has been frequently pointed out. . . . In short, poverty in modern society is fundamentally a state of mind rather than a state of stomach."[56]

Riggs called the mental exhaustion of commercial leisure "fear-neurosis," something that Roosevelt himself had highlighted in his celebrated 1933 inaugural speech, stating that "the only thing we have to fear is fear itself."[57] Recreation reformers thereby equated economic decline with the physical and psychological decline and inertia of the modern citizen. George Barton Cutten, psychologist and president of Colgate University, stated that "The Pace Is Driving Us Crazy," arguing that people ended up with mental problems "because they were unable to stand the strain of present conditions." The cost to personal and national coffers was immense, he noted, for "if the present rate [of hospital admissions] continues, in seventy-five years, one-half of the population will be working to support the other half which will be insane."[58] Walter Pitkin, professor of journalism at Columbia University, concurred with this assessment of the prevalence of "feeblemindedness" and mental illness in his book *Take It Easy*. Using the findings of the President's Research Commission, surveys by *Fortune* magazine, and newspaper articles, Pitkin claimed that science and technology had created "this earthquake," which left men vulnerable to nervous breakdown, tension, desperation, and madness: "Now look at those who cannot cope with the world of reality. The President of the American Medical Association, at its October, 1933, meeting, reported that 'The number of commitments to institutions for mental diseases almost parallels the increases in matriculation to colleges.' Almost half of the hospital beds in this country are occupied by people having mental disorders. . . . During the past fifty years the population has a little more than doubled; but there are nine times as many admissions to state hospitals as there were half a century ago."[59]

Most leisure writers concurred to some degree with Pitkin, claiming that some form of social maladjustment and mental ill-health was the result of machine living and misused leisure: "the degradation of personality, the danger to health, mental balance and vitality, and the consequent social deterioration are obvious perils of misused leisure."[60]

Pathologizing the perceived weakness of the American body (and economy), Nash saw misdirected energy, or lack of wholesome play, as

the result of "spectatoritis," which causes "a particular kind of fatigue."
Nash's view that fatigue was caused by the stimulation of modern commercial leisure metaphorically described male impotency and sexual dys-
function, where inhibited activity results in "incomplete combustion."
Although Nash didn't say exactly what the effect of this "incomplete combustion" might be, the implication remained that, without the proper
use of leisure, the sluggishness of the nation would increase rather than
decline, and the likelihood of a quick recovery from the Depression
would similarly disappear.[61] Degeneration of the social order through
exhaustion was to be avoided at all costs by participation in properly
organized national leisure programs.[62]

With the saturation of the mass media by new visual technologies, fears
that the visual tendencies of crowds would lead to unthinking passivity,
and by extension mob rule, were common. Nash described how misdirected energy creates criminals whose "crime was largely play."[63] Leisure
was so commonly linked with crime that one columnist in *Recreation*
claimed, "I suppose I need not speak of crime. Leisure time easily lends
itself to the prosecution of crime; and easily lends itself to the development of certain unsocial recreation so that anybody looking at the general question of leisure can see immediately that if we leave it alone . . .
this increased leisure time may become a serious liability in the whole
social structure."[64] At the height of a perceived crime wave, this made
leisure reform even more important. Many commentators agreed, however, that it was not the lack of recreational facilities that was to blame
for increases in crime, but the *misuse* of leisure. Youths who spent their
free time in pool halls and bars, as shown in Figure 1, were one symp-
tom of this wasteful use of time. Leisure was not something with which the
uneducated could be trusted. Improving the mind, however, would allow
for wise use of leisure—enabling the citizens to appreciate opera above
jazz or read good literature instead of picture magazines and comics.

Many books and articles written on leisure and recreation, appearing
from the burgeoning "mental hygiene" movement, also saw the Depression as a problem of mass psychology. For example, Austen Riggs's *Play:
Recreation in a Balanced Life* argued that, while the Depression was comparable to personal physical decline, it could be overcome through controlled leisure: "The disease is called Depression but is not just a matter
of dollars, nor of over-production. It is chiefly a psychological disorder,
a question of morale, of lost courage, of shaken faith. It must run its
course, and there is much suffering entailed, even though the patient,
in this case the nation, will surely survive. Months—perhaps years—are
consumed in recovery. First there is paralysis—the weak, unfit organizations that flourished in the atmosphere of false prosperity perish. The
patient's recovery depends upon remodeling his life, upon rebalancing

his time budget as well as his financial budget and upon recasting his values."[65]

To many, the Depression was a "sickness" of capitalism, in part caused by the acceleration of technological culture that had outstripped human ability, or "cultural lag." Social scientists had subscribed to this view since the midtwenties, and the Depression provided fitting evidence that they had been right all along. These social scientists believed that by changing the way Americans used leisure, cultural lag and the psychological problems of the Depression could be cured. Properly organized leisure should supplant mass leisure, argued Neumayer, not by "smashing the machine, but by building up a strong leisure life of the people. The world cannot afford to have its leisure life corrupted."[66]

As many writers saw machine living as something that had disabled the ordinary American, they feared that the return of prosperity would only make matters worse. Material wealth and easy living had created citizens who did not know how to play. The time to act was now, before the Depression ended and citizens forgot the lessons their restricted

1. Recreation (pool). At midafternoon of a sunny Saturday, a typical group of small-town high school youths idling in the local pool hall. Courtesy National Archives, Still Picture Branch, RG119-Cal-183.

circumstances could teach them. The "abundant" life could be rede-
fined through leisure pursuits, they stressed, so that adaptation to the
new circumstances of modern leisure could be successful. Neumayer
claimed that the abundant life was possible by a two-pronged approach,
which involved "a) the progressive development, in ourselves and in
others, of rational and rich personality, functioning with efficiency and
satisfaction in wholesome co-operative living; and b) the establishment
of social order conducive to this end."[67] Most agreed that the reconstruction of the individual through leisure would counteract degeneration.
Balance between social and technological advancement was seen of paramount importance for the future survival of America and its people.
Fitting humans to their new physical and cultural environment and
equipping them with new abilities and skills was seen as vital for the
future of American civilization.[68]

Despite their interest in working-class use of leisure, of particular interest to professionals was the effect of mass culture on the middle class. At
the same time that rocketing unemployment hit the middle classes for
the first time, threatening their secure incomes and lifestyles and undermining theories of meritocratic ascendancy through education, training,
and intelligence, Lundberg and associates argued that commercial leisure now posed real dangers for the middle classes. Class boundaries
were difficult to maintain in the new environment of downward mobility, and heterogeneous leisure and blatant fears of racial decline among
whites fueled a survivalist rhetoric that was barely masked in many reports.
Although the suburban dweller appeared to have the most promising
prospects for leisure, according to sociologists he or 'she was under the
growing threat of "bad leisure" emanating from the city. The new physical mobility of all Americans, due to the automobile, made it impossible
to maintain traditional class barriers. The suburbanite needed "protection" from urban influences: "Protection against the leisure activities of
our neighbors as well as recreational opportunities and facilities for ourselves can be attained only through community action."[69] The problem
of leisure for the suburbanite appeared to consist solely of this danger
of urban influences for, as Lundberg and associates noted, Westchester
County was a wealthy New York suburb, significant for its political stability, its public parks and golf courses, and the abundance of facilities
provided by regional groups and businesses.

Books examining the problem of leisure emphasized the importance
of professional guidance, equating intelligence with leadership and success. The cycle between earning money and consuming leisure, he explained, were "activities suitable rather to the brain of a squirrel than to
that of man" and had a "hypnotic centripetal power" that holds all in its
sway other than "some preachers, professors, artists and others who won't

work according to the formula." Identifying themselves outside of the business class and as part of an intellectual and moral elite, leisure professionals, academics, and intellectuals attempted to invest themselves with status and authority to guide and reeducate people "to other wants, other tastes, other ideals." Establishing themselves as disinterested and neutral observers, by being outside of the "centripetal" power of popular, or mass, culture they positioned themselves to look calmly and "scientifically" at the whole problem of leisure.[70]

The Depression revived and enhanced the age-old debate over the influence of technology and popular amusements on society, a debate in which the inertia of the economy could be personalized and blamed on the inertia of the American people, and the apparent decline of America as a producing nation could be attributed to the stagnation of the intellect in the face of a shift from traditional culture to modernity. How ubiquitous these discussions had become by 1934 was shown by sociologist Arthur Pack in 1934:

And precisely because this newly discovered leisure promises to become the universal fate of man, it has been widely and diversely discussed in editorials and magazines. It has become news. It has even become a political issue, one of the various features of the New Deal that can comfortably be discussed without the bitterness inherent in other current problems. The New Leisure has become a subject for the appointment of committees, the compiling of statistics, the conducting of nation-wide surveys. As a slogan for advertising, it has even been widely publicized—and with good reason. That simple phrase "New Leisure" comes to depression-worn mankind with almost irresistible seduction.[71]

The perception that leisure time was not simply a product of unemployment, but had become a permanent feature of modern industrial democracy, led nearly all writers to demand some sort of federal policy on leisure time. As criticism of laissez-faire industrial economics grew, laissez-faire attitudes to nonindustrial aspects of society also came under scrutiny. With leisure becoming a permanent feature of modern society, its assessment, regulation, measurement, and analysis assumed an unprecedented urgency, because the types of commercial amusements people enjoyed continued to grow despite the Depression. Control over the economy necessitated deeper understanding of the individual effects of modern industrialism, and many new statistical surveys were undertaken that would examine the impact of technology on the role of leisure in the everyday lives of Americans.[72] For the first time, social scientists attempted to analyze and quantify leisure by class, gender, race, and age—dividing the leisure experience into groups that would reveal how best to manage and control them. Responses and feelings were elicited using new theories of psychology and technical equipment in an unprecedented attempt to discover the peculiar attractions of mass leisure. Social scientists thus employed rigorous scientific analysis to perfect national planning for leisure.

In this way, play time now came under the same scrutiny that work time had under earlier scientific management. As discussed in the following chapters, the new government responded quickly to these calls for planning and control over nonwork time, implementing federal recreation programs as part of a broader national policy toward planned welfare and security for all. As leisure experts had shown, the key to recovery was deeply interwoven with the way Americans used their newfound leisure: although leisure was the problem, it was also to become the solution.

Chapter 2

Preparing for Spare Time

In 1931, few could imagine federal intervention in the new machine-made leisure, even if they could see its potential to rebuild the defeated nation. Concerned about the peril of this new leisure on the laboring classes, journalist Ralph Aiken of the *North American Review* discussed the double-edged view of leisure, where "likelihood is that those who lose their jobs to machinery will form a large class of parasites and accomplish nothing but degeneracy in their idleness," even though leisure was a "golden opportunity if the unemployed are now and in the future tactfully encouraged and influenced." Yet workers, "moping in breadlines and on street corners," were not visibly taking up the chance to use their "golden hours in the pursuit of learning," and government along with other authorities had a responsibility to make workers utilize their free time in ways profitable to both the individual and the nation. How this was to be done left Aiken wondering, for "people cannot be driven" in a democratic nation and so the possibility of making the unemployed use their minds remained in the realms of fantasy: "Can we imagine a system of doles wherein the recipient must be required to exhibit some intellectual proficiency or some crude work of art before he may receive his subsistence from the government? We can imagine it, but that is about all."[1]

Anxiety over the new leisure problem had reached fever pitch by the time Roosevelt was elected president in 1932. As reports and statistics had shown, the solution to the problem of leisure could be found in federal control: "Another problem . . . is the devising of ways and means of better governmental supervision and control of commercial amusements. This involves suitable measures of control over motion pictures and radio broadcasting, and the regulation of dance halls, pool and billiard rooms, cabarets and road houses, burlesque theaters, horse-racing and other forms of amusement provided on a commercial basis."[2]

In the summer of 1932, however, economic and social control appeared lost as more than twenty-thousand destitute war veterans assembled in Washington, D.C., to demand early payment of their army service bonuses. These "bonus marchers" became symbols of modern

America's "Forgotten Man." Veterans of a war where technology turned machines into mass murderers, the men had returned to a world where machinery had apparently rendered them useless and unemployed. As these anxieties began to show, the problem of leisure also became a problem of changing gender roles. On the one hand, because traditional femininity had become inscribed with an ideology of idleness and non-work, men now appeared emasculated by worklessness.[3] On the other hand, the very technologies of mass production appeared to have weakened the male as the primary producer; the "rudderless" American male could clearly be equated with the "rudderless" nation. Men displaced by machinery were visible everywhere, on the roadside, in soup kitchens, and stooping in breadlines. These widespread images of idle men confirmed the specter of revolution, middle-class job insecurity, and lack of political direction. Fears that modern Fordist methods of production had emasculated workers paralleled the fear that the traditional authority of the patriarch was in decline.

These fears were paramount in the crusade to purify recreation and create a "stronger" race of people who could physically and mentally bring the country out of the Depression. The need for strong leadership, a "rudder" to steer the aimless ship, appeared paramount to the survival of America as a powerful economy. The Forgotten Man thus became the symbol of the decade, a human victim of the waste that technology, war, and capitalism had created. "Unproductive" leisure, then, had by the 1930s escalated into a crisis of the highest order, where moral issues surrounding free time were pathologized into a disease that was manifested in the body and stoop of the Forgotten Man.[4] Franklin Roosevelt, in his radio address of April 1932, claimed that organizing for the needs of the Forgotten Man in the Depression was parallel to the organization of troops during the first world war: "It is high time to admit with courage that we are in the midst of an emergency at least equal to that of war. Let us mobilize to meet it."[5]

American intellectuals and social scientists pointed to the nation's free market economy as the primary cause of the economic catastrophe that had occurred. Fissures appeared in the Fordist dream of American welfare capitalism, leaving citizens vulnerable to a system based on ever-increasing consumption. Roosevelt promised a "new deal" for America. The new direction in government prominently utilized a gaming metaphor to describe the change in policy. Indicating that it could no longer be left to whimsical economic games—the spin of the wheel of fortune or the random acts of card playing—to decide the fate of the nation, the New Deal government sought to control work and leisure as a part of providing social and economic security for all. Michael Szalay has described how Roosevelt borrowed the "new deal" metaphor from a political

cartoon of 1931, which showed a farmer, a worker, and an "honest busi-
nessman" at a poker game, demanding a "new deal" from dishonest spec-
ulators and politicians.[6] Roosevelt used this expression to criticize the
insecurity of stock market speculation and to offer an alternative to the
haphazard playlike policies of his predecessors. As Szalay points out,
"Roosevelt believed that the American people were tired of games," and
in New Deal political thought "gambling epitomized laissez-faire economics" that many believed had led to mass unemployment and the
Depression. One aspect of this re-creation of government was a new
approach to recreation itself.

The limitations imposed on laissez-faire capitalism by the New Deal
government therefore provided reform professionals with the ideal environment in which to practice benevolent social control in line with earlier
play movement goals. Writer Harry Overstreet illustrated the conjunction between leisure reform and government through his objection to
laissez-faire leisure: "We have imported this *laissez faire* conception into
our treatment of the leisure activities of the unemployed. But it is obvious that where individuals are mentally and emotionally disintegrated
by worklessness, there is an obligation upon society to come to their aid
both with guidance and opportunity. We are beginning to be ready now
to believe that the body politic should take upon itself this new function
of organizing ways in which the leisure time of the unemployed can be
utilized."[7] Overstreet thus showed how this new function of government
to prevent irregular activities offered opportunities for change.

While severe unemployment made the issue of leisure a national crisis, the enactment in June 1933 of the National Industrial Recovery Act
(NIRA) intensified concerns. One aspect of the act was a limit on working hours, as Roosevelt attempted to cut surplus goods and provide employment for all by reducing the hours worked while increasing hourly
wages. In many ways, this measure signaled the administration's acceptance that unemployment had been caused by the overefficient machine
and that the "new leisure" was a permanent feature of modern industrial society, as so many sociologists had argued. Confirming this, the
sociologist Martin Neumayer stated that it "has been pretty well established that no matter how complete recovery may be we will never be
able to make full-time jobs for the entire working population of the
country."[8] Thus, the legislation also indirectly prompted a new recreation
policy, for with so many workers on limited hours, even those in employment had to have provisions made for their increased leisure time. Refer-
ring to the direct impact that the Recovery Act would have upon leisure,
George Cutten, sociologist and president of Colgate University, warned
in 1933, "With the N.R.A. enforcing a 35-hour week in industry, and
shorter hours coming, we have something real to consider. There are 112

waking hours in a week of seven days, 16 hours each. Subtract 35 hours for gainful labor and 21 for meals and there remain 56 hours with which a worker may do as he pleases. It will take something more than games or radio to keep 45,000,000 adults happy for 2912 hours a year, each."[9]

The sheer quantity of these hours enumerated by Cutten appeared alarming. Such expert warnings from sociologists and experts were heeded, for without guidance the new leisure—being something that the working classes did not know how to deal with—could result in crime and dissolution.

Popular magazines and periodicals fed these concerns back to the public. In August 1933, *The Literary Digest* concurred that one of the problems of the new leisure was the dearth of accurate statistics with which to operate. Underneath a picture of vast crowds on the beach at Coney Island a caption read: "It is impossible to obtain an accurate estimate of the number who seek recreation at New York's world-famous seaside playground during the summer months. On one Sunday in August no less than 259,251 passed through subway turnstiles to seek relief from city heat at Coney. The total is said to approach the million mark."[10] *The Literary Digest* stated that amateur statisticians totaled the new leisure hours at "some thirteen million per week" and summarized the reactions of the professional classes: "Keenly awake to the problems involved, ministers, social workers, psychologists and educators are devising 'first-aid' programs for the new leisured classes."[11]

Although there are no official documents to confirm that these articles and sociological texts were read by those in government, it is no coincidence that one week after the *Digest* article appeared, the President's Emergency Reemployment Campaign created the New York Committee on the Use of Leisure Time.[12] The popular clamor over leisure time and the increasing concern of sociologists had meant that one of the first acts of the new government, following the establishment of the National Recovery Administration (NRA), was concerned specifically with the problem of leisure. The committee held hearings at which professionals such as police officials, social workers, and educational and religious leaders gave evidence about the effect and use of leisure time. Chaired by Raymond B. Fosdick, the committee and its research received financial subsidy from the Rockefeller Foundation.[13]

Anxious not to create confusion, committee members were at pains to make it clear that the new leisure was not a clever metaphor for unemployment; real leisure could only come from better controls over employment, members claimed, and the New Deal, which had provided this leisure, would also provide guidance in, and make provisions for, the availability of right sort of recreational opportunities. The committee claimed that it was not there to dictate how people should enjoy their leisure but to listen to needs and help "men make handsome uses of their leisure." Working-class use of the new leisure time was a primary concern of the committee, illustrated Grover A. Whalen, New York city chairman of the President's Emergency Reemployment Campaign, in a *New York Times* article describing the effect of the NRA maximum hours ruling on various employees:

For instance, a large percentage of garment workers, who have been toiling in sweatshops as high as seventy hours a week, are about to return to work for a maximum of thirty-five hours weekly. What are they going to do with those thirty-five hours saved? In the gasoline field hundreds of thousands of men will be putting in not more than forty-eight hours instead of from sixty to seventy-two a week. Think of the countless small shops throughout the country in which salesmen and women have been putting in from fifty-four to sixty hours, who will now work no more than forty. Multiply these few illustrations by thousands and you begin to see the enormity of this problem of how we Americans are to use our new found leisure. . . . [The Committee on the Use of Leisure Time] may well affect the lives of 120,000,000 people of this nation for the years to come.[14]

Not everyone saw the importance of organized leisure, and many were affronted that intellectuals, sociologists, clergymen, and business leaders would deem themselves the new leaders of the nation's leisure activities at a time of chronic unemployment. The New York Committee on the Use of Leisure Time thereby came in for much ridicule in the popular press. Some of the resulting objections and comments were recorded in *Recreation* magazine, formerly called *The Playground,* the official voice of the playground and recreation movements. According to Howard Braucher, editor of *Recreation* and a committee member, the national response to the committee was disdain and indignation, ranging from outrage at attempts to Stalinize leisure to mockery at the pomposity of so-called recreation professionals.[15] Publishing some of the responses in *Recreation,* Braucher hoped to teach recreation leaders that their purpose was not to control but to respond to people's wishes and needs. Democracy in leisure was fundamental, he asserted, and the leisure leaders of the New Deal had their work cut out for them, showing people that they were there to respond to the protean needs of the American leisured masses, not to control or dictate.

One article reprinted in *Recreation* responded to the leisure committee by noting the hypocrisy of values, which sees "one class in society [as] a fit guardian of the leisure time of others," and a letter to the *Boston Herald* stated that the title of the committee sounded "like a public welfare satire."[16] An editorial in *The Nation* claimed that the devil "certainly has found work for idle hands to do," manifested in the time-wasting activities of the committee. "Leisure, it appears, has become a 'problem,'" the writer added, although the academics and social scientists "did not find it appropriate to consult the unemployed or the insufficiently employed as to the disposition of their leisure time, any more than the NRA Labor Board and the President could permit the automobile workers to control their jobs by establishing the closed shop." One consequence, it was ironically added, may be a "wave of strikes against this 'use' of leisure time, rivaling the present wave of industrial strikes; a kind of holy war against both the 'made-leisure' and 'used-leisure' activities." Conjuring up imaginary slogans that such strikers might employ, the article finishes with militant chants of "Down with Rockefeller-financed leisure!" and "Rhythmic dancing, my eye!"[17] Another *New Yorker* article ironically claimed that one use of the new leisure could be to serve on leisure committees.[18]

Less satirical responses to the issues raised by the committee were also widespread. Labor organizations had long been fighting for shorter working hours, and the NRA had brought this about. Many pointed out that more leisure would satisfy a "strong impulse for self-improvement among people whose experience has been limited."[19] Workers could compensate for limited educational opportunities by attending evening classes and undertaking further study, it was argued. Matthew Woll, vice president of the American Federation of Labor, stated that the Recovery Act was received with enthusiasm by the labor movement because it represented "a trend and a social philosophy to which Labor has promulgated for a generation and more." Seeing the gains in leisure time as a direct result of the victories of the labor movement, Woll emphasized that the fight for fewer hours was not just for rest and recuperation, or to help balance the economy, but to enable "the development of a full and rounded life" for all workers. His comments reflect the history of socialist self-betterment and equality that inflected the leisure reform movement around the turn of the century. Woll commented that the workers were less unprepared for leisure than many commentators held, arguing that, through its support of public schools, worker education, and union-sponsored recreational activities such as choruses and orchestras, art exhibits, work theaters, and library facilities, it was the labor movement that had shown New Deal officials the way forward.[20]

In fact, the support given to unions by the NRA and New Deal labor policy enabled the development of union-led cultural and recreation policies in an unprecedented way. As Michael Denning illustrates, although a few unions had developed recreational or educational programs prior to the Crash of 1929, the Congress of Industrial Organizations (CIO) cultural activities in the thirties turned the welfare capitalist programs of the 1920s into CIO-driven activities. Adopting these earlier programs, unions backed avant-garde theater, art exhibits, sports events, dances, and social events.[21]

Despite this, recreation experts claimed that the provision for recreation was woefully limited, and those out of work would not have access even to union-sponsored events. New philosophies concerning leisure, it was argued, necessitated increases in training and education of recreation workers so that programs would be properly organized. In many ways this professionalization refuted the ability of union officials to provide adequate facilities. *Recreation* magazine, as the official journal of recreation workers, argued that professional guidance in the new leisure was the most crucial way to maintain and enhance social stability and the general welfare. In contrast to earlier recreation policies, recreation workers were encouraged by the magazine to believe in a new interpretation of recreation that could contribute to the development of a "wholesome personality" even late into adulthood. Influenced by new theories of popular and mass psychology, and excited by the challenge of the new Depression-made leisure, *Recreation* contained articles describing the new crucial role for that previously neglected person, the recreation worker. As a social force, recreation could balance the personality and work to help people cope with the "storms of life," such as bereavement and financial ruin. As a salve to the condition of modernity, the proper use of leisure could aid the "mental hygiene" movement and act as a preventative of mental illness and other social ills.

Physicians and other medical experts concurred with *Recreation*'s outlook, publishing articles that claimed that the proper use of leisure would lower blood pressure and prevent "undesirable complexes" such as "neurasthenia and psychasthenia" and "Americanitis," disorders attributed to the intensity of modern technological living as well as unemployment.[22] One writer claimed that the introduction of hobbies to six boys in a reformatory suffering from hip disease and infantile paralysis enabled them to be "finally discharged, fully cured, six months before boys [without a hobby] similarly afflicted."[23] Aiding "personal engineering" by creating socially adjusted personalities, planned leisure along with planned communities could increase national capacity for useful and productive workers and citizens.[24]

Recreation gave broad sanction to the NRA's leisure policy and was clearly enthusiastic about the adoption of a national leisure program. Always interested in professionalizing the recreation worker's role into that of a social worker, psychologist, play specialist, teacher, and all-round community leader, the recreation movement celebrated its new alliance with federal government. The new relationship between the National Recreation Association and the National Recovery Administration, for example, was proudly pointed out in the magazine in a transcript of a radio broadcast by John H. Finley, associate editor of the *New York Times* and leisure committee member:

It is a coincidence which others must have noticed that the National Recovery Administration and the National Recreation Association have the same initials. They are both N.R.A. movements in that they both have a national construction and reconstruction purpose—the one an economic recovery primarily, the other a personal development or recovering of strength and of spirit. The second has a very definite and sequential relationship to the first. The National Recovery Act will shorten for millions the work period in the day and week. The National Recreation Association seeks to make possible the most beneficial use of the longer periods of leisure which the codes have suddenly provided. Having been devoting itself for a quarter of a century to this very problem of making joyous, creative and especially recreative use of leisure time for whole communities, it is prepared to be of service in this new era of man's freedom due to his enlarged free time.[25]

Finley's comments appear to respond to Aiken's desire to make workers utilize their free time in educational and cultural pursuits, yet to do so in ways that were fully compatible with a democratic society. These goals were at the forefront of government thinking as it began to search for models for New Deal recreation. Whatever way you looked at it, it was time for the government to take action. Only two years after Aiken's article, the New Deal government thus began instituting an unprecedented national leisure program that responded to the epidemic of Depression-made free time.

Mobilization and planning, however, was no simple thing. Many governments around the world had been trying to bring their countries out of severe Depression for much longer than America. At the same time, they had also been experimenting with national planning for mass leisure, some with apparently impressive results. The economic emergency that beset the nation required extensive social planning, and Europe, with its social experiments, welfare programs, and a longer history of deeply entrenched economic depression, could provide instances of the best, and the worst, models for recovery and reform. New Deal administrators thus turned to Europe for examples of national planning for mass leisure just as they were beginning to institute their own national leisure policy.

European Models for New Deal Leisure

Early in the formation of the New Deal, in order to get a better idea of the effects of welfare reform, Roosevelt sent Harry Hopkins (who would later head the Works Progress Administration [WPA]), to Europe to "look over housing and social insurance schemes in England, Germany, Austria and Italy, because I think you might pick up some ideas useful to us in developing our own plan for security."[26] Although Hopkins would have found that the problem of leisure was as crucial an issue in Europe as it was in the United States, he would also have found a variety of leisure and welfare models to choose from. Whereas the leisure policy of the WPA was later to become uniquely identified with the Roosevelt administration and democratic welfare government in general, alongside the twin domestic influences of progressive reform and corporate welfare, the experiments of left- and right-wing European governments, both totalitarian and democratic, provided interesting examples of state organized mass leisure for New Deal planners. Looking at these experiments in more detail sets into greater relief their impact on New Deal leisure programs.

ITALY

In the early thirties, Italy provided the most notable model of state organization for capitalist welfare. Following Mussolini's coup in 1922, the fascist dictator began a program of recreational organization that enabled him to centralize control over production and workers throughout Italy. Mussolini's rise to power and the fascist takeover in Italy during the 1920s provided a striking illustration of the battle to assert control over leisure time. Mussolini's nationalization of leisure, however, was modeled on the rationalization of American industrial systems such as those developed by Ford. As historian Victoria De Grazia demonstrates in her detailed study of the Opera Nazionale Dopolavoro (OND; National Agency on After-Work), "As an idea, the *dopolavoro* was the American-inspired invention of a technocratic reformer" and was influenced by the ideology of American technocracy and social engineering in the post-World War I period.[27] State-sponsored recreation facilities were developed that were initially modeled on Henry Ford's sociology department, but that eventually went further by aiming to become centers of "uplift," of recreation and instruction, for entire communities.[28] From 1925 onward, the goal became no less than the creation of a nationalized leisure network for "reeducating the laboring masses of all Italy."[29] By 1935, "Fascist Sunday" was introduced, which ended the work week at 1 P.M. on Saturday to allow an afternoon of "instructional activities."[30]

The OND expanded immensely between 1927and 1929, becoming involved in a whole range of social services: "instruction (divided between popular culture and vocational training), artistic education (with subsections for amateur theatre, music, cinema, radio and folklore), physical education (including sports and tourism), and assistance (concentrating on housing, consumer affairs, health and hygiene, social insurance, and company recreational facilities)."[31] Women were targeted with special leisure programs for producing fitness in the home, producing babies, and performing industrial work when required. Two kinds of programs were developed to target both working women and housewives that would consolidate state policy to ease women from the industrial workforce and into the home and to facilitate the scientific management of the home while countering falling birthrates.[32] The OND also concerned itself with consumer education and control, aiming to restore the economy and enable economic planning of the growing mass market through simple methods of control. Gradually, the fascist organization of leisure penetrated all forms of popular recreation as well as reviving others: "Activity by activity, fascism after 1927 gradually developed a de facto policy toward all existing popular recreational pastimes, from choral singing to bowls. An incessant publicity on behalf of formally organized activity was accompanied by vigorous promotional efforts to engage groups in outside events sponsored locally and nationally by the OND."[33] Folklore sections were created to "revive" nationalist sentiments, and cheap day trips, bicycle tours, and "popular trains" were subsidized to stimulate tourism and invoke national pride through pleasure.[34]

In America, Mussolini's program received general admiration, which lasted until Hitler's takeover and Mussolini's undeniably aggressive foreign policy in Ethiopia. *Fortune* magazine dedicated a whole issue in July 1934 to Fascist Italy, claiming that "the Corporative State is to Mussolini what the New Deal is to Roosevelt."[35] As Benjamin Alpers has noted, reform-minded liberals in the 1920s, including Charles Beard, Horace M. Kallen, and Herbert Croly, fleetingly considered Italian fascism as a possible solution to the problems of modern society. At the start of the Depression, during fears of total social collapse, Mussolini's apparent restoration of order to Italy made a number of American conservatives also sympathetic to the idea of dictatorship.[36] Both nations were in the depths of economic recession, and Roosevelt wrote to the American-Italian ambassador in 1933 that "there seems no question that he is really interested in what we are doing and I am much interested and deeply impressed by what he has accomplished."[37]

Germany

Although the Third Reich was still in its infancy during Hopkins's visit, Hitler's mass organization of leisure in the 1930s came to surpass the system organized by Mussolini, so that by the time Roosevelt commissioned a study of Hitler's leisure policy in 1938 the Nazi doctrine had incorporated a fully fledged system of totalitarian nationalized state leisure.[38]

Shortly following his ascension to power, Hitler formed the Labor Front, a nationalized employer and labor union, and the only legal union organization allowed in the Third Reich. Controlling working conditions, wages, and all aspects of the production process, the Labor Front set about to control the nonwork time of the entire nation. Leisure and physical fitness formed an underlying ideology in the formation of the Labor Front, which aimed to "build up Germans mentally and physically" and to secure their good health. Louis Bader, sociologist at New York University, explained to Americans in 1937 that "undernourished, broken-down, and tired women and children are given vacations in the country where they can receive good air, light, and plenty of good food which it is hoped, along with rest and recreation, will restore them to good health."[39]

While banning other trade unions, the Labor Front appropriated the tradition of organized workers' sports and leisure that had emerged from socialist organized leisure in the nineteenth century.[40] Kraft durch Freude (KdF), the Strength Through Joy leisure program, was funded through compulsory deductions from workers' wages, assuming the cultural activities of the Nazi Kulturgemeinde (the Propaganda Ministry). Through a network of subsidies and organizations, the KdF controlled nonwork activities throughout Germany. With 20 million members, the program organized activities in five distinct areas: excursions and travel; sports facilities and activities, cultural activities such as theater and cinema, "popular" and worker education, and the development of a low-priced automobile, the KdF-Wagen—eventually known as the VolksWagen, or people's car. One of the KdF's most famous projects, the KdF-Wagen (or the "Strength Through Joy Car") illustrated the direct influence of Ford's corporate welfare strategy. The people's car, like the Model T, was to be offered for payment on an installment plan and made in such quantities that all Germans would be able to own one.

The Strength Through Joy program was split into two offices—the Office for Leisure Time and the Office for Popular Education—both of which worked together to offer low-paid workers access to the same recreational and cultural activities as the elite. At the same time, the office monitored and enforced higher safety and work conditions from employers. Like Mussolini, Hitler used the form and organizational style of free labor unions to penetrate further into the popular culture of German society and, like Mussolini, he combined this strategy with aspects of corporate welfare policy that offered higher wages, fewer hours, and worker welfare. This two-pronged approach to the productive process appeared, by 1938, to have led Germany from economic disaster to become the world's leading industrialized nation. Yet, for the price of increased leisure and welfare, the German worker had to forego the right to free labor organizing.

Still interested in the German "experiment" with leisure in 1938, the American ambassador to Germany, Hugh R. Wilson, commissioned an extensive report for Roosevelt of the Strength Through Joy program and activities. The report was conducted by the embassy's "Mr. Beam," who took part in Strength Through Joy activities and excursions as research for the document, under supervision from the KdF office. The lengthy document produced a fascinating description of the extent to which the Nazi government had taken control of leisure. Funded by worker contributions, albeit compulsorily, the system meant that workers were in fact paying for state-funded amusements under the guise that leisure was centrally subsidized. Wage increases, the KdF claimed, would only be spent foolishly, and the KdF control of leisure would provide value-for-money beneficial leisure that was good for productivity and the community. Despite this, the program had mass appeal and appeared, at least on the surface, to be more philanthropic than political. The Office for Travel, Hiking and Vacations, for example, offered subsidized travel and holidays at one-fourth to one-fifth of the cost of ordinary travel and enabled workers, who had the legal right to annual paid vacations, the chance to go on a number of trips. Mr. Beam found that in 1937, "Strength Through Joy trips attracted over 10,000,000 participants, the shorter trips being particularly well patronized. Strength through Joy owns five ocean-going ships (including two luxurious vessels built to its specifications), charters six more, and possesses as well a vast bulk of other facilities in its own buses, vacation villas and a giant sea bath for 20,000 workers now being built on Rugen."[41]

While the KdF sponsored luxury cruises to the Mediterranean as well as the Norwegian fjords, many workers could still not afford the longer trips, and a class system of travel was still fully present despite Nazi claims to have created "classless" travel and tourism.

Strength Through Joy also participated in the promotion of national health through the sponsorship of sports activities and facilities. In 1937, about 8 million workers took part in these sports. Factories were required to provide sports fields and athletic facilities, create competitive leagues, and offer instructional classes to the workers. Large numbers of sports teachers and instructors were trained and employed by the KdF, who provided the physical accompaniment to the mental improvement offered by the Office for Popular Education. Like sports, popular education often took place within the factory itself, supplemented by "popular education stations" outside of the factory gate. Workers could learn a foreign language, practice amateur photography, and have lessons in music, painting, or sculpture for a nominal fee. Lectures on German history and world politics and cultural visits to museums, art galleries, and factories were also intended to instill the precepts of Nazi philosophy and German national pride.

Cultural stimulation was also available in the huge quantity of subsidized theater and cinema. Strength Through Joy helped to organize "factory concerts, community singing, costume and dance festivals and broadcasts by amateur musicians; to send traveling theatrical companies and motion-pictures out into the country districts; and generally to help workers spend their spare time pleasurably and profitably."[42] Of "special interest" to the American embassy was the way in which the KdF was "bringing about a kind of back-to-the-theater movement," where ordinary workers were offered cheap access to all types of performances.[43] The variety of performances varied from burlesque and slapstick to "the Peoples' Opera" and the Reich Orchestra in Berlin. In village locations citizens had access to performances and motion pictures made available by traveling "automobile trains," sponsored by the KdF, "giving them the latest news reels, dramatic, cultural or political films at a cost of 20 or 30 pfennigs."[44] Likewise, local talent was employed by the KdF to provide radio broadcasts of amateur hours and other volunteer performances such as community singing, folk-dancing festivals, musical recitals, and fashion shows. Hobby and handicraft circles were also encouraged by the program, resulting in local exhibitions of arts and crafts. As a result of the huge growth of revenues from the combined attendance at such cultural events, performers were able to obtain social benefits "such as sickness insurance and old-age pensions which are in part paid for by the surcharge of 5 pfennigs on every theater ticket."[45]

On September 3, 1938, Roosevelt wrote to Hugh Wilson to thank him for the KdF report, at one point remarking, "I am making it the basis of a broader study from our own point of view over here. . . . [T]his helps us in planning, even though our methods are of the democratic variety!"[46] The ambassador's report was then sent to Hopkins for summary analysis. The official response to the report came from Aubrey Williams, Hopkins's deputy administrator, in a memorandum that highlighted the differences between the leisure policy of the WPA and the KdF, despite certain similarities: "The activities described in this report are, for the most part, in themselves desirable and many of them are a part of our own leisure time program as carried on through federal, local and private agencies and more particularly through the WPA recreational projects in this country. It is the motivation, method, and goal that is different."[47]

Williams's response emphasized that the differences were significant in that the leisure-time activities operated by the Nazis were to compensate workers for low wages and lack of free labor organization, and the Nazis restricted membership of the group to Aryans, while the leisure activities of the WPA were enabling to workers, making them aware of their capacities as citizens and allowing wide participation of all groups, classes, and people of all political and religious affiliations. Nevertheless, he concluded, "disagreement with the fundamental philosophy of National Socialism should not blind us to the interesting aspects of their activities in the recreational field. It should be possible to adapt what is good in their leisure time program to our own democratic institutions without confusion of purpose, so long as the fundamental distinctions outlined above are clearly recognized. Actually, most of their activities have been simultaneously developed in this country, without dominant stress on centralized control and standardized practices."[48]

Nazi Germany provided an example of organized mass leisure that went unrivaled by any nation in the 1930s. By 1936, the KdF hosted the World Congress for Leisure Time in Berlin and provided a leisure model for all industrialized nations. Yet, while increased productivity and industrial peace appeared to reign in the apparently conflict-free German factory, the success came at the high cost of worker freedom, racial exclusion, and democracy. The control of after-work activities in Germany illustrated the extent to which culture had become politics, and the U.S. response illustrated that the way a nation planned its state-organized leisure had become a benchmark of democracy.

Soviet Union

The covert politicization of leisure in Germany and Italy appeared, on one level, in total contrast to the cultural policy of the Soviet Union, where culture was openly treated as an arm of the state and a weapon of the masses in the fight for freedom. Since Lenin's proclamation of an eight-hour day following the 1917 Bolshevik Revolution, there was little question that class action would lead to more leisure time for all workers.[49] Marxists around the world saw the Soviet Union as the model nation, providing workers with true opportunities and facilities for noncapitalist leisure pursuits. In the optimism of the post-Bolshevik Revolution era, the Soviet experiment promised to provide the first example of mass social engineering based on Marxist principals, and with that provide new forms of proletarian leisure that enhanced, rather than diminished, workers' freedom.

From 1928 to 1940, Stalin intensified a program of state monopoly over cultural entertainment and leisure activities, prioritizing fitness and leisure through official sponsorship for the first time. In tandem with a huge industrialization drive and farm collectivization, rational leisure and worker fitness was encouraged by new physical culture programs. The public and ceremonial nature of this new fitness regime was illustrated in 1931, when the first Physical Culture Day parade was held in Red Square.[50] Beginning in 1933, compulsory physical education was introduced into schools, and "exercise programs printed in Soviet newspapers and magazines" appeared, along with exercise programs on the radio.

By 1936, Stalin had formed the All-Union Committee on Physical Culture and Sports. As Lynn Attwood and Catriona Kelly have put it, "The culture of the Stalin period required not only the reconstruction of cities . . . but also [of] the human body," where "public parades by trim young *fizkul'turniki* [gymnasts] with their human pyramids and mass exercises were also intended as powerful representations of a fit new society, of the healthy state of the Soviet body politic."[51] During the reurbanization of the Soviet Union, Stalin created a new official Soviet culture, building free leisure parks with state-approved rational entertainment for the masses. Like his dictatorial counterparts in Western Europe, he requisitioned and fetishized folk culture to the utility of the state, with leisure reform underpinning his drive to increase productivity and nationalist sentiment. Imported capitalist forms of entertainment were censored or banned. The workers' freedom to self-expression and right to human fulfillment—so central to Marx's writing—was subsumed in the pressing of culture into the service of the state and constituted a complete denial of the brutality, famine, murder, and misery that had become a dominant feature of Soviet life.

The Depression in America acted as a catalyst for increased interest in Stalin's first five-year plan (1928–33), and, at least until the Nazi-Soviet pact and the revelation of Stalin's atrocities, the Soviet example continued to have currency for many left-wing Americans. Many social scientists whose research underpinned the ideology of the New Deal were favorably impressed with developments in the Soviet Union. Economists Stuart Chase and Rexford Tugwell, among other intellectuals, reported positively back from the Soviet Union, following a visit in 1927. At the end of his 1932 book, *A New Deal*, Chase asked, "Why should Russians have all the fun remaking the world?" The Soviet example underlay many suggestions for economic planning by American socialists.[52]

Solidarity with the Soviet Union was expressed in the United States during the 1930s as social experimentation with forms of anticapitalist and noncommercial leisure and culture. Broad left-wing alignment under the antifascist Popular Front during the second half of the decade had a huge impact on the development of welfare and the cultural policies of the WPA.[53] Influenced by socialist precepts over the role of culture, "art with a purpose"—in other words, art and culture that pushed forward a broad proletarian agenda—became a dominant theme of cultural production at this time. Commercial leisure was always problematic for the Left, who saw it as alienating and balked at the profit motive behind it. Proletarianism and social realism became prominent forms for the avant-garde, and state-sponsored art projects featured figurative murals and folklore themes that would not have seemed out of place in

Stalin's Moscow. Despite significant, and fundamental, historical differences between the two nations, the influence of the Soviet experiment with alternative modes of cultural production remained strong on American intellectuals' views of leisure and culture throughout the 1930s.

BRITAIN

Not all experiments with leisure came from welfare capitalism or fascism. Like other European nations, Britain in the 1920s and 1930s saw the rise of all forms of leisure in commercial, voluntary, and public spheres.[54] Socialism, trade unionism, and worker cooperatives played a significant role in the development of sport and leisure in Britain. The labor movement always saw leisure as an important feature of working-class life and attempted to offer worker education and uplift in broadly Marxist terms. Marxist summer schools, for example, offered bathing, boating, hiking, socials, popular lectures, and worker outings. Unions planned leisure to consolidate worker solidarity as well as to provide an alternative to capitalist "distractions." Socialists offered critiques of capitalist leisure in all its forms as a tool that worked to solidify the power of capital. A planned socialist system of production, it was believed, would inevitably lead to better provision of free leisure activities.

In many ways, Britain's democratic experiments with unemployment insurance, welfare, and the socialization of leisure and recreation provided America with a test case for its own welfare programs. Yale social scientist E. Wight Bakke went to Greenwich in East London to study the effects of unemployment insurance on workers' lives and attitudes. Bakke reported that the insurance had not led to an increase in "pauperization," or idle loafing, and that insurance provided security that offset the dangers of fear over unemployment. His positive response to welfare, published in America in 1933, emphasized the importance of leisure for helping the unemployed adjust to new roles in the family and society.[55]

Ideologies of leisure formulated from the left offered workers the chance to participate in non-capitalist or non-commercial leisure. For example, the active communist, socialist, and labor movements led to the formation of the British Workers' Sports Federation in 1923 that enabled workers to participate in sport on an international basis. Formally associated with the elite "leisure-class," many of these sports became available to the working classes for the first time. Promoting worker fitness and the ideology of brotherhood, participation in sport helped to fulfill socialist agendas for full citizenship. Keeping workers mentally and physically fit for the class struggle—and later as a way of maintaining a united front against fascism—recreation reform ideology functioned equally well in a variety of political contexts.[56]

The 1920s and 1930s were "halcyon years" for the formation of cooperative societies that in turn spawned recreation societies—offering those on low incomes access to swimming, gymnasiums, football, cycling, tennis, and rambling. The socialist alternative to the Boy Scout movement, Woodcraft Folk, was established in 1925, and recreation and sociability was frequently linked to capitalist critique.[57] Class struggle fed the growth of rambling associations, for example, where workers fought the landed elite for access to the countryside. While socialist and communist ideologies differed, the labor movement operated to counteract the effect of "bourgeois" leisure practices on the workers.

While commercial recreation, corporate recreation, and labor recreation all increased, so too did state regulation of sport and leisure. As an outgrowth of welfare capitalism, recreation expanded an arm of national and local government. By the 1930s, sports and recreation were a compulsory part of the British school curriculum, and by 1937 the Physical Training and Recreation Act instituted a national plan for recreation, forming the National Fitness Council. The following year, the Holidays with Pay Act gave workers the legal right to paid vacations. In 1938, the Trades Union Congress president called for an agency of the state directly concerned with leisure, saying, "I should like to see a Minister of Leisure appointed, who would have under his control, all problems of leisure time: recreation, educational and cultural."[58] Although union organizing and campaigns for lower working hours had been successful, the benefit to the state of having a fit workforce in preparation for a possible European war was not insignificant.[59] This bureaucratization intensified as governments recognized the role of national leisure for propaganda, and its part in foreign affairs was highlighted when the British government, in an act of appeasement to Hitler, instructed the English football team to give the Nazi salute in 1938.[60]

While fascism and dictatorship took hold in much of Europe, however, Americans looked to Roosevelt, not for military dictatorship, but for strong leadership modeled on traditional patriarchal family roles.[61] Thus, the Forgotten Man was also a lost child who would be brought to manhood through welfare and state planning. In this context, leisure-time activities were seen as fundamental to rebuilding the family and reinvigorating strong leadership, all necessary to make America internationally, as well as nationally, strong again.

When Harry Hopkins returned from his European trip in August 1934, he had decided that the social experiments in the rest of the world would not fit the New Deal policy: "It is clear that we have to do this in an American way," he stated, and "instead of copying foreign schemes we have to devise our own."[62] Democratic leisure, while organized, broadly reformist, and funded from tax revenues, had the tricky tasks of distinguishing itself from the organization of totalitarian leisure, of providing free but noncoercive leisure for the poor and unemployed, and at the same time allowing private industry to recoup the losses from the 1929 crash. Yet, despite Hopkins's exceptionalist rhetoric, many of the same principles lay beneath the New Deal "Americanization" of leisure as had underpinned those "foreign schemes."

Compared to European provision and planning for leisure, America appeared woefully lacking. Organized recreation schemes sponsored by private industry had gone into decline since the start of the Depression, and sociologists strove to fill the gap with more permanent, more scientifically based government-sponsored efforts. In her WPA training manual for recreation workers, Dorothy Cline pointed out the limitations of the recreation movement of the 1920s. Even though local governments were spending increasing amounts on playgrounds, swimming pools, and parks, municipal recreation programs were confined mostly to big cities, employed few trained recreation professionals, and provided inadequate education. Despite the money being poured into the construction of new facilities, programs were limited in scope, and little qualitative or scientific assessment of needs and benefits took place. Recreation mostly involved children, sports, and playgrounds. The scale of unemployment during the Depression made these facilities appear barely adequate for children, let alone the adult population with so much time on their hands.

Cline pointed out the dearth of leisure facilities and national provision. Up until the Depression, public recreation had been mostly the concern of charities, churches, and municipal governments. The only federal agencies that had been involved in recreation were the National Park Service, the National Forest Service, and the Extension Service of the Department of Agriculture (which provided volunteer leaders in rural recreation programs). The onset of the Depression brought a simultaneous halt to any locally sponsored efforts and a growing need for more geographically and socially comprehensive programs for small towns and rural areas, as well as big cities, that included adults as well as children. The unprecedented amount of leisure time prompted by mass unemployment created new problems that local and private organizations were unequipped to deal with, and the government thus stepped in. Describing the creation of the New Deal recreation programs, Cline stated, "There were two major reasons why the federal government turned the spotlight on recreation leadership with the initiation of a works program. In the first place, policy-makers appreciated the urgent need for providing decent and respectable jobs for white-collar workers. Second, the people who directed this program saw in it an opportunity to tackle the problem of leisure, an opportunity to expand the frontier of American culture by giving expression to the natural and basic interests of the American people."[63]

Many publications in the early 1930s echoed Cline's view that leisure would play a crucial role in the economic resuscitation. As I have discussed in the previous chapter, technocrats called for more planning in leisure as well as the economy, while educators saw the new leisure as way of combating mental and physical breakdown associated with unemployment. Thus, New Deal rhetoric calling for federally funded economic safeguards dovetailed with recreation reform rhetoric about the proper use of leisure. "When the young folks are taught the worth and ways of recreation," said reformer Charles Loomis Dana, "they are taking out an insurance policy against nervous disorders, and in middle-age, when they come to collect, they will find themselves reimbursed a hundredfold."[64] Social security adopted the same paternalistic imagery of a caring society that was a mainstay of official recreation publications, where statistics of accidents during unsupervised play, for example, were used to gain increased funding for leisure facilities and justify organized programs.[65] With proper New Deal planning Americans could expect safety and security in their non-work as well as working hours.

The New Deal thereby implemented the most extensive recreation program that had ever been seen in America, by funding, via the Federal Emergency Relief Administration (FERA) and WPA, the first federal recreation program. Although never going so far as nationalized leisure on a European scale, the program aimed at encouraging the unemployed to use their free time to improve their physical, artistic, and intellectual capabilities. In line with federal plans to improve economic security of all Americans, properly used leisure became a way to provide insurance against the pitfalls of laissez-faire capitalism but also to counter the totalitarianism of the sort gaining momentum throughout Europe. National security and economic stability, some argued, was established by the proper use of leisure, which balanced the extremes of individualism and totalitarianism: "It is leisure that saves us from the impossible choice between two equally unacceptable alternatives—complete regimentation and suicidal individualism. . . . Leisure is the best guarantee of security because it tends to make some degree of regimentation tolerable, always provided leisure itself is not regimented but left for the free expression of the individual within us."[66]

While wary of dictating the leisure activities of a democratic society, recreation experts, sociologists, economists, and reformers, both religious and political, demanded some kind of intervention and increased funding for recreation programs from the federal government in order to create a new national security through educating for leisure.[67]

Although attempts to direct the proper use of leisure were not unique to this decade, the scale and degree of government and professional involvement in those efforts were. Despite fears of fascism and totalitarianism, a significant commitment now existed to the idea of officially sanctioned and regulated mass leisure. Thus, understanding the social and economic functions of leisure became a central concern of the state during this period. The expansion of leisure time needed forethought and planning, many argued, as well as effective social control of recreation trends. Leisure professionals focused on the crucial question "How far is it possible to develop among the mass of the people leisure time interests that would lead to a wise use of leisure?"[68] To ensure that this question was addressed, the leisure professional assumed the increasingly important role of devising the "ways and means of better governmental supervision and control of commercial amusements."[69] Far surpassing previous notions of the trained professional teaching individuals the skill of play, this new governmental role demanded that skills of statecraft and policy making be brought to bear in the pursuit of a proper national leisure policy. In an era of welfare and constructive national planning, the leisure of the New Deal appeared to offer not only more amusement but an opportunity to harness nonworking time to public service.[70]

Chapter 3

National Recovery of Recreation

The New Deal government began a massive plan for recovery by funding huge programs to rebuild and remake the nation. Although many of these were labeled as "work" relief, they often had as much to do with the new use of leisure time as with work. As a sign of the new government's commitment to leisure and recreation, funding was soon made available for the more "nonessential" leisure and cultural programs that characterized the New Deal era. Recreation was of central importance to WPA administrator Harry Hopkins, who allocated at least 30 percent of the WPA budget (around $11 billion in all by 1943) toward recreation projects. While New Deal construction projects worked to repair or build more than two thousand swimming pools and create parks, playgrounds, stadiums, grandstands, bleachers, fairgrounds, athletic fields, tennis courts, golf courses, ice-skating rinks, ski runs, and bandstands, the recreation projects were concerned chiefly with organizing leadership programs so that facilities could receive proper use and supervision.[1] State-sponsored recreation projects, begun by the Civil Works Administration and Federal Emergency Relief Administration in the early 1930s, were continued and expanded by the WPA in 1935. Despite the abandonment of the NRA in 1935, debates surrounding leisure continued to remain pertinent, for, as one sociologist remarked, the "demand for a six-hour day and a five-day week again came to the front and has been made a paramount objective by organized labor."[2]

By 1938, employment on recreation projects averaged thirty-eight thousand people, including supervisors, leaders, and custodial and clerical workers. Programs were conducted in every state apart from Maine and in more than half of the three thousand counties of the country. During one week in February 1939, WPA recreation projects were in operation in 7,085 communities and thus covered nearly 70 percent of all urban areas and just over 35 percent of all rural communities.[3]

The attempt to coordinate leisure led to a complicated system of leisure management that was officially sanctioned but not dominated by federal policy. However, leisure activities organized by a wide variety of groups were offered centralized planning and support via the WPA.[4] This did not mean complete standardization. Rather, WPA workers were sent out to develop local grassroots networks so that existing community recreation projects were given support and guidance, while new projects were initiated where provision was seen as negligible. Coordination of the various New Deal agencies concerned with public works, education, and art allowed for a more effective network of leisure facilities throughout the United States—where workers from the Federal Theater Project, for example, would be loaned to the recreation division to improve the provision of "informal dramatics" in leisure projects.[5] Other projects such as the Civilian Conservation Corps and projects run by the National Youth Administration also included educational and recreational programs, adding even greater numbers to those involved in New Deal–sponsored leisure. The "manly" pursuits promoted by the recreation managers of the Civilian Conservation Corps are good examples of how leisure was to be ideally used by young men. Single-sex sports and games, manual crafts, and some formal education—all supervised by recreation trainers—were heavily prescribed.

Increasing leisure hours had created the need to instruct youth in constructive leisure-time activities, claimed educator Howard Oxley, and "in Negro CCC camps, arts and crafts, music, dramatics, the reading of books, discussion groups, sports and hiking parties have been introduced as leisure-time pursuits."[6] Youth learned the arts of leathercraft, woodwork, metalwork, and furniture making, visited towns to entertain civic and social organizations with their "glee clubs" and orchestras, attended lectures on social diseases, personal hygiene, and diet. Social evenings, where young women were invited, were used as the "basis for instruction in social etiquette."[7]

The education system also reflected this new significance of leisure. With increased sponsorship of leisure programs, there developed new university courses for training leisure leaders.[8] The new social function of leisure and recreation also necessitated planning new school curricula.[9] Educational sociologist Henry Harap wrote new programs that enabled schools to cultivate wise recreational habits among young people by encouraging active recreation, hiking, dramatics, folk dancing, arts, and crafts. Most notably, the recreation habits to be formed were those that provided an antidote to commercialized recreation. In all areas of welfare and education, recreation became the vital way to transform society. The formation of the Society of Recreation Workers in the mid-thirties was a sign that recreation had truly come of age.[10]

The New Deal recreation projects served many purposes. On one level, they created construction work and, when finished, provided cheap and healthy leisure for both the employed and unemployed. On another level, they provided unemployed white-collar workers and professionals with jobs and training in leadership and management skills.[11] Leadership initiatives were set up to recruit and train recreation professionals such as the "well-informed leader" at the 1939 Golden Gate International Exposition, shown in Figure 2.

Moreover, in conjunction with WPA education programs, the projects aimed to involve more adults in community recreation and to encourage cultural, social, and educational amusement rather than solely physical recreation. Recreation, it was claimed, was the panacea for modern society at all levels, an antidote to crime, disease, fascism, and social instability.

"The chief function of the State recreation programs," claimed youth expert Katherine Glover, "is to provide employment for recreation workers whose services are available to agencies, such as State departments of education, welfare commissions, park boards, etc."[12] Training conferences and programs were held throughout the country to advise

2. Leadership initiatives were set up to recruit and train recreation professionals such as this "well-informed leader" at the WPA stand at the Golden Gate International Exposition in 1939. Photo from *Report of WPA Activities of the Golden Gate International Exposition*. Courtesy National Archives, Pacific Region, NRHS-69-NCWPA-BOOK.

recreation leaders on setting up local recreation councils. Experts trained by the WPA were made available to other federal agencies in a nation-wide effort toward closer cooperation in recreational developments. Group recreational activities were undertaken by a number of federal agencies alongside the WPA, such as the National Youth Administration, the Civilian Conservation Corps, the National Park Service, and the Department of the Interior.[13] The WPA projects, however, provided "a splendid opportunity to bring America's cultural and recreational activities into closer harmony" and became a national effort toward recreational uplift and improvement.[14]

By 1938, most recreation projects operated in a devolved way, managed on the state level, with one official sponsor—usually the state department of education or public welfare or the state university—and numerous local cosponsors, such as municipal commissions who worked in close cooperation with advisory councils or lay committees. The official state sponsor of the program had to furnish one-fourth of the cost of the program, with the rest coming from the WPA, though all but 3 percent of the WPA money had to be used for the wages of relief workers employed on the projects.[15] One WPA report that year claimed that "over 2,500 such committees are now active in helping to determine community leisure-time needs, in promoting public participation, in planning programs, and in training workers." WPA trained leaders organized recreation councils composed of private individuals and representatives of groups such as churches, fraternal lodges, boys' and girls' clubs, schools, libraries, park boards, and trade unions and acted to make the program an integral part of community life.[16] In the state of Wisconsin, for example, the WPA divided the state into five regions, placing a qualified recreation supervisor in each to promote and coordinate all activities in the region, as well as assist in setting up municipal departments of recreation. The duty of the recreation department was also to supervise and train for recreation programs in all state institutions.[17]

As antifascism gained momentum, this type of organization was increasingly emphasized in comparison to fascist European leisure programs. Eduard Lindeman, director of the WPA Recreation Division and professor of social philosophy at the New York School of Social Work, increasingly emphasized the role of community: "The true whole is the local communal or community where people live life, where experience is a kind of flow of events in which specialists play their part but in which people don't think of each other primarily as specialists . . . where experience takes the form of a kind of rhythm of detail."[18] Photos taken of WPA recreation show very few crowds or large groups and emphasize the activities of artisans and community dancing rather than group gymnastics or athletics, which were so prominent in images of fascist Europe.

Individual self-control through leisure rather than the regimented crowd came to illustrate America's democracy of leisure—a Popular Front of leisure activities—where personal expression was directed for the benefit of the community.

In this way, recreation projects attempted to diffuse accusations of government interference in community leisure and to create a "grassroots" approach to the national problem. For, as recreation professionals had counseled, superimposed models of recreation generally received little enthusiasm or interest.[19] "Such control as there is we want as self-control," stated Howard Braucher in *Recreation*, as "some of us would rather live in a bad world than in a world made good by compulsion."[20] Other sociologists, however, admitted that proper leisure could only be taught with some form of social control in place. "To provide facilities for wholesome recreation, to control and redirect the tendencies to promote undesirable amusements . . . can be achieved without seriously thwarting or hampering freedom of action," stated Martin Neumayer, "for social control . . . aids individuals in their search for legitimate pleasures."[21]

Thus, one of the major problems facing federal recreation programs was directing and disciplining the uneducated masses at leisure and at the same time fashioning a democracy of leisure, where individuals could use leisure time as they wished. Trying to avoid comparison with fascist programs by their detractors, recreation professionals trod a careful line between guidance and control. Proper management was crucial to maintaining this balance, and professional leadership training became a priority of the federal projects. The goal was to create managers who would then organize community recreation projects along professional lines. To that end, the government set up training programs for recreation professionals, who were in turn instructed to single out natural leaders from the communities in which they operated who could guide and instruct their peers. Leadership was of utmost importance during this "peculiar period," according to Eduard Lindeman, because otherwise "governorship gets into the hands of irrational people as it has in so many places in Europe today," and "whole groups of people lose their rational basis, and that is what is happening now."[22]

In contrast to many of their contemporaries in Europe, leisure professionals in the United States attempted to fit their views on beneficial mass leisure into a peculiarly American democratic framework, which validated personal rather than communal freedom. Quoting Emerson and Tocqueville in his speeches, Lindeman evoked an image of community leisure based on the founding principles of American democracy. Standardized "automatons" created by mass leisure and propaganda programs were not the aim of democratic leisure, Lindeman claimed in 1939, but opportunities for individual growth through leisure had become a prerequisite of a democratic society. "Democracy and recreation are alike in spirit, and each tends to promote and strengthen the other," stated George Butler in his expansive review of community recreation published in 1940.[23]

While arguing for increased government involvement in leisure, many other recreation professionals also insisted that this did not mean "mass production" of community leisure. Believing that once people were given the opportunity they would follow the "natural" path that was so apparent to the professional, the role of government was to provide for "healthy" and "appropriate" leisure pursuits while limiting undesirable diversions and temptations that were not "natural."[24] Mental breakdown en masse, instability, and imbalance were partly caused by modern life, Lindeman claimed, as "life becomes more artificial where you use automobiles, street cars and trains. When your relationship is no longer directly with nature, your physical development becomes unsymmetrical."[25] Thus, in an unnatural world, the "natural" art of playing needed to be taught by experts working with the community. Organized activities that brought participants closer to nature were heavily promoted as one way of readjusting the unbalanced individual. Society was compared to an organism that would evolve more organically once the unnatural influences created by consumerism and industrialism were removed or negated through recreation. Professionals attempted to inspire activities by evoking the image of the traditional, rural, and communal past where such pursuits were enjoyed.

At the same time, however, recreation projects were seen as vital in rural areas as much as in cities. By 1936, the National Recreation Association held recreation institutes in the training of rural leaders at the request of the Department of Agriculture. Two workers held full-time posts at these institutes, which ran programs that trained in music, drama, folk games, social recreation, and dancing. Archery, wood carving, handicraft, amateur photography, games, singing, and metal craft were other activities promoted by these rural recreation institutes, fearing that local handicrafts and skills were on the wane.

Yet teaching people the lost art of play and community leisure under the professional eye of the government employee was not always so simple. Some small, farming, or religious communities saw the government-sponsored schemes as an anathema. Leisure projects in migratory labor camps, for example, met with suspicion and disdain from the "old-fashioned" women and laborers for whom they were intended. "We are gradually breaking this condition," social worker Tom Collins reported from Kern Migratory Labor Camp in 1936, where mothers and children could learn to "play" together despite their religious objections to many forms of entertainment. Having applied for two playground supervisors from the National Youth Administration, Collins counseled caution to overcome the suspicions of the migrants: "We learned that it is useless for some outsider to come to camp and organize sports, playgrounds etc . . . therefore the camp management organizes the various activities of the camp, arouses interest, supervises and conducts the activities for some time and then solicits outside agencies to assist. . . . We exercise extreme care in the selection of the playground supervisors."[26]

As this shows, not all responses to the recreation programs were positive. The recreation division in Washington, D.C., received a variety of complaints, from the poor quality of the art such programs produced to complaints about working conditions from recreation leaders. One female participant wrote to say that she felt humiliated by the training program, which required her to spend her training playing children's games, where "even the neighbors of the settlement poke fun at the sight of grown men and women cavorting around the outside playground on their hands and knees."[27] Complaints about hours and pay also revealed that some felt the recreation projects did not provide equal opportunities for all. Letters were received at the recreation division with complaints about the racist treatment of non-white recreation workers in the South—many of whom were classed and thus paid as unskilled, despite having equal training—or about the paltriness of the recreational facilities for African Americans compared to those provided for whites.[28] Other members of the public wrote in to say that recreation projects were employing married women with working husbands or that employees were communists who were paid for doing nothing.

Despite these criticisms, the ideology of recreation reform continued to inflect official publications. To many, the road to mass happiness was a return to "traditional" activities by a system of state-organized educational programs that offered citizens the chance to restore "organic balance" and augment a "natural impulse" toward play through leisure programs.[29] WPA training programs identified the "attainment of a genuine folk culture" as common to the interests of both artists and the community.[30] The return to crafts and folk leisure patterns was not only a manifestation of nostalgia for a preindustrial world, but it dovetailed with new popular human sciences of the mind and body that were being applied to society in an attempt to "restore" balance, order, and "normality." As discussed in Chapter 1, the belief that men were becoming mechanized by their contact with machinery was widespread; writers on leisure viewed the Depression as an opportunity to wrest the individual from the hands of the monster machine. By encouraging handicrafts and simple leisure, the sociologist believed he could return dignity, humanity, and virility to the American worker. WPA Recreation Division director Eduard Lindeman wrote about this loss of physical power where the majority of workers, he claimed, performed their tasks sitting down or operated machinery with just hands and feet, so wherever machinery was employed, the physical organism was employed to a lesser degree. Lindeman stated, "Millions of modern workers do their work sitting on chairs, or operating machines which require the use of the accessory muscles of the forearm and fingers and occasionally one foot; or dictate letters, messages, and memoranda; or take papers from one place and deposit them in another; or tabulate figures on sheets which are later bound into volumes. . . . I can see no way by which organic balance can be restored to future generations except through appropriate exercises engaged upon during leisure time." Divorced from a primal use of the body, men were losing control over their lives, and only through healthy leisure-time pursuits—that would "develop a symmetrical body which can function in a wide variety of ways"—could balance and control be restored.[31]

Like many recreation experts, Lindeman invoked "traditional" folk leisure pursuits as antidotes to the influence of commercial modernity. While realizing that it was important not to "Stalinize" mass recreation, the directors of the recreation projects attempted to popularize what reformers saw as "wholesome" popular folk-style traditions. Lindeman saw leisure as a way of "revamping" the democratic process by providing each individual with "a guided and self-directed experience based upon personal needs and the needs of democratic society."[32] The "folk art" revival of the 1930s played a significant part in the recreation programs of the WPA; it provided a tradition that was both radical and stable and that was noncommercial and yet symbolic of "the masses" and the "popular."[33] Ironically, this fetishism of the "folk" also inflected the state leisure and culture programs of Germany, Italy, and the Soviet Union— all dictatorships from which reformers were trying to distance themselves, especially Lindeman. Unlike the Aryan nationalism of the Nazi folk revival, however, the folk revival of the recreation programs provided a new pan-nationalism that represented the variety and difference of a unique American "melting pot" and had broad appeal. Playing together, it was assumed, was a way of crossing divisive class and race boundaries.[34]

Not wanting to be dogmatic about controlling leisure, project leaders were encouraged to find traditional culture that was assumed to be already within a community, albeit buried by modernity and urbanism. Lindeman saw the enjoyment of nature as a "mark of culture," evidenced in the writings of Audubon and Thoreau, an enjoyment that "everyone can and should share," he remarked.[35] Clarence March, educational director of the Civilian Conservation Corps, called the educational program a "great American Folk School," which grew out of "the native culture of a people but develop[s] and expand[s] that culture by helping the people to learn the things that are of most interest or importance to them."[36] Working close to nature, traditional manual crafts, nature walks, and hikes were seen as ways to restore natural balance. (See Figure 3).

This leisure was not only "wholesome," but it was invariably cheap and simple to provide. Programs were not permitted to compete with commercial ventures and thus had no choice but to offer alternatives to commercial leisure activities. Programs included hikes, picnics and outdoor games, festivals and plays, community singing, various forms of folk dancing and country dancing where "the only music necessary is furnished by the piano," community nights, and spelling bees or other group games requiring little or no equipment.[37] (See Figures 4 and 5).

"Poverty of play has been as great, if not greater, than poverty of work" for America's youth, Glover claimed. And "a plan for a youth recreational program, therefore, must consider what kind of world the young live in

3. Learning to enjoy the outdoors. WPA recreational supervision was provided in approximately twenty public schools and nursery schools of Portland, Oregon. Courtesy National Archives, Still Picture Branch, RG69-MP-C-191.

today and must counteract those influences that are most threatening. Surely in this day among those influences in their *environment* are speed, mechanization, the pay-entry or commercialized type of entertainment, and passive amusements; in their *personal* life it is frustration, lack of the stimulus of accomplishment, of normal association and social contact, which last they are accustomed to think cannot be had without money."[38]

Program activities were divided into four categories so that participation could be properly analyzed and quantified—as well as to enable further statistical evidence of the effectiveness of the programs. "Physical recreation" included swimming, athletics and sports, hiking, camping, and other outdoor activities. "Social recreation" included game-room activities; ballroom, tap, folk, or square dancing (never jazz); and special events such as parties, carnivals, parades, and pet and fashion shows. "Cultural recreation" described arts and crafts, drama, music, lectures and discussion groups, art appreciation and history, education in literacy, and nature or folklore study. "Therapeutic recreation" covered all activities

4. Coffee County, Alabama, April 1939. A recreation evening at the community school under the direction of the Works Progress Administration recreational supervisor. Photo by Marion Post Wolcott. Courtesy Library of Congress, Prints and Photographs Division, FSA-OWI Collection [LC-USF 34-51464-D].

5. Visalia, California, March 1940. The Farm Security Administration Tulare
camp for migrant workers. Men in the recreation hall. Photo by Arthur
Rothstein. Courtesy Library of Congress, Prints and Photographs Division,
FSA-OWI Collection [LC-USF 34-24236-D].

carried on for "the benefit of disabled, maladjusted, or other institutionalized persons."[39]

Recreation for "out-of-school" young people, organized by recreation
committees with the help of bodies such as the YMCA and the YWCA,
included activities such as dramatics, bridge, "and a course on marriage
and the home."[40] Other activities organized were cooking schools, garden
clubs, wood carving, handicrafts, folk dancing, community singing, dramatics, games, and metal craft, as shown in Figure 6.

Describing the training offered by the recreation institutes, Katherine
Glover illustrated the kind of recreation that trained leaders would be
offering young people:

The program each evening consisted of a 40-minute period on community
singing, followed by a 40-minute period on hobbies conducted by the Director
of the Rochester Museum. Special demonstrations of folk dances in costume
were arranged to demonstrate the possibilities of folk dancing in community
programs. These dances were given by the Polish Centralia, and by groups of
German and Ukranian young people. This part of the program was followed by
a more active program of recreational games, including rhythmic activities and

folk dances. . . . One evening a member of the department of rural social organization conducted a demonstration of a progressive game party and showed
how to make simple home-made puzzles and games.[41]

The desire to control leisure-time activities in order to create a more
stable society was aided by a back-to-roots philosophy that became widespread by the end of the decade.

As an apparent revolt against modernism and technology, the "folk"
movement temporarily received broad cultural sanction, satisfying the
cultural imperatives of both the Left, who read "proletarian" for "folk,"
and conservative recreation reformers, who read "folk" as "tradition."[42]
Yet WPA recreation programs did not initiate the revived interest in dis-
covering an authentic indigenous culture—as a reaction to industrialization it had been ongoing since the nineteenth century. Neither was
the revival based solely on socialist or labor movement utopianism.
National folklife and historical preservation projects that were taken up

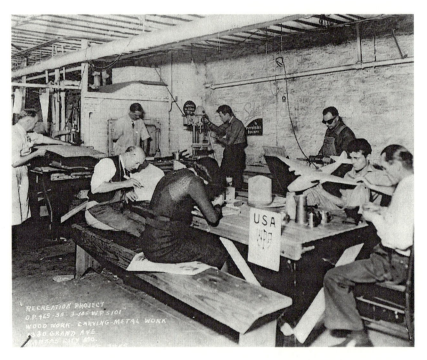

6. Woodwork and metalwork are activities carried on by the WPA Recreation
Program in Kansas City. Courtesy National Archives, Still Picture Branch,
RG69N-19678-C.

by the WPA were founded on the bedrock of welfare capitalism, offering leisure opportunities that enabled the visitor to contemplate history or the achievements of Americans in the past. Over the twenties and thirties, corporate money spearheaded some of the more prominent of these projects. Preservation projects created historic districts in Charleston and New Orleans; Jefferson's former home, Monticello, was saved from ruin; Colonial Williamsburg was funded by J. D. Rockefeller Jr.; and Greenfield Village—Henry Ford's open air "living history" museum, dedicated in 1929—was opened to the public. One distinct feature of these educational programs was a desire to instill national pride and combat "foreign" influences such as socialism and fascism.

These "living history" sites were just a part of the boom in new recreational activities—which involved motoring and touring to visit designated monuments (both natural and historical) throughout the country. Few of the newly designated historic sites were rebuilt with any plan to include public transportation. Paradoxically, Ford even rerouted a road that went around the Greenfield Village site at Dearborn in order to preserve the setting and help create an atmosphere of authenticity. Automobiling, however, was a major form of recreation during the Depression and very often the only means of access to the newly created recreational and leisure facilities.[43] Like many other paradoxes of the decade, while encouraging Americans to enjoy "natural" and preindustrial leisure, the motor car—and by extension commercial and industrial culture—was boosted by such developments in the leisure industry.

As a backlash against the shortcomings of capitalism, however, the folklife trend escalated with the support of the Left during the 1930s, receiving broad sanction under the Popular Front umbrella. The sense that society was out of control was prevalent, and the urgency to restore social stability acted as a catalyst for the proliferation of educational programs that bore a direct influence on the leisure problem. As shown in Figure 7, the WPA recreation projects continued the industrial welfare model by encouraging Americans to spend their leisure time in folk rituals that many had to learn anew.

In their hunt for a "useable" past, the WPA followed in the wake of industrialists such as Ford to provide leisure that enabled national pride in the history of American democracy. During the 1930s, the federal government heavily sponsored projects with preservation and recreation goals, some directly related to the WPA Recreation Division and others working alongside it. In 1934, the National Park Service was established to coordinate efforts of the 48 states concerning scenic, health, historical, and recreational opportunities.[44] WPA art projects also functioned to catalog and eulogize past American achievements to distinguish them from their nondemocratic or corrupt European roots. Like Ford's museum, the Index of American Design was a project that attempted to make and preserve a record of "native" arts and crafts and to keep a record of as many indigenous inventions and objects of "American" origin as possible. Holger Cahill, director of the Federal Art Project, worked out the plan for the Index following his experience working on the restoration of Colonial Williamsburg. According to McKenzie, Cahill "expected the Index to preserve a rapidly disappearing part of Americana" and claimed that the project would "clarify our complex heritage for the expert" and "recreate the past in human symbols for the average citizen."[45] Yet the "average citizen" and indigenous design did not include the Native American, and it was decided that Native American design should be included in projects on ethnology instead.

Interest in folk art initiated a folk-craft revival during the Depression, which was sponsored by official bodies including "folk schools and settlement houses; Agricultural Extension, Works Progress Administration and other governmental agencies; [and] educators in many places and physicians."[46] Education in traditional skills and crafts was seen as a way to combat the highly mechanized style of modern living that had left

7. WPA recreation—folk dancing. This photo was taken in Louisiana.
Courtesy National Archives, Still Picture Branch, RG69N-10492-C.

workers weakened and emasculated. Arts and crafts blurred the boundaries between work and leisure and gave the former a domestic feel. Leadership training manuals echoed this point and began from an assumption that "bad" leisure was urban, industrial, commercial, and disintegrated the home as a unit, whereas "good" leisure reintegrated the community and family, was simple, and involved social interaction or proto-industrial artisanal skills. Leisure, many claimed, could rebalance the family and the community. A directed and "fatherly" approach to the recreation projects emerged in the language of studies and reports made about current and advocated uses of leisure. Out-of-work fathers, for example, could regain some of their standing as head of the household through organizing family recreation.

While most experts claimed that the pressure of modern commercial leisure caused the family to disintegrate, putting the home and community under threat, many surveys and reports actually showed evidence to the contrary. In 1934, the National Recreation Association commissioned a survey, *The Leisure Hours of 5,000 People: A Report of a Study of Leisure Time Activities and Desires.* This survey found more of concern in the desires of participants than in their current leisure activities. The survey found that, because of the Depression, the home had become more significant as a center for leisure activities, rather than less, and that people chose low-cost, locally available leisure. Among the top-ten activities listed, reading was first, followed by listening to the radio, conversation, gardening, and visiting. Despite this, their expressed desires were for activities away from the home that usually involved considerable expense. When asked what they would like to do, respondents chose more sports, automobiling, or attending "legitimate" theatre. According to the survey, the unemployed were "pathetically lacking in variety or richness of opportunity," and only through community leisure programs would their leisure needs be realized.[47]

Just in case these surveys were not as compelling as the social scientist hoped, they usually contained more suasive material. As testimony to the transformation that leisure programs could make on the individual and community, the NRA survey concluded with some examples of "typical" cases that illustrated the benefits of properly used leisure:

The father of three young children with a new babe on the way, who had been out of work for many months and was disheartened and discouraged even to the point of threatening suicide, at the suggestion of a friend dropped in at a public recreation center in his neighborhood. His interest in craftsmanship was soon discovered and the idea of making a crib for the expected newcomer proved his salvation. Another somewhat older man without children, driven to the point of desperation because of no funds and no occupation, learned to cut out jig-saw puzzles in a recreation center class and later turned his new found craft interest to good account by cutting out puzzles and selling them from door to door. His wife said of him, "His whole attitude is changed."[48]

Other "typical" experiences also illustrated how curtailed circumstances keeping people at home had, according to the sociologists, made them better parents. A housewife, forced to sell her car and give up traveling and picnicking, was doing more canning and preserving, had "increased interest in the care and welfare of her two year old baby," and was improving her garden. Similarly, men were learning how to be fathers again after too much time away from the home: "Others say they are staying at home more with their children. A number of fathers are making things with their children; there has been particular mention of spending more time with their boys in home workshops."[49]

In one *Recreation* magazine editorial, Howard Braucher underlined the vital necessity of rebalancing the power dynamics of family relationships thus: "Families fret with all family traditions overturned, with the man about the house all the day, every day. The man feels he has lost standing with his children, with his neighbors. Yet there is much that the father can do for his children if in this period there can be built up a neighborhood tradition of 'whole family recreation.' Recreation workers have a special challenge now to take the lead in helping to train fathers in recreation leadership with the family."[50]

Advocating the extension of adult recreation because of the growth in adult leisure time, one WPA circular commented that the recreation leader's role should include improving "the manner in which whole families use leisure" by teaching skills that can lead to hobbies, arts and home decoration, and family games.[51] "By extending the influence of the adult recreation program into the home, much can be done to make family life happier and more successful," the author claimed.

These experiences conformed typically to the professionals' demands for the right use of leisure and appealed to their professional and meritocratic outlook. In the ideal scenario, the parents were happy to stay at home with their children more, using their homes as preindustrial hives of productivity to develop proto-work skills that made them useful members of society once more. The Recreation Association saw positive gains for the family out of the straitened circumstances of the Depression, and sought to consolidate these gains with programs that would absorb leisure desires and interests even when prosperity returned.[52]

Leisure and Time Management

These "folk" and simple leisure pursuits, however, belie how much the technological vision of the future had been recuperated by the mid

1930s. A cohort of writers, planners, scientists, and New Deal techno-crats began to envision a new future of machine-made leisure, where machines took over production, leaving everyone to reach their highest potential. Now that technology could provide people with every need, it was time for them to take back control of "the monster." The role of the leisure expert was to guide the working classes so that this sudden "excess" of leisure—"a truly magnificent opportunity for progress"— would not be misused. Ralph Aiken wrote, "There are many indications that we are approaching a time when the machine will release practically all men from the necessity of physical labor; when freedom in its most dangerous form, an excess of leisure, will be given to the human race."[53]

So while earlier writers blamed machinery for the disaster, many con-sidered that the root problem could now become the cure. During this time, many writers viewed technology as having "cut the drudgeries of life," redistributing the means of leisure to the masses. Rather than being enslaved by the machine, "the machine is our slave,"[54] if used to enable citizens to enjoy a nonmechanical leisure. Leisure thereby became cen-tral to visions of mechanical progress that dominated the modernity of the 1930s. For example, in his book discussing the two-hour workday, Yale professor Clifford Furnas wrote, "When the working day gets down to two hours, we can feel that at last the machine which once threatened to enslave us had freed us and cut the drudgeries of life to a negligible quantity, leaving us our time to do as we see fit. Being freed by technol-ogy would leave humans to rediscover their humanity and to become more human or more "natural" again."[55]

While federal programs and the recreation reform movement worked to promote this vision of a more organic culture operating outside of production, increasing numbers of nonfiction writers contributed to and supported this ideology. Self-help manuals began to tutor men in regain-ing their lost social standing through the proper use of leisure in the hope that their position as "natural" leaders and cultural authorities could be regained—not through the work they did but through the way they played. "What must you do to be saved?" asked Walter Pitkin in *Take It Easy*, to which he responded, "You must first of all, study yourself from head to foot, inside and outside. Next you must study the world you live in. This done, you turn to the toughest task of all: you must fit yourself to your world as ingeniously as possible," or re-create yourself as a balanced, normal person through adjustment and acceptance of the social order.[56] As Lundberg and colleagues stated in 1934, "The ultimate objective [of leisure] is the adjustment of the individual to the desired social order. This can be achieved by a process which has two phases: 1) The manip-ulation of the environment. 2) The conditioning of the individual."[57] These two phases were certainly addressed by the recreation programs.

Similarly, many leisure books argued that the primary meaning of the word *recreation* foregrounded this (re-)creation of the self. Harold Rugg argued that "our chief cultural goal is not goods but men."[58] Machine-made leisure could be used to rebuild the musculature weakened by lack of manual labor, and mental capacity could be increased in leisure hours. Feeblemindedness and mental illness could be overcome by new methods of control over leisure time, which in turn would create an improved race, one equipped for leadership and authority in the new world.

These visions illustrated how the problem of technological unemployment could be turned into the solution, harnessed to create a new ideal society. Sociologist Paul Frankl claimed that the "machine is introducing a new communism more profound than man-made doctrines" and that it would be possible to create out of the chaos "a new unity, a unity of thought and art, of leisure, of life, and the new art of life."[59] Not opposed to the "folk" revival but part of it, the technological vision of the future became more deeply entrenched, recuperated through the proper use of leisure.

Taking inspiration from these visions of mechanized leisure, economists, historians, architects, sociologists, and philosophers all began to develop theories of modern society based on leisure. Systematic and scientific study was recommended, which necessitated the division of leisure and consumers of leisure into various categories and types. For economists, leisure was now a commodity. L. C. Walker referred to leisure as the new American product, claiming that "we here in America face the necessity of studying our new product, leisure, and finding a way to make it more attractive by making it more usable—by putting it in acceptable packages and selling it to ourselves much as we sell ourselves the goods produced by our industrial machine."[60]

Leisure was thereby a human resource that was quantifiable and contributed to the personal and social economy (if well used): "Even though most people may not use leisure to their degradation, they are not prepared to use it most proficiently. Proficiency in the art of using leisure may be acquired, however, by careful attention to and application of the principles of economics which pertain to its use."[61] To one economist, W. Lou Tandy, maximizing the right use of leisure was important to the common weal, "for an unwise use of leisure may give rise to evils of inconceivable magnitude."[62] Optimizing leisure time could be both an art practiced naturally and something to be studied and taught. Tandy drew up charts that would enable "people to become more rational than they are at present" by applying economic principles to their leisure time, creating efficiency out of proficiency in the art of using leisure. He concluded that "if rationality in the use of leisure is to be attained, it is essential that the principles of proficiency in the use of leisure should be followed, and that hindrances to both the maximizing of leisure and to the best use of leisure should be offset insofar as it is possible."[63]

These writers recommended the scientific management of time in order to prevent wasteful leisure. Applying the precepts of time and motion studies to argue for a new control over nonwork time, sociologists paradoxically used the industrial metaphor to invoke a nonindustrial use of leisure. Attempts to carefully measure hours, minutes, and seconds of free time became one way that the nonproductive hours could be made more effective. Time had to be counted and accounted for. As "personal engineer," Frank Cheley wrote in *Investing Leisure Time*, training for leisure was "a new attitude towards life which will very greatly increase your own personal happiness and consequently your usefulness."[64] Planning, training, and educating for leisure were ways to combat the "greatest menace to civilization," cheap commercial amusement. "Make each minute serve a purpose," he advises, describing leisure time in terms of stockbroking, accountancy, and time management: "You have just such a bank, and its name is Time. Every morning it credits you with 86,400 seconds. Every night it writes off as lost whatever of these you have failed to invest to good purpose. It carries over no balances. It allows no overdrafts."[65] In a similar style, leisure writer Gove Hambridge suggested, "Every day the Teller of the cosmic bank hands us twenty-four freshly minted hours—and not a second more—as our time income for that day, with which to purchase what we can or will of life. How do we spend it?"[66] And Frank Cheley advised taking an inventory of the collective family time as if it were a material belonging like other household objects: "First be sure you recognize the 'new leisure' when you see it. Look over your day as you would your pantry shelves or your bureau drawer. Examine your family as you would had you never seen them before. Take an inventory of your time, and theirs, and what you actually do with it."[67]

Recreation magazine supplied similar advice in an article titled "Budgeting Your Spare Time," advising people to work out a daily schedule that accounted and planned for all spare time. Many writers attempted to persuade Americans that they needed to quantify and measure their leisure time so that they could get the proper balance of rest, fun, and education, claiming this balance was as important to mental and physical health as the proper balance of vitamins in a diet.[68] Illustrating the importance of time management, a WPA poster advertising a leisure exhibition, titled "March of Leisure Time," was illustrated by a clock that segmented the various leisure activities into bands of color radiating from the center of the clock.[69]

As a way of redefining success and bringing happiness into unemployed lives, this type of studied self-control was advocated by many

popular psychologists and sociologists. It recommended not only looking at self and family but judging oneself in relation to the mass, and the
mass in relation to oneself. Cheley recommended counting mass loss
of hours in mass amusements: "No doubt the modern radio is a great
invention and essentially a blessing, but just stop a moment and com-
pute the billions of wasted hours it is now party to. Think of the armies
of supposedly intelligent folk who have nothing to do but waste pre-
cious evenings listening to the poorest or utterly useless jazz—being
conditioned to utter dependence on someone else for their simplest
enjoyments."[70]

Hobbies

One way of using time "properly" grew in an unprecedented fashion
during the thirties: the adoption of a hobby. Hobbies, in fact, provided
the perfect solution to the often conflicting aims of New Deal programs:
they fulfilled the need for a private and autonomous world of domestic
leisure and the public goals of community improvement. Self-controlled,
the hobby fitted the need for individual psychological self-adjustment
and, as a way of maintaining mental health, functioned to provide a
sense of purpose in an unpredictable world, for "the unemployed man
who occupies himself with some task, even though he receives no pay
for it, or who cultivates a hobby of some kind, or who takes part in some
organized recreational or educational activities in his community, is taking a long step towards keeping his mind from rusting and his personality from growing crabbed."[71] One WPA recreation circular, for example,
strongly recommended teaching hobby skills such as "arts and home
decoration . . . skills for outings and for home games such as croquet,
table tennis, badminton, and shuffle board" that would extend the influence of the recreation program into the home, making "family life happier and more successful."[72] The circular recommended family-minded
recreation such as "camps, outings for families, family tours, family hobby
nights, family dances, shows, orchestras, and singing groups" as a way of
contributing "toward a greater degree of family unity and to a more
complete enjoyment of the family association."[73] Handicraft guilds and
hobby clubs were given support and sponsorship from a variety of New
Deal agencies including the WPA, the Tennessee Valley Authority, the
Farm Security Administration, and the National Youth Authority.[74]

From the stock market crash in 1929, there was an increased public
acceptance and encouragement of hobbies, illustrated in the sudden
plethora of hobby shows, articles, magazines, programs, and clubs, where
previously there had been none. State recreation departments supported
hobby workshops, and the National Recreation Association argued that

"every man should be encouraged to find one or more hobbies."[75] Hobbies were encouraged as ways of maintaining prowork values and job skills, yet they also functioned to bridge the gap between definitions of work and leisure—conflating the two, hobbies were "a job you can't lose."[76] Hobbies were also seen as a way of maintaining individuality (e.g., creating unique collections of objects or developing idiosyncratic talents) and as neo-artisanal—an antidote to everything that mass commercial leisure stood for. Hobbies fulfilled the needs of democratic leisure, for they entailed all people having self-expression and not just an elite of trained artists or artisans who produced for a passive consumer.[77] The hobby combined the spheres of work and home—fusing the meanings of work and leisure—and combined new pastimes (e.g., jigsaw puzzles) with old "folk-craft" traditions. The hobby craze of the 1930s benefited greatly from the legitimizing process undertaken by professionals and politicians of the era, who set up groups, published articles, established "leisure leagues" and hobby clubs, and ran hobby shows on the radio; as Gelber notes, a "group of self-professed experts surfaced in academia and journalism to join the hobbyists themselves in a lively discussion over the definition and merits of hobbies."[78]

Hobbies also provided the solution to another conundrum of the New Deal leisure policy: how to increase consumer spending without creating unrealistic consumerist desires. As the hobby trend became a commercial fashion, it provided some entrepreneurs with a way of recouping losses from the crash. *Business Week* magazine noted in 1932 that "We Spend About As Much for Fun As for Running the Government," and again in 1935 that "increase in spare time engages attention of business as well as of sociologists, leads to staging of a New York hobby show to launch the drive on new leisure market." Illustrating how hobbies had become a Depression-era phenomenon, the "Hobby Round-Up," promoted by the Leisure League of America, combined the commercial needs of industrialists with the leisure problem of sociologists. As *Business Week* put it: "Continued development of labor saving machines means that Americans are going to have even more time to kill. Here is the situation that worries sociologists and interests various industries. Both are determined that the surplus of workless hours shall not be employed in stagnant loafing. It is not good for man to bite his nails and think overmuch on his troubles. Industries catering to the leisure demand already are pushing their wares, others observing the signs are wondering whether they ought to move in, preparing sales forces for rapid mobilization."[79]

As leisure professionals began to quantify and judge the new leisure as a form of personal and national wealth, as a "commodity" that "must be taken into consideration just as fully as the world reckons with food supplies and monetary standards," many directly equated the new moral and social benefits of coordinated leisure with the personal gain that could be made from it.[80] The new leisure of the New Deal could be used to create "wholesome" personalities and could be morally as well as practically profitable to the individual, according to one writer in *Catholic World*. Making use of work relief programs to learn a new skill or study something that there was previously no time for could help to keep an individual from despair and enable him or her to get a job more easily. In contrast to this, a girl who did not make use of the programs was now "in a state of moral collapse and the dark wings of contemplated suicide shadow her wherever she goes."[81] This writer describes how another woman successfully solved "her unemployment problem as a result of her determination to keep busy and use her leisure time constructively," making the "leisure problem" solvable from an ethical as well as political angle.

By 1938, a survey of WPA recreation projects claimed that the recreation division had demonstrated the "desirability of making recreation a permanent responsibility and function of government."[82] Although it may have been hard for Aiken in 1931 to imagine workers having to perform a work of art or put on a show in order to receive unemployment relief, by 1934 the notion of a "secretary of amusement"—a government official who would help people sing and dance their way out of the Depression—was presented, mockingly or not, as part of the film narrative in *Stand Up and Cheer*, Shirley Temple's first film. Indeed, popular perceptions of the Roosevelt administration's "fatherly" intimacy with the populace presented a newfound notion that the happiness of the masses and their psychological well-being was now definitely one of the government's responsibilities. Eduard Lindeman stated that "for the first time in America people are talking about recreation as part of the good life. That is what the Government program has done. It has pushed the whole concept onto a sociological level. Now it is no longer recreation to save people from crime and delinquencies, no longer for body building alone, no longer recreation to keep them out of minor mischief. Now it is recreation as one of the essential ways towards a good life."[83]

Recreation programs throughout the decade had aimed at this ideal: the young man expending his energies on useful projects; the young woman learning her role as social butterfly within acceptable limits; the married mother learning homemaking and child-care skills, while spending her time with other married women; the married man "puttering" about the house with an absorbing hobby that kept him happy and indoors, near his family and head of the household. Ironically, young children were the least of the recreation manager's problems, despite the image often promoted that recreation was about children's play and that programs were created to satisfy children's needs. Satisfying multiple needs, the government recreation programs provided amusement and yet managed to promote the work ethic at the same time—keeping the workforce useful for more prosperous times.

To many, the need to regulate leisure was perceived as crucial to the proper functioning of society and was fueled by stories and images perpetrated in the mass media. Ironically, with the help of the new philosophy of leisure, the Forgotten Man needed not bonuses and relief but a new identity and personality to match. Having established the "fact" of a leisure problem, social scientists developed answers that presented themselves as neutral and apolitical, as scientific discoveries equivalent to other health and educational programs. The discourse of the leisure problem thus emerged in a way that bypassed divisive political affiliations—either left or right. The provision of cheap mass leisure and training for self-improvement on a mass scale was an amalgam of reform and conservatism, of modernity and tradition. To those on the left, commercial leisure meant social exclusion for the working classes, who, without a leisure program, would not reap the benefits of increased free time made available to them by machinery and their own labor. To others, the provision of noncommercial leisure for the masses provided a popular route to back-to-basics social philosophies that put family stability and patriarchal control firmly back on the map. The two approaches were not mutually exclusive, and in many respects the New Deal programs provided a synthesis of tradition with innovation in their provision of cheap leisure and recreational facilities for ordinary Americans. Thus, while the official discourse beneath the problem of leisure appears distinctly antimodern and anticommercial, somewhat paradoxically it was also an act of modernism itself, a drive toward state management based on a streamlined, modern, and scientifically organized state.

As much of this shows, the traditional moral imperatives of the recreation movement in the nineteenth century were merged into the new vision of the technocratic future—both free and controlled, both advanced and "natural," both playing and working. As this indicates, recreation programs apparently spanned the divisions and bridged cultural battles that seemed to be affecting all other aspects of society. Despite this, conflicts emerged that revealed how indebted many professionals were to earlier theories of social control and the management of poor and working-class lives in a very political way. Debates over the proper use of leisure that emerged within the mass media were encoded with gender, class, and race presumptions, and as such were met with objection, as well as approval. The notion of a "problem" of leisure encompassed and included all other perceived problems in American society and culture of the time: fears over the disintegration of traditional communities, fears of mass uprising, race and class anxieties, gender anxieties, poor educational standards, and fears of the dissolution of "high" culture into "low." The way that writers, artists, filmmakers, journalists, and critics interacted with these "leisure debates" provides an important and unexamined adjunct to other cultural histories of the Depression. Ordinary "pleasure seekers" also ignored the reformers' censure and developed their own response to commercial leisure at the height of Depression. Many different groups reacted to the question of the "leisure problem" in a variety of ways, responding to it outside of "official" programs and activities. In many ways, this very heterogeneous response to the appearance of "official" leisure was where America emerged as most distinctly different from Germany, Italy, or the Soviet Union. The particular contours taken by these debates is examined in the following chapters.

Chapter 4
The March of Culture

Too dull to think, people might read: too tired to read, they might look at the moving pictures: unable to visit the picture theatre they might turn on the radio: in any case, they might avoid the call to action: surrogate lovers, surrogate heroes and heroines, surrogate wealth filled their debilitated and impoverished lives and carried the perfume of unreality into their dwellings. And as the machine itself became, as it were, more active and human, reproducing the organic properties of eye and ear, the human beings who employed the machine as a mode of escape have tended to become more passive and mechanical. Unsure of their own voices, unable to hold a tune, they carry a phonograph or a radio set with them even on a picnic: afraid to be alone with their own thoughts, afraid to confront the blankness and inertia of their own minds, they turn on the radio and eat and talk and sleep to the accompaniment of a continuous stimulus from the outside world: now a band, now a bit of propaganda, now a piece of public gossip called news

—*Lewis Mumford*, Technics and Civilization

It is only when you are torn from your mooring, when you drift like a rudderless ship, that I am able to come near you

—*Sherwood Anderson*, Perhaps Women

The issues and problems of national leisure soon spread beyond the social scientific and governmental worlds. The discourses of leisure and the definition of its proper use reached out into the cultural sphere through books, periodicals, and newspaper articles. Writing in the context of a "national wrangling over the deposition of American bodies at work and at rest," fiction writers and artists, in addition to social scientists and other experts, engaged with the leisure problem as a crucial social question more actively than has been previously examined.[1] Influenced by developments in psychology and sociology, writers and intellectuals responded to the leisure debates in a variety of ways. For one thing, the "cultural" use of leisure featured more centrally than ever as the role of the cultural producer came under increasing scrutiny. If culture could help rebuild forgotten men, then writers were more central to the use of leisure for social improvement than ever before.

This chapter looks at the ways in which many writers of the thirties perceived the threat of the new leisure and analyzes some of their fictional responses to the changing role of leisure in mass culture. Looking at the correspondence of thought between social reformers and writers, this chapter also illustrates how integral the leisure debate was to writers' perceptions of self and society and how these were reproduced within the fiction they produced. While fearing the debasement of culture through new leisure formations typified by Rugg's "problematic" pursuits, writers engaged with mass leisure semantically in the narratives they produced. The meaning of leisure to American culture in the Great Depression was thus rewritten not only by social scientists but also by cultural producers whose work relied integrally on the new leisure of the New Deal, or the march of spare time.

The reaction of writers to the shifting perception of leisure in the thirties was crucially affected by a new relationship emerging between writers and social science professionals at this time. William Stott has written extensively on the relationship between documentary fiction and social studies in his *Documentary Fiction and Thirties America*. The style of writing that produced documentary fiction came from a marriage of two genres that alone seemed inadequate to portray the shock of Depression in American culture. At the start of the Depression, fiction appeared to lack the necessary facts and realism to give it social meaning, and sociological case studies or reports on poverty lacked the imaginative intensity that would move readers into action. Taking Clinch Calkins's *Some Folks Won't Work* of 1930 as the first example of a marriage of sociological with fictional styles, Stott illustrates how the social worker/poet author appealed to the emotions of a middle-class audience with a new realism constructed from her imaginative engagement with sociological case studies, and not from any firsthand experience at all. The use of social science data and evidence was only one aspect of the new merging of fictional styles. As Stott points out, sociological texts became more influenced by fictional modes as sociological studies began to adopt a less scientific and quantitative approach and started using stylistic touches more in keeping with methods of fiction or journalism.[2] So as many writers tried to distance themselves from the "romantic" fictions of mass culture by adopting social scientific method, they also found themselves implicated even more deeply in the fabrication of sociological narratives. In this way, fiction writers reiterated and confirmed—sometimes even fueled—the concerns of the social science professionals concerning the new leisure of the Depression.[3]

The new role effected by this relationship meant that many writers in the thirties found themselves negotiating the contested terrain of the leisure problem in their statements about the role of the writer in

American culture, in comments about writing styles, in perceptions about the meaning and importance of words in culture, and within the narratives of the literature they produced. The problem of leisure as a problem of American culture and values reemerged throughout the literature of the period, both "proletarian," or political, and mainstream, expressed through concerns with mass culture, commercialization, capitalism, and working-class and bourgeois leisure.

In the early thirties, many intellectuals appeared to concur with the sociological view of mass culture and leisure. Like social reformers, critiques of capitalism by radical writers apparently rejected popular culture as false consciousness and social waste. To writers with a new awareness of the political role of writing and culture, commercial leisure and culture often appeared antagonistic to the environment of revolution and working-class struggles up until the formation of the Popular Front in 1935 and could be blamed for anything from the decline in culture to the failure of socialist revolution.

The "weakening" effect of mass culture, or the emasculation of culture through capitalist commercialism, reappeared in the cultural criticism of left-wing writers. Michael Gold, editor of the journal *New Masses,* claimed, for example, "Factory girls in America wear silk stockings but have no class consciousness . . . [and] . . . the workers now . . . were bribed by radios and Ford cars, and are therefore essentially members of the bourgeois class."[4] Much left-wing rhetoric argued that writing should function to reconstruct cultural consciousness corrupted by the decadent bourgeoisification of both upper- and working-class culture.[5] Despite the fact that many women were successfully involved in strikes and labor protests (to an unprecedented degree), the communist editor of *New Masses* relegates working women and their "silk stockings" to the realm of effeminate bourgeois culture.[6]

Throughout the thirties, *New Masses* contained many similar references to this weakening effect of effete bourgeois culture, erecting a set of gender-inscribed terms with which to attack capitalism. Work was male, and, consequently, the proletarian experience was male. In attempting to align themselves with the working class, to reinscribe writing as a labored rather than a leisured activity, and to revalue the role of the writer in American culture, many writers saw themselves reinvigorating a weak and effeminized culture. In *New Masses,* a criticism of Sinclair Lewis as a humanist writer stated that he was "deprived of masculine experiences."[7] One of the foremost writers who seemed to come under attack with regularity was the modernist Marcel Proust (despite his influence, along with James Joyce, on writers such as Farrell) who was accused of effete "bourgeois angst" and "verbal acrobats" and whose writing was described as "a sedative for sick Americans."[8] As Rita Barnard has pointed

out, "The virile posture expresses, at least in some measure, an opposi-
tional response to the new promises of abundance and leisure" that
characterized America "when all kinds of newly invented home acces-
sories and time-saving devices combined to make life more comfortable
and aesthetic, but also more "weightless" and "unreal."⁹

Likewise, the Forgotten Man, enfeebled and alienated from nature,
featured prominently in much artistic output of the thirties, where the
displacement of people by machines became entrenched in cultural productions, such as New Deal art or photo essays such as *An American Exodus: A Record of Human Erosion in the Thirties*, photographed by Dorothea
Lange and written by sociologist Paul Schuster Taylor. Taylor's commen-
tary accompanying Lange's photos depict a people "eroded" by machines,
just as the land was being eroded by drought. One caption stated that
"mechanization is invading the Delta," another that a tractor could now
do the work of eight men and eight mules and that tractors "cultivate to
the very door of the house of the men they replace."¹⁰ The rapacious
machinery became responsible for the displacement of the farm worker,
who in turn became disconnected from the land, cut loose to join the
increasing numbers of mobile unemployed. Federal government docu-
mentaries such as *The Plow That Broke the Plains* (1936) and *The River*
(1937) also blamed machinery and modernity for the era's problems.
Machines had made men obsolete, they suggested.¹¹

Along with the belief that man had been made impotent/unemployed
by machinery was the sense that machinery had developed beyond
human control. In this view the machine became a living organism that
overpowered individuals. This was not a new vision of the modern world;
since the Industrial Revolution similar representations of the machine
had been made, yet writers and intellectuals during the Depression re-
cycled these popular perceptions, which fed into the discourses about
how leisure was created and how it should be utilized. Although man
was to blame initially—"he is carried away by his mechanical genius and
allows his life to be mastered by his inventions rather than holding them
wisely and firmly to his service"—machines had gained autonomy from
man.¹² Fiction corroborated this sociological view of technology. In *The
Grapes of Wrath* (1939), John Steinbeck describes tractors as uncontrollable monsters, which also turn the men who operate them into machines:

The man sitting in the iron seat did not look like a man: gloved, goggled, rubber dust-mask over nose and mouth, he was part of the monster, a robot in the
seat. The thunder of the cylinders sounded through the country, became one
with the air and the earth, so that earth and air muttered in sympathetic vibra-
tion. The driver could not control it—straight across country it went, cutting
through a dozen farms and straight back. A twitch at the controls could swerve
the cat, but the driver's hands could not twitch because the monster that built

the tractor, the monster that sent the tractor out, had somehow got into the driver's hands, into his brain and muscle, had goggled him and muzzled him—goggled his mind, muzzled his speech, goggled his perception, muzzled his protest.[13]

Confirming male impotency, the giant tractor seeds the land that no man has touched ("no man had crumbled a hot clod in his fingers and let the earth sift past his finger-tips"), giving him "no connexion with the bread" that he eats.

Other writers similarly used sociological findings on technological unemployment to structure the themes of their books. Sherwood Anderson, for example, found new vigor and potency in this theme at the onset of the Depression. Excited by the possibility of new styles and subject matter, Anderson, like many other writers at the time, went "on the road." Out of his travels and interviews with ordinary folk came two documentary-style books—*Perhaps Women* (1931) and *Puzzled America* (1935). *Perhaps Women* was constructed around a series of ruminations upon Anderson's visit to a South Carolina mill. Despite this contact with workers and his own political awakening, his style is doggedly apolitical, and the central theme is the prevalence of male social and cultural impotency as a result of the machine. Anderson was fascinated by the topic and found that the Depression gave new justification for his argument that "modern man was losing his ability to retain his manhood in the face of the modern way of utilizing the machine."[14] Finding new direction and fresh impulses from the weary and downtrodden world he uncovered, Anderson's writing became a quest to discover and describe the Zeitgeist of the Depression.

As the quotation at the start of this chapter reveals, Anderson felt that only when a working man had become "rudderless" could the writer make contact with him, perhaps to help or work with him in some way. As I discussed in Chapter 2, the image of the Forgotten Man underwrote many cultural enterprises of the Depression, including popular fiction, literature, film, and photographic documentary. This image of the impotent male permeates the entire text of *Perhaps Women*. It was, however, not unemployment (the men in the mill were still working) nor the Depression that rendered men impotent, but technology that caused the loss of male power in the modern world. Machinery, he claimed, had not only replaced men in the workplace but had unequivocally and irreversibly transformed their role in the modern world. Men no longer had ascendancy over women—physically their bodies were rendered useless by machinery, and women could do the work of men—and the machine had humiliated men into a subservient position. His impressionistic sketches and literary wanderings in *Puzzled America* claimed that it was the most important thing of all to "understand and appreciate" the new role of the American workman, "thrown out of their place in our social and economic scheme by the modern machine" and consequently "robbed of something peculiarly vital to their feeling of manhood."[15] Despite his involvement in the labor movement at the time, his attitude toward machinery was organic and naturalistic: machines had evolved to replace man, and he must now begin to find a new place for himself, a new ascendancy. This organic view of unemployment and displacement, as a breach in a prior "natural" harmony, concurred entirely with sociological perceptions of machine-made leisure and sidelined economic and political analysis in the same way that the rhetoric of the Forgotten Man universalized the problem of the Depression.

Anderson's fears were thoroughly in keeping with the sentiments of leisure reformers at the time, and his writing shows strong parallels with social scientists' concerns over technology. In *Puzzled America,* he described the American workman's love of the beauty and speed of machines as a hypnotic lust, as if "there were actually a kind of devil sleeping down in these so-gorgeously beautiful masses of steel in action."[16] Described with words such as *gorgeous* and *beautiful,* machines were not only demonized but feminized. A similar description of the machine as a siren could be found in sociologist Paul Frankl's *Machine-Made Leisure* (1932), where the machine is described as woman needing control: "Twentieth-century man is in the toils of a new mistress. This new mistress is the Machine. . . . We love her. The old fear that the Machine is destined to enslave Mankind is supplanted by an attitude that approaches breathless adoration. . . . The Machine has awakened and intensified all of Man's insatiable drive for domination. We must tame this shrew or be enslaved by her."[17] Like many others, Frankl claimed that "this new age of ours is the inevitable and organic outcome of a series of developments" beginning with the printing press. Later he asks, "Can she [the machine] ever be converted into a willing wife?"

Moreover, like WPA Recreation Division director Eduard Lindeman, Anderson emphasized the importance of men creating with their hands: "The machine has taken from us the work of our hands. Work kept men healthy and strong. It was good to feel things being done by our hands. The ability to do things to materials with our hands and our heads gave us a certain power over women that is being lost."[18] Male impotency in *Perhaps Women* is the result of machinery, and male productivity is contrasted with women's role as consumers who, as leisured, live symbiotically with modernity, technology, and mass production.

This attempt to reinvigorate the Forgotten Man was paralleled by the reinvigoration of the writer at the start of the Depression. Though many artists had been involved in left-wing and revolutionary politics well before the Depression, the crash in 1929 came as, in the words of one historian, "a momentous symbol of failure through which to assemble the images of a decade."[19] The Forgotten Man—or his literary equal, "the bottom dog"—would perhaps now be persuaded to change his fortunes and fight back at the system that was oppressing him. Writers, too, effeminized and emasculated by mass-produced, syndicated art, could fight against the new leisure that threatened to reduce them to bourgeois lapdogs. Like the professional middle classes, writers and artists interpreted the Depression as the failure of capitalism and the beginning of a new, albeit uncertain, era of opportunity. As in Anderson's case, the Depression became a catalyst for new political outlooks, the impetus for new styles of writing, and presented new and fresh material from which to draw. Like other intellectuals, the crash confirmed their prior fears and criticisms of American society, presenting writers with a new opportunity to reinvent themselves and transform their role in society as cultural and intellectual leaders. Edmund Wilson later spoke about the exciting potential that the Depression laid open for writers: "Yet to the writers and artists of my generation who had grown up in the Big Business era and had always resented its barbarism . . . these years were not depressing but stimulating. One couldn't help being exhilarated at the sudden and unexpected collapse of that stupid gigantic fraud. It gave us a new sense of freedom and it gave us a new sense of power to find ourselves still carrying on while the bankers, for a change, were taking a beating."[20]

Edwin Seaver appeared to confirm this view when he claimed at the American Writers' Congress in 1935 that the cultural movement provided a new beginning for writers that rejuvenated them and made even older writers feel young again.[21] At the same meeting, communist literary critic Joseph Freeman listed the benefits of the revolutionary movement to the writer, saying that it "offers them an audience," gives them "a whole new range of subject matter," gives "the artist a perspective on himself," and "allies the interests of writers with those of a class that is rising, instead of with the interests of a confused and futile decaying class." In short, it "gives them a new source of strength."[22]

Despite this, the Depression, along with other trends in mass culture, left many writers feeling threatened, and because of the rise in visual or passive amusements—or Nash's term "spectatoritis"—writing itself seemed a form in danger. Writers suffered from unemployment with the collapse of literary publishers, markets, and traditional forms of patronage. Fiction writing was highlighted as something dispensable (even frivolous), and many fiction writers were forced to justify their writing in new ways, as socially useful or potentially revolutionary. Much left-wing literary criticism of the 1930s used new utilitarian values to judge fiction, illustrating a climate of ambivalence toward the role of the writer in American society. While the Depression gave the writer new subject matter, it also created a climate of threat; never before had writers been viewed as so integral to political and social life, and never had they been viewed as so alien from it.

Alongside new critical expectations of the writer that made traditional subject matter seem obsolete, the culture of mass entertainment threatened to put writers out of business unless they were capable of reinventing themselves. Relying on a culture of print and word, the development of new visual entertainment threatened to make the writer a cultural anachronism. Nash's statement that "spectatoritis has become almost synonymous with Americanism and the end is not yet" would have done little to ease the worry. Predicting how technologies would provide the passive viewers with a surfeit of entertainment, in a parallel with the way that the machine had provided the American worker with a "surfeit" of produced goods and leisure, he foresaw that "the stages will get small and the rows of seats mount higher. Magnifiers and lights carry the messages to the far corners and one can perform for ten thousand as well as ten." To this notion he added despairingly, "Twenty-five million people go to the movies daily at a time of the worst depression known to man."[23]

Nash's prediction of a nation of screen watchers was perhaps partly due to a nascent television culture that was beginning to take hold in the public's awareness. Regular television programming first took place in 1928 but remained an amateur hobby with little to offer as entertainment. In the early thirties, there were no complete television receivers on the market—an enthusiast would have to buy a "televisor" or "radiovisor" unit to use with a short-wave receiver. Programs remained based on radio entertainment, such as singers, dancers, and comedians, or on the novelty of the moving image—silhouettes, cartoons, and half-tone images. While being little more than a scientific novelty, awareness of the new visual mass medium was growing. In 1933, the film *Men Must Fight* had a futuristic scenario with television screens and video telephones. On June 30, 1936, the *New York Times* reported that field tests from the Empire State Building had created a huge demand from the public, and telephone operators were "swamped" by the widespread interest in the test, many of the inquirers asking where they might go to view the "performance." "It is understood restaurant, department stores, night clubs and other public gathering places have requested that receivers be installed so that their guests and clients may look in on the experimental 'entertainment.'" By 1939, RCA advertised the first television sets and the New York World's Fair was notable for the presence of this mass-produced visual "radio."[24]

Inventions other than the movies, though related technologically, were also appearing to change the way that culture was produced and consumed. Technology in the form of microphotography that appeared to turn books into films was heralded in 1937. *The Literary Digest* explained how a "full-sized newspaper can be reduced to a foot of movie film" and that the machinery involved resembled movie cameras.[25]

Other technological developments in printing and photography were also challenging the space that words had traditionally occupied: picture magazines had become a fad by 1937, and publishers were presenting news stories visually with only a minimum text to guide reader's reactions. In 1937, *The Literary Digest* reviewed the recent development of *Life*, *Time*, *Fortune*, *Mid-Week Pictorial*, and *Look* magazines, all produced from advances in print technology. From the midthirties, beginning with *Life* magazine, the public demand for these new or revamped titles grew prolifically. *The Literary Digest* claimed that within days of selling out, the first issue of *Life* magazine in 1936 had become a collector's item and the sole excuse for having a cocktail party. Anxiety over the low standards of some of these pulp magazines accelerated with the appearance of "pixies"—picture magazine "spinoffs" catering to the public's insatiable demand for images. One lurid example was the first issue of *Highroad*, a monthly published in January 1937, where two pages were devoted to the "horrors of automobile accidents." The photos for the article were selected from the news photos taken by the Highway Department and freelance photographers and haughtily titled "Thou Shalt Not Kill." *The Literary Digest* ended the review with speculation on how far this trend for visual sensation and "candid" photography would go—warning that it could go a lot further yet.[26]

Radio listening also gave writers cause for concern as the thirties witnessed rapid radio commercialization, with the introduction of soap serials and a huge rise in levels of corporate sponsorship.[27] Radio listening and ownership underwent a phenomenal growth, boosted by technological enhancements, cheaper sets, and hire-purchase schemes. From an amateur hobby in the twenties, by the midthirties radio broadcasting had become the fourth major industry in the United States. In a 1938 *Fortune* poll, asking readers which industry best met public demands, radio was voted second only to the automobile—motion pictures came a distant fourth.[28] By 1939, "86 percent of all households owned at least one set, and the average listener tuned in for four and one-half hours daily."[29] Six and a half million cars also had radios installed. Popular radio shows were piped into cinemas and stores so that they would not lose patronage, as a result of the enormous, and apparently addictive, popularity of serial shows and dramas. Many programs attracted repeat listeners by running quiz shows and offering prizes that were linked to the sponsors' products.

In July 1932, *Business Week* analyzed the consumer market for leisure in an article titled "We Spend About as Much for Fun as for Running the Government." Claiming that Americans spent as much on the consumption of leisure products as "it costs to operate the federal government," the article noted that "the outstanding feature of the picture of pleasure expenditure by the consumer over this period is the dominant and relatively increasing importance of the commercial or professional kinds of recreation as contrasted with the private, personal, or individual varieties." Confirming Nash's judgment on the passivity of the American consumer, the article stated that "Americans are apparently vicarious sportsmen, preferring to pay and see rather than to indulge actively themselves." Claiming that "passive recreations" had increased fourfold over private ones and that "outlay on private recreation apparently drops more sharply in depressions than that of the commercial variety," *Business Week* appeared to confirm the diagnosis that America had become a nation of passive listeners, movie addicts, and sufferers from the condition of "spectatoritis." Especially notable was the claim that money spent on movies "even increased continuously in depression years" and that "in 1930 there were about 21,000 motion picture theatres, two-thirds of them wired for sound, and with an average number of paid admissions per week of about 100 millions," which showed that almost the entire population, excluding infants, apparently attended the movies once weekly.

Although educators and social workers followed in the footsteps of earlier reformers on the problems of "passive" leisure, the Depression added a variety of new dimensions to previous concerns. In particular, it was assumed that new technologies sparked increasing competition and lowered income, with the result that cultural standards were driven down to their lowest possible point. If technology in general was to blame for the decline in American vigor, then visual technologies in particular were perceived as a threat to mental capacity. This would most certainly impact on the popularity and sales of more serious and "difficult" writers. This "dumbing down" was part of the "thrill" of the movies, according to journalist Alice Ames Winter, and relied on the public's "resentment" of words: "The audience resent words, words, words. Something doing and real people doing it is the demand. Not talking about it but acting it. The average picture can hold not more than 500 or 600 words to a reel, say 6,000 to a ten reel movie. Not many words tell a complicated tale with enough variety of action and of character to satisfy its much asking public. And that public has generally a very limited vocabulary."[30] With a disappearance of words into film, an increasing movie-going public, and the imitation of movie speech by youths, assumptions that a limited vocabulary was as "catching" as the disease of spectatoritis were widespread by the midthirties.

Because of the perception that mass culture was becoming dangerously visual, reading experienced new attention from reformers. Educationalist

Edwin Embree claimed that libraries were "pressing their wares on every-one as aggressively as a Fuller Brush salesman," and no one "in America has any excuse for not reading except his own laziness or his own stu-pidity." Books "are the greatest inheritance of the new generations," he claimed. "They preserve the wisdom and the beauty of the race, and carry it as a living, ever growing stream." There was also commercial gain to be made. Rather than simply borrow books, the wisest readers were "those who would really enjoy and enrich their leisure" by purchasing them, for they "will not be content simply to borrow their reading. They will want to own a part of this literary wealth. A book these days costs no more than a fat dinner. And happily both wisdom and brilliance are being made up into beautiful units of type and binding and format. In the new era mental foot and emotional raiment are quite as vital as fodder and overcoats. In the rapid upswing of the market, books are commodities in which each of us with great profits may make investments."[31]

Publisher's Weekly emphasized how the new leisure could in fact be a boon for the book trade, and yet it must be "in the thick of this compe-tition" with "theatres, movie houses, beer gardens, game manufacturers [and] magazine publishers," both "for its own survival and because of the great wealth that books have to offer."[32] Advertisements indicating the benefits of reading became common: in one advertisement for cor-respondence learning, for example, the popular writer Booth Tarkington stares intently into the readers' eyes with the caption above him saying: "Fall in Love with Words and You, too, May Climb the Ladder of Fame."[33] According to this, words could lead to power, fame, success, and money. Another article emphasized the wealth of the pulp writer who "may be putting out the lights of his chateau" on the French Riviera after having "written 10,000 words at two cents a word."[34]

Of great concern to writers was Nash's fear that "spectatoritis" now defined the experience of being American, and this was compounded by a general sense that standards of literacy, education, and intelligence were also declining. With the predominance of the visual over the liter-ary, even greater emphasis on the importance of written language was made to combat the lazy-minded habits of the public. Much advice to the unemployed tacitly personalized the nationwide problem by advis-ing the jobless that they needed to improve their minds in order to find employment—almost as if it were low literacy levels that had caused mass unemployment in the first place. Advertisements for correspondence education in popular magazines correlated employment with educational success and offered the chance for the working man to improve himself during leisure in readiness for productive employment, arguing that reading was a productive way to make the most of "The March of Spare Time."[35] Reading was promoted as one way that a worker could make himself more valuable to his employers, or as one way the unemployed could step back into employment.

Reading was also promoted as a leisure pursuit that could reunite the nuclear family broken apart by commercial leisure pursuits. As the cover of *Leisure: The Magazine of a Thousand Diversions* for December 1935 showed, a father could keep his family happily close to his side by reading to his children in his leisure (Figure 8). WPA photographs similarly captured men reading to their families at the hearth and working-class men learning to use libraries for self-improvement.[36] The power of words to rebuild a man's confidence, gain control over his family and friends, and to win respect and love were emphasized in contrast to the enervating and emasculating effect of passive commercial entertainments.[37]

Such concern over declining mental capacity was paralleled in the widespread fear that society's traditional leaders had been confounded by the challenges of mass culture. In the early years of the Depression, intellectuals and social scientists no longer appeared in control of the nation, and their cultural authority often seemed undermined by the social stresses and the instabilities of modern commercial culture. One writer in the *American Sociological Review* in 1936 summarized the crisis in this way: "For the past three years, news stands and book shelves have creaked with essays on business recovery. Within this period . . . The Brain Trust rose, staggered and fell before the supreme court. The professor in Washington became a theme for cartoonists. People began to ask, 'who are the intelligentsia and what do they know about steering a nation?'"[38]

Fearing that culture itself was under "threat of extinction," socialist novelist Waldo Frank said in his foreword to the *American Writers' Congress*, "We were drawn together by the threat, implicit in the present social system, to our culture and our very lives as creative men and women." Allying themselves with the interests of the "propertyless and oppressed," many writers agreed that the "alliance of writers and artists with the working classes" was key to their mutual survival. Writers attempted to create a style that would revalidate the role of the writer, that would be anticapitalist and anticonsumerist, and that would reinvigorate the role of literature as instrumental to social transformation. In the attempt to create proletarian literature, where writers could effect social and political change and where writing was "work" for the communal good, writers adopted styles that were heavily influenced by sociological and "scientific" methods. The role and image of writing as a "leisured" occupation had to change. Idleness, waste, and frivolity were eschewed in the very adoption of this literary style. Mass culture was frivolous, whereas writing had to be serious or with a serious purpose. Writers had to be involved in the collective social process and forego their bourgeois individualism;

8. Cover of *Leisure*, December 1935, shows Dad keeping the family happy in difficult times. *Leisure* magazine suggested thousands of diversions for family entertainment. Courtesy Library of Congress.

like industrial workers, they were expected to join a union and define themselves in similar terms as workers.

For the writer, mass culture, commercial leisure, and the growth of mass-produced amusements often presented a more persistent threat than even fascism or capitalism. Author John Dos Passos outlined how the "belt conveyor factory system of production" threatened the writer, putting him "in a position of increasing danger and uncertainty": "Newspapers, advertising offices, moving picture studios, political propaganda agencies, produce the collective types of writing where individual work is indistinguishable in the industrial effort."[39]

While Dos Passos's statement hits at capitalist modes of production, his worries over individualism illustrate an anxiety that the role of the writer was becoming circumscribed by all forms of "collective" writing, including those coming from the government-sponsored programs or communist dictates. However, he omits the complicity of, and benefits from, the writer's connection with the industrial process. Not just victim but creator of mass markets and a middle-class readership, the writer was almost entirely reliant on the prosperity and leisure of the middle classes. Yet, in allying themselves with the proletariat, many writers and artists spurned notions of bourgeois and commercial leisure by emphasizing work, utilitarian values, and precapitalist or communist modes of existence.

The dichotomy between intellectuals and mass culture was thereby not as simple as some of the rhetoric implied. The relationship of writers with mass culture was becoming more symbiotic, and the collapse of art into commodified culture was something that writers could hardly ignore, especially as their role was instrumental in making this happen. As Barnard states, "All artistic practices were becoming commodified or 'mass' in the way that they were produced, or consumed, or marketed, or distributed, or discussed."[40] Cultural production in the thirties was "often the product of a dialectic between the proletarian avant-garde and the culture industries."[41] Yet, by using the same methods employed by industries—such as mass production, syndication, and mass consumption—the avant-garde and WPA projects aimed to create a public culture as an alternative to the commercial culture industries.

Although recent cultural historians have examined the relationship between writers and working-class politics in this period, and more recently between writers/artists and popular culture, few have looked at how the writers negotiated their role within the professional classes at this time. Michael Szalay provides a corrective to this, describing a complex formulation where "writers assimilated themselves to an emergent professional-managerial class in a way that belied the often radical content of their writing."[42] Illustrating how writers and their productions became inwrought in New Deal thought and culture, Szalay explores how they emerged during this period as salaried cultural workers and "agents" of New Deal, albeit avant-garde, government projects. As cultural representatives of government policy, many writers engaged deeply with the reconstruction and redefinition of "work" and "leisure" ethics during this period. In opposition to the vulnerability of free market economics writers adopted a new role of "professionalized proletarianism" that secured or enhanced their position in society, yet it was a role limited by its relationship to the new bureaucracy of New Deal liberalism. At the same time, New Deal recreation programs that employed writers and encouraged "good" reading complemented the radical approach to mass culture. However, despite this new security, writers remained ambivalent about their new functional role.

As Szalay notes, writers reinvented themselves as "workers" and "producers" and professionals as part of a wider movement to provide security from the haphazard tropes of "bourgeois" patronage and the laissez-faire publication market. Writers and artists could benefit directly from that reinvention by rejecting individualism and turning art into "cultural work" for the social good of all. Turning writing into "work" that was performed for a wage, literary productions directly engaged with the anti-gambling/play metaphors of a "new deal" in order to regulate literary markets and counteract the uncertainty and insecurity of the capitalist marketplace.[43] Through the New Deal, "art would become not a system of commodities at all, but an administratively coordinated process of production" and as such would become "a form of recreation that all might perform . . . making consumption and production one and the same process."[44] The pivotal choice at the American Writers' Congress in 1935 to change radical rhetoric about "the worker" to the less class-based "the people" also signified a shifting concern from production to consumption, and thus from work to leisure.

In the same year, accommodation between writers and the machine also appeared to be taking place. Writer and critic Robert Forsythe wrote in *New Masses*, "As writers and critics we'll have to get over the notion that the Machine is an evil and that all workers are slaves of the Machine. . . . The Machine can be an oppressor but it doesn't need to be. That fact makes all the difference in the world."[45] The survival of the artist and writer in the climate of the New Deal seemed somewhat ensured by the progressive emphasis on the cultural primacy of art, education, and literature as an antidote to "machine" living. In fact, eclectic writer and social planner Lewis Mumford predicted in 1934 that "control" of machine living would return to the "masters" through a new philosophy of art and cultural expression: "Like an old-fashioned menial, the arrogance of the machine grew in proportion to its master's feebleness and folly. With a change in ideals from material conquest, wealth and power to life, culture and expression, the machine, like the menial with a new and more confident master, will fall back into its proper place: our servant, not our tyrant."[46]

Mumford suggested that traditional authority could be regained by social and cultural leaders through the improvement of education and culture, by using intelligence and "social discipline," "sounder forms of recreation [and] greater opportunities for the natural enjoyments of life" in place of passive dependence on machines.[47] The metaphor incorporated the notion of impotence and weakness—the "feebleness" and "folly" of social and cultural "masters"—and indicated that meritocratic hierarchies could be established with the adoption of intelligently led leisure programs. The more time that machines created for leisure, the more time that ordinary Americans could now devote to becoming both consumers and producers of "real" culture.

With New Deal funding of cultural projects, then, writers became central to this reconstruction of nonwork time. The new role of the writer as government official and social worker was highlighted by the Federal Writers Project (FWP). In fact, the FWP epitomized the marriage of sociological and creative efforts toward the proper use of leisure. The project had a utilitarian impetus from the start: creating indices, encyclopedia, historical, regional, scientific, and economic studies. Writing became "work," even a form of sociology, and folklore studies were modeled on sociological investigations and methodologies. Henry Alsberg, director of the FWP, claimed that "the most creative writing of the times was being done in the field of non-fiction," adding that perhaps one of the most stimulating and imaginative of contemporary writers was "not a novelist, like Hemingway, but an economist like Veblen."[48] Despite having published his most famous text—*The Theory of the Leisure Class*—more than thirty years previously, Alsberg obviously saw Veblen as more significant in the world of literature and writing than either creative writers, or more recently popular social scientists. More importantly, the use of Veblen as a model indicated the centrality of leisure theories in the production of literature at this time.

In fact, the reinvigoration of the cultural producer involved him or her in the new use of leisure for positive or productive purposes. As such, federal art projects like the FWP were seen as having a double use—while amusing the unemployed and employing unemployable artists and writers, the artists themselves acted as community educators and social workers. In keeping with the leadership goals of recreation reformers, writers and artists also became community and recreation leaders. Not only did this keep them from turning to revolutionary politics, as many had already done, the FWP functioned to keep writers busy and employed in more useful roles of social and leisure educator. At the same time, projects that involved community education for the new leisure helped to keep the unemployed out of "trouble." In his essay "The Artist as Social Worker," WPA artist Irving Marantz described his work in a community boys club: "It is a source of personal satisfaction to me and to other teachers that the artistic merit of the production of our art classes has been widely recognized and is often publicly praised. But far more significant is the social value of this work in terms of human rehabilitation. Experience has clearly demonstrated that the Abe Levines and Johnny Langs are what they are because of their family surroundings and social environment have made them so—and that art is a great therapy which can in many cases turn them into useful social beings, often into sound craftsmen, and even sometimes into distinguished artists."[49]

Marantz's essay is unintentionally ironic, as the two boys mentioned were not exactly success stories; Abe Levine went off the rails during Marantz's sick leave and ended up in "a school for delinquents," and Johnny Lang "is now institutionalized" after the supply of art materials was exhausted. The essay functions as a plea for increased funding for relief programs rather than a straightforward example of the success of such projects.

Yet the social role of the artist continued to feature as justification for the cultural projects, showing that the funding did not get wasted on "art for arts sake." Showing this, WPA artist Lawrence Jones stated how his employment with the Federal Art Project (FAP) gave him "a vivid realization of my social responsibility towards the underprivileged, and in New Orleans I have since followed the example of many of my race who in the North have been taking an active part in the WPA/FAP art work for many years."[50] In New York, evening classes "frankly aimed at taking young people from the frequently disastrous influences of the street" made similar claims of reducing crime and delinquency.[51] Occupying both artists and unemployed youths in their free time, WPA art projects fulfilled a multitude of the goals of traditional leisure reform.

Like other WPA projects, the FWP also played a significant role in encouraging the "proper" utilization of leisure. Its major project, the American Guide Series—a series of state-by-state guides—was intended to introduce Americans to American culture and history, on one level controlling how readers should read the history and landscape of the past and present. Leisure time that was used to learn about the democratic opportunities and roots of American culture was leisure functioning for democracy itself. However, limiting opportunities for creative expression, the FWP directors became increasingly interventionist: "The national editors issued a series of manuals to state offices, eighteen in all, which dictated collection practices, filing systems, the flow of copy through the editorial office, textual organization and style."[52] Despite getting paid to work on the FWP, some writers found the strict application of utilitarian values and sociological methods somewhat limiting. Some expressed dissatisfaction with the restrictive practices of the project, including the overall editorial control from Washington, D.C., complaining of a lack of creative opportunity and overbearing management from nonwriters and bureaucrats.[53]

Despite, or perhaps because of, the new security that the cultural program offered, artists and writers remained skeptical about the potential of the bureaucratic machine to reinvigorate the Forgotten Man and prescribe for cultural rejuvenation. Regardless of their concerns over mass culture, many writers also found it impossible to ignore the way that leisure had become an arena of struggle, where hegemonic social forces merely replaced the earlier and more obvious forms of industrial control of the worker in the workplace. This awareness came about precisely because of the relationship that had arisen between government and party politics, social scientists, and writers. Uniquely placed to understand the role of leisure in the production and consumption of texts, writers' negotiation with the problem of leisure often reflected ambivalence to mass culture as well as social authoritarianism. Writers during this period were therefore more fully aware than ever of their complicity with, and alienation from, the role of government and social control. Central to this issue was the role of the new leisure in creating a bureaucratic and homogenized American culture. While many writers had struggled with the notion of a degenerate mass leisure, their fictional reactions came to represent a different response to that of the leisure professionals. Although there are many parallels between the social scientists and the writers who adopted their stance, there were also fundamental differences between the two, which prevented "correct" leisure from becoming a panacea in the fiction of the era as it did in most of the social science texts on leisure.

These doubts over bureaucracy and the imposition of cultural imperatives from above triggered new anxieties. Over the course of the decade these anxieties about modern leisure often commuted into anxieties over social control and fascism. The most fitting example of this is Sinclair Lewis's 1935 novel *It Can't Happen Here*, charting the fictional rise to government of an American fascist dictatorship where leisure becomes a conduit for the introduction of control and suppression. The novel followed the rise of fascism in the United States through the personal experiences of Doremus Jessup, a liberal, rather effete (his wife calls him Dormouse), newspaper editor. Over the course of the novel, Jessup's initial indifference to conservative trends, which he originally supports, transforms into opposition to the resulting oppressive dictatorship. In it, Lewis satirizes middle- and upper-class attitudes to leisure and reform, indicating how the conservative views of the wealthy toward leisure and reform could function as a precursor to authoritarianism and dictatorship. The novel begins at the meeting of the local Rotary club where speakers are giving patriotic addresses; in a satirical sketch of Adelaide Tarr Gimmitch at this meeting, the conservative reformer is used to illustrate the evolution from benevolent leisure reform to social control. Gimmitch imagines she saves American soldiers from European/sexual corruption by the imposition of "suitable" and approved occupations: "no more renowned for her gallant anti-suffrage campaigning way back in 1919 than . . . for having, during the Great War, kept the American soldiers entirely out of French cafes by the clever trick of sending them ten thousand sets of dominoes."[54] This portrait of Gimmitch parallels the real-life experience of Raymond Fosdick, chairman of the Committee on the Use of Leisure Time, who "formulated and executed the great program of recreational opportunity and activity for the American Army" when the armistice left "two million men in France" who were "surrounded by every inducement to misconduct and almost no opportunity for wholesome behavior."[55] As previously mentioned, the mobilization needed for recovery from depression involved planning for leisure and work comparable to wartime arrangements, all of which necessitated some form of social control.

Later in the novel Gimmitch gives a speech arguing for "Discipline," "Will Power," and "Character," all major objectives of leisure reformers.[56] Jessup is stirred into conservative meditation by these speeches on the way home and bemoans the effeteness of mass culture: "The youngsters today. . . . Oh, the aviators have plenty of nerve. The physicists, these twenty-five-year-old PhDs that violate the inviolable atom, they're pioneers. But most of the wishy-washy young people today. . . . Going twenty miles an hour but not getting anywhere . . . not enough imagination to *want* to go anywhere! Getting their music by turning a dial. Getting their phrases from comic strips instead of from Shakespeare and the Bible and Veblen and Old Bill Sumner. Pap-fed flabs!"[57] However, he later regrets the call for strength and direction, equating that with the fascism that had come to dominate the country. The consequences of reform and censorship over leisure practices is presented as far worse than the haphazard, random, and freewheeling nature of modern commercial leisure, of which he had been critical. He despairs about the "sudden diminution of gaiety" caused by the bureaucratization and control of leisure: "The Corpos found nothing more convenient to milk than public pleasures. After the bread had moulded, the circuses were closed. There were taxes or increased taxes on motor cars, movies, theatres, dances and ice-cream sodas. There was a tax on playing a gramophone or a radio in any restaurant. . . . Even the most reckless youngsters went less and less to public entertainments. . . . It was impossible to sit in a public place without wondering which spies were watching you. So all the world stayed home."[58]

At this stage Jessup, a "former gossip," no longer dares to talk openly; his role as a writer in the community is circumscribed and controlled by the fear of the dictatorship in power. Lewis's novel points out the way that anxieties over modern leisure and attempts to control it, even for the collective good, are connected to the possibility of repression and even violence.

The significance and importance of modern leisure were also explored in stories by the working-class writer William Saroyan. These stories are the apparent antithesis of social "realism": rambling, self-reflexive, and ambivalent. For Saroyan, leisure is essential to the creative process, and he continually reminds the reader that it is in his leisure that the writer is writing and consequently in the readers' leisure that his words are read. This awareness of the cultural nourishment afforded by leisure is a direct rejection of the work ethic, the idea that writing is a form of "production," and the notion that the role of leisure is to reinvigorate the worker for the industrial process. For example, his story "Myself upon the Earth" is essentially a preamble to a story, something that the writer is in the process of creating, a rambling that "may seem pointless and a waste of time, but it is not." "There is," he claims, "absolutely no haste." Later he again insists, "There is no hurry, I am a story-teller, not an aviator," disassociating the process of writing from the commerce and production of machine-led capitalism. Eventually he explains that the purpose of the story is to tell that he now has his typewriter back from the pawnbrokers, and that is how he has come to write the story. Explaining that he went to the moneylender and received fifteen dollars for his typewriter, he confesses that "I put my typewriter in hock and I began to spend the money," going to a movie theatre and then a restaurant. Saroyan's writer acts in a way that leisure professionals feared, against all values of thrift and accumulation. Spending "irrationally," Saroyan indicates the need for working-class leisure and pleasure despite poverty. High culture and middle-class values of propriety hold little meaning in a life of poverty, he indicates. High cultural values and educational improvement, in this respect, is a deferred use of time that is empty of meaning to the poor: "No one, not even the greatest writer, can go on being poor hour after hour, year after year. There is such a thing as saying to hell with art. That's what I said."[59]

Unlike "proletarian" realist and naturalist writers, Saroyan labors constantly in his short stories to undermine the assumption that writing is "work" in the way that other jobs are. In "Seventy Thousand Assyrians," for example, the narrator meets a young man looking for work in the lettuce fields of Salinas and compares his own hard-luck tale in an ironic tone: "I wanted to tell him how it was with me: rejected story from *Scribner's*, rejected essay from *The Yale Review*, no money for decent cigarettes, worn shoes, old shirts, but I was afraid to make something of my own troubles. A writer's troubles are always boring, a bit unreal. People are apt to feel, *well who asked you to write in the Wrst place?* A man must pretend not to be a writer."[60]

Like Saroyan, the limits of the writer and words to represent a transparent "truth" was something that concerned many writers of this decade. Words were not, in this case, productive economic units that were paid for or that could be harnessed for practical use and self-improvement. Words, insubstantial and mutable in Saroyan's stories, are compared with the need for "real" sustenance of the poor and hungry: "Water and prose were fine, they filled much inorganic space, but they were inadequate. If there were only some work he might do for money, some trivial labor in the name of commerce."[61] The death of the writer at the end of the story "The Daring Young Man on the Flying Trapeze" reflects not only the failure of words but the failure of the new bureaucratic culture to allow him pleasure and life. He dies having spent his last few hours attempting and failing to write "An Application for Permission to Live"— the very notion of writing having become "unpleasant to him" as "there was nothing to say."[62] Not only do words fail the writer, but he cannot use them to justify his existence in a world devoid of pleasure—a world where words are instructions or applications to bureaus rather than forms of entertainment and pleasure. The writer dies failing to comply with regulatory and bureaucratic expectations and definitions, as an individual whose citizenship and "permission to live" involves a literacy based on bureaucratically defined requirements.

Writers also expressed ambivalence about the role of the author as "authority" within the text, indicating that the role of art was less concerned with cultural ascendancy than with questioning such traditional hierarchies. Aware of their role in the new world of leisure and commerce, writers sometimes slipped into a self-reflexivity and parody to represent this new "reality," less a position of power than a deconstruction of the politics of power and objectivity that anticipated notions of literary failure and collapse. In "Seventy Thousand Assyrians," for example, Saroyan writes more about what the story is not, and what it can never be, than what it is: "I am not using great material for a short story. Nothing is going to happen in this work. I am not fabricating a fancy plot. I am not creating memorable characters. I am not using a slick style of writing. I am not building a fine atmosphere. I have no desire to sell this story to *The Saturday Evening Post* or to *Cosmopolitan* or to *Harper's*.

I am not trying to compete with the great writers of short stories, men like Sinclair Lewis and Joseph Hergsheimer and Zane Grey, men who really know how to write, how to make up stories that will sell."[63]

Saroyan's story is the antistory, the story not of literary usefulness and production but of purposeful waste, of leisure and uselessness. Also addressing the new utilitarianism of cultural outlooks, where leisure becomes a time for self-improvement and productivity, he mocks the authority of the new supervised culture in his short story "A Curved Line," showing that in everyday experience "high" culture and supervisory intentions are often meaningless. Writing from an awareness of the intended didacticism of thirties cultural programs, he literally cuts up the letters from the "Pelman Institute of America," which tell him he could have a "big fine brain" and is propelled by boredom with such didacticism to attend an art class in the high school next door: "It was a place to go at night. I was tired of the radio. I had heard NRA speeches, excerpts from Carmen, Tosti's "Goodbye" and "Trees" every night for over a year. Sometimes twice a night. . . . The pattern was the same. It was the same with symphonies even. Once a lady conducted, but it was the same. Beethoven's Fifth, "The Sorcerer's Apprentice" and "The Blue Danube Waltz." Its been going on for years and years. . . . It's gotten so that when the music isn't played, we hear it."[64] Saroyan's narrator is aware that "proper" educational leisure—signified by the repetitious playing of classical music over the radio—is intended to "improve" the individual. The big fine brain offered to him by the Pelman Institute connects to anxieties over educational standards and psychological well-being that underpinned many leisure programs. While eugenic and scientific studies purported to show that brain size illustrated the degree of culture and civilization, he cuts up this vision of himself with scissors. His encounter with "high culture" leaves him bored rather than educated. He attends an art class as "something to do for a while" and not to improve himself. Saroyan gently undercuts the intended didacticism of reformed leisure, illustrating that, for some at least, leisure programs merely offered a warm shelter, some company, and were sometimes used in a way that subverted reformers' goals of improvement.

Similarly, other productions criticized the apparently homogenous "folk revivial" so central to recreation reformers' ideals. In fact, the paradox of folk art as an antidote to industrial oppression provided fuel for some satirists and writers. Upton Sinclair, in his book *The Flivver King: A Story of Ford America* (1937) provided a literary perception of the relationship between "organized" folk leisure and the violence of the industrial process. Describing Henry Ford's anxiety over modern trends such as short skirts and listening and dancing to jazz, Sinclair wrote, "As part of his crusade against the new America, Henry declared war upon that dreadful style of [jazz] dancing which the international Jews and Bolsheviki had taught the American people for their undoing. Henry liked the clean and jolly 'square dances' which the farm people had known when he was a boy."[65]

In the book, Henry's "war" on the new America begins as a leisure reform that creates joy and community cohesion through play: "America, the world, needs understanding of each other, the spirit of play."[66] Yet the violence behind such reform is indicated by a later scene, where a quadrille danced at one of Ford's parties is intercut with a scene of Ford "gangsters" beating up labor organizers:

> The gangsters were making a professional job of it. They had Tom on his side and were kicking him in the small of his back to loosen his kidneys.
> "Chassez out," called the prompter; the old-timers always pronounced it "Shashay." And then, "Form lines." The dancers moved with perfect grace, knowing every move.
> The chief executioner was now kicking his victim in the groin, so that he would not be of much use to his wife for a while.
> "Six hands around the ladies," called the prompter. Such charming smiles from elderly ladies, playing at coquetry, renewing their youth.[67]

The respectability of the dance is compared with the underlying violence of social control and the repression of labor organizers, indicating that the call for a "spirit of play" was imbued with the violence of class control. Sinclair thereby equated Ford's impulse to re-create "folk" leisure pursuits with the control over nonwork time that characterized new forms of industrial and state management of workers.

Even when thoroughly influenced by social scientific rhetoric, many writers subtly critiqued the authoritarian goals and methods of leisure reform. In his chapter from *The American Earthquake*, "Hull-House in 1932," writer Edmund Wilson reiterated the analysis of mass consumerism so dominant in books by Lundberg and Lynd: "A relief worker's cross-section of an industrial suburb shows the sinking of the standard of living. The people are mostly Poles. Every pressure has been brought to bear on them to induce them to spend their money on motor-cars, radios, overstuffed furniture and other unattractive luxuries: and they are caught now between two worlds, with no way of living comfortably in either."[68] Although Wilson saw the "unattractive luxuries" of the poor in sociological terms, observing how their purchases were a result of mass-culture brainwashing ("pressure . . . to induce them"), he also highlighted the way reformers used the spaces of leisure and recreation for their education programs and social control. In his assessment of a flophouse he claimed that Tarzan movies are "provided to keep them out of the hands of the communists" and that music is played to entice the homeless men into the recreation hall, where they were then subjected to a talk by a policeman who tells how he was "saved" by religion. The use of culture or art (in this case music) by social reformers serves the reactionary purpose of tricking the men into a forced moral and religious lesson.[69]

In contrast to the idea of a leisured technological utopia, where time freed by the machine was spent in self-improvement via noncommercial pursuits, Saroyan's play *The Time of Your Life*, performed in 1939, celebrated human victory over the machine within commercial leisure. Willie, a young Assyrian obsessed with beating the pinball machine in Nick's bar, finally wins: "Himself vs. The machine. Willie vs. Destiny. His skill and daring vs. the cunning and trickery of the novelty industry of America, and the whole challenging world. He is the last of the American pioneers, with nothing more to fight but the machine. He is the last challenger, the young man with nothing to do in the world."[70] Idle Willie's leisure has become work, a struggle not only for revenue but for meaning and identity in a mass-produced world. Willie's triumph, though small, impresses the other characters, as they didn't believe the machine could be beaten; his identity is confirmed and his self-belief invigorated. Throughout the play small amounts of money are lost into machines through gambling, gaming, or entertainment. Willie's victory is a qualified one—his six nickel reward only balancing the amount he puts into the machine—that shows that the economic relationship between work, leisure, and machinery is one negotiated by human decisions and acts, where identity and agency become possible. Pleasure and agency, it poses, are possible negotiations despite mechanical and commercial leisure.[71]

The growth of popular leisure activities as an industry that involved the commodification and appropriation of the working body was also perceived by other writers at the time. If leisure was work, then work was sometimes a form of "leisure." In his memoir, Albert Halper, a young working-class writer during the thirties, described spending a summer "servicing" an adult summer camp. Working at a country leisure resort as a waiter and host, he equated the work itself with performing a sport where the jogging waiters were "like panting runners in a marathon race." In another simile, Halper describes being commanded to dance with guests once the shift had ended: "We took off our damp clothes and flopped upon the beds like exhausted swimmers, cursing the management, the guests and the surrounding mountains. Soon the strains of dance music drifted in from the casino on the lake. A flunky from the office appeared in the doorway: 'Okay boys. Mrs You-Know-Who wants you to get dressed pronto and dance with the female guests.'"[72]

The collapse of clear definitions between the meaning of work and leisure is further illustrated by the unceasing "round of cultural and athletic events in the camp." "Guests ran from event to fresh event, as if to extract the last ounce of value from their stay," he writes: "Each Saturday morning we waiters watched new guests piling out of the buses that had hauled them like so much freight from the city. They arrived pale and wan from a year's work in offices or show-rooms, many of them loaded down with tennis rackets and golf clubs, the girls carrying bulging suitcases of sports clothes and evening dresses they had skimped all year to buy."[73]

The leisure of these city dwellers is described as part of the industrial process, the workers as freight, shipped in en masse, enjoying an endless and exhausting production line of leisure activities, leaving them tanned and tuned for a return to the productive process. Clearly, here, Halper saw leisure as no less than an adjunct to the production process and in many ways as a replacement for it in a time of economic breakdown. Halper's descriptions of the summer camp undermine the association of leisure with good health and illustrate how too much organization of leisure merely re-creates the industrial stresses that it is supposed to alleviate. Like the suggestions of leisure professionals to make good use of every moment available in the day—in a parallel to the time and motion studies of industry—the summer camp provides a wearying parallel to the industrial process and at the same time creates low-paid, nonunionized jobs for those who service it. Halper shows how the leisure industry not only purchases the labor of workers but purchases their bodies for consumption. By equating work with sport and leisure, Halper collapsed the notion that they are discreet entities, reconfiguring the blind assumption that a leisured society automatically entailed leisure for all.

The intersection of social science with art produced interesting correlations surrounding the ideology of modern leisure, yet the debates over culture that emerged at the time indicate there was little real consensus on which to base any single program of cultural reform. Although writers were centrally involved in the cultural reconstruction of America through leisure during the thirties, they also expressed ambivalence over the use of culture for bureaucratic and federal control. While patriarchal discourses of leisure reform and left-wing criticisms of "effete" consumerism often overlapped, fundamental differences between cultural producers and state officials or social scientists emerged over individuality, freedom of expression, and creativity. Further, anxieties over changing gender roles extended this conflict over leisure and culture even more, for where men were "emasculated" by the Depression, women, it seemed, were simultaneously empowered to let loose all their irrational excesses—to the possible detriment of family, morality, and masculinity. The problem of leisure, then, extended way beyond the battle over cultural representations of leisure or the political and social organization of the New Deal. In Anderson's view, male impotence was caused by a relationship to modern machinery, but it was women, uniquely adapted to modern life and consumption, who apparently gained most from it. Reconstructing women's leisure, then, became a distinct feature of the new leisure of the New Deal era.

Chapter 5
Shopping for Leisure

> *In our complex system of division of tasks, consumer purchasing has largely fallen to the women. While men earn about 80 percent of the money income in the United States, women do about 85 percent of the consumer purchasing. When, as consumers, we "vote with our dollars" women's suffrage comes into its own.*
>
> —*Roland Vaile*, Income and Consumption

> *But woman's greatest weapon against the forces of depression is her buying power. Regardless of which side of the house the earning power comes from, women are reliably estimated to do 85 percent of the nation's retail buying.*
>
> —*National Recovery Administration*, Handbook for Speakers

In a chapter on consumers in *Recent Social Trends,* Robert Lynd and Alice Hanson noted that leisure was increasingly tied to consumption: "The growing margin of leisure in the American family, with the increasing variety and availability of leisure time . . . affects the consumption of a wide group of goods and services."[1] That same year, Harold Rugg claimed that a "fever" of consumerism had led many to resort to leisure that was "little less than sheer anaesthesia." "Witness the daily milling about of restless crowds in city squares, the herding together in athletic fields, the experimentation with new concepts and mores of sex life, the gin parties and the petting parties in which all ages and all social classes indulge," Rugg declared, confirming the fear that the consumption of leisure in commercial culture led to degenerate pursuits. Rugg, Lynd, and Hanson saw that rationalization of the economy was reliant on the rationalization of leisure.

Americans, Rugg argued, "lacking both the disposition and the racial experience for quiet reflection, contemplation, or personal creativeness" would, instead of "creating the contemplative artist," evolve "more rigidly than ever into his restless, uncultivated mold."[2] The uncultivated mold, in fact, was more typically female than male. Women played a central role in the new "fever" of consumerism, and while the Forgotten Man fought for a place in cultural output, social studies that confirmed the decline of patriarchal family structures heightened concerns over what women did with their leisure. Despite attempts to remedy it, the image of the weak male clearly persisted throughout the decade. This image was heightened by studies that indicated women's growing influence and ascendancy in a culture based increasingly on consumption and leisure, which in turn fueled attempts to control women's leisure activities and bring them into line with traditional recreation reform ideals.

Following research for Lundberg's *Leisure: A Suburban Study*, sociologist Mirra Komarovsky went on to write her doctoral thesis on the effect of unemployment on the status of the man in selected families, noting the breakdown of "authority relations," increasing control by women over finances, entertainment, and sex, all contributing to marriage breakdown and changes in the balance of power in the family.[3] This study reflected general perceptions on the changing gender roles precipitated by the Depression.

As early as 1931, Sherwood Anderson reflected extensively on this new balance of power, where "modern man is losing his ability to retain his manhood."[4] Anderson's book discussed contemporary American society while observing a night shift in a factory. Watching men and women working on the production line, he ponders on gender relationships, concluding that "American life had passed into the control of the women, I did not resent the fact. It had come about because we men of America had fallen down on our job."[5] To him, women seemed immune to the enervating effects of the machinery by virtue of their "hidden inner life" and ability to bring children into the world. Because they bore children, he assumed, they felt no compulsion to produce anything else and were thereby supremely adapted to consumer culture. As a result, America had become the "land where women rule."

I am trying to proclaim a new American world, a woman's world.
The newspapers are all run for women, the magazines, the stores.
The cities are all built for women. Whom do you suppose the automobiles are
    built for?
Practically all the American men I know have surrendered to women.[6]

Present-day life "humiliates men more directly," he claimed, as they have no territory. Anderson, like many recreation experts and social planners, felt that men needed to "go back to nature more," whereas goods were women's territory: "It seems to me that the goods are mostly for women. Women are the great consumers. They have a passion for possession. The passion for possession is feminine."[7] Although observing female laborers in a factory, he concluded that their position was one of power and that their ascendancy revolved less around their ability to produce than to consume goods.[8]

These concerns over male "impotency" in the face of machines, and the displacement of human agency in a system of mass production, were underwritten with desires for the reassertion of patriarchal control. Leisure manuals and federal programs followed this call with support for traditional leisure occupations or proto-work hobbies—which necessitated traditional gender roles—and advised against too much "machine-made leisure." As such, Anderson's view of machinery and modernity was part of a wider response to the Depression, where men were seen as "castrated" by unemployment. In contrast, all women, it appeared, had emerged as a new "leisure class," whether working on not, whose primary role as the consumer of household and luxury items led many to consider that modernity had led to an emergent matriarchy—visible even on the production line. While it was feared that men were in danger of being feminized and weakened, both physically and mentally, by their contact with the female sphere of leisure and consumption, women appeared to have become ascendant.[9] Anderson, like many other observers in the 1930s, saw consumer culture as a new form of matriarchy—one in which women held the purse strings and the key to ending the Depression. Thus it was women, through their leisure, rather than men, through their labor, who appeared to have the power to shape the future. These claims combined a fear of both women and modernity, which influenced how political and cultural leaders would react to the Depression and the cultural representations made of it.

Changes in women's roles in the interwar period fueled anxiety that authority over women was being lost. Not only had women gained suffrage in 1920, their presence in social and political life had substantially increased. The Depression often reversed accepted gender roles and this, it was assumed, depleted male confidence and authority while giving women new confidence and control. Robert Lynd, for example, noted on his return to Muncie to study the effect of the Depression, that "it is the world of male roles that has been under most pressure" but that for some women the Depression "brought temporary easement of tensions."[10]

Multiple representations in mass culture of the 1930s substantiated Anderson's image of the acquisitive and consuming female. He used the example of a popular comic strip, "Bringing Up Father," to corroborate his view that women were now more powerful than men. In it the self-made millionaire father is physically beaten and abused by his wife and daughter, who spend his money recklessly for any whim that enters their heads. "Bringing Up Father" illustrated a new female power; as male power was represented by accumulated wealth, women embodied the disintegration, through consumption, of male dominance and prosperity. In mass culture at least, the humiliation of the male was blamed only partly on the Depression, overproduction, or machinery; women, it appeared, could consolidate and enhance male impotence through their furious and irrational consumption. Visual representations expressed similar ambivalence to the newly "powerful" female consumer; paintings by Reginald Marsh showed women shoppers as "energetic sexualized female[s]" who packaged themselves for the male gaze and yet posed a liberated and "defiant threat to masculine claims to social and economic power."[11] His paintings juxtaposed siren shoppers in close proximity to physically crippled men, helpless drunks, or exhausted marathon dancers.

Fears of a new "matriarchy" of shoppers controlling the purse strings of the nation thus permeated popular discourses. In *Recent Social Trends,* the consumer was referred to primarily as the housewife, easily seduced by advertising campaigns to purchase unnecessary baubles during her leisure hours. According to the president's committee, relying on her untrained mind as a way to make "our habits of consumption more rational and of getting the maximum satisfaction made possible by our technical progress" was not a bright prospect for the future stability of the economy.[12]

A spate of films released in the early thirties confirmed the view that women were irrational or volatile consumers and that given more leisure they would be more so. While movies about society matrons may have "implied that given leisure, women lounged about in salons, titillating their imaginations and libidos with illicit liaisons," many films portrayed even more dire consequences of too much leisure for women.[13] Without meaningful and appropriate occupations, it was feared that women would become bored and seek new sensations and thrills. The film *Three on a Match* (1931) indicated precisely the effects of this fall into sensation hunting. The narrative follows the fates of three girls from the same school: one a "bad" girl who does a stint in a reformatory for women, one a bright but poor girl who becomes a stenographer, and one an upper-class society girl who marries a rich lawyer. When they meet up in a beauty salon in 1930, it is the rich woman who is most unhappy with her life and who envies the other two. Money and material comfort have only served to make her increasingly dissatisfied. Soon after this, looking for thrills and adventure, she falls into dissipation, drinking, drugs, and becomes the mistress of one of the mob. Her son is neglected and abused and eventually kidnapped and ransomed for more drug money. Finally she redeems herself by throwing herself out of the top floor window with a message written in lipstick on her nightdress to indicate her son's whereabouts before the mob kill him. The dramatic ending served to remind the viewer of the serious consequences of women's ennui, and that the problem of leisure was one that could affect all classes of women.

Abundant leisure and consumer desires, at least in the movies, led to infidelity, greed, and promiscuity. It was also a realm where the siren or harpy ruled. As a rich socialite in *Platinum Blonde* (1931), Jean Harlow emasculates her writer husband, publicly humiliating and dominating him. In *The Easiest Way* (1931), an avaricious woman heads for downfall after her greed forces her to become a mistress to a dress seller. In *Transgression* (1931), a wife turns siren once her husband goes to work, illustrating that women of position, wealth, and leisure "went bad" as easily as the hard-up working girl or gold digger. Jean Harlow in *Red-Headed Woman* (1932) played a gold digger who marries for wealth, sleeps with and blackmails her husband's friends, and shoots her husband, only to become a concubine of a European nobleman. In *The Bride Walks Out* (1936), Barbara Stanwyck follows a similar fate as a materialistic woman working as a model who sells herself in order to acquire dresses. In *Sensation Hunters* (1933), a woman's adventurism and career as a dancer drive her to the edge of prostitution. Women, given abundant leisure and an array of material goods, were thereby seen to be easily driven to acts of criminality. In *Born to Be Bad* (1934), Letty Strong fraudulently sues for faked injuries, and in *Accidents Will Happen* (1938), driven by greed and materialism into acts of criminality, a woman threatens the safety of even those she loves with her uncontrollable urges for acquisition. In Hollywood films at least, women's careers and ambitions appeared driven by urges for consumption and possessions, often conspicuous display, that lead her into criminal dissipation and low-life occupations.

Woman's lack of rational control over her own acquisitive nature and impulses was a common theme in mass culture and mass media at this time, confirming the need for benevolent male authority to take control. Popular social science texts corroborated the view that women's greed and ambition had become a pathological trend. Consumption, or acquisitiveness, was treated as an illness with a spiraling pathology, something that could only be satiated by more consumption. As a result, it was assumed that women could never be happy until an external force had ended the cycle of desire and consumption for them. In movies at least, a man or legal authority was usually forced to intervene and make choices for a woman's own good.

According to such popular representations, poverty rarely had anything to do with women's desire for goods; in fact many of the films implied that the more a woman had, the more she would desire—inferring, of course, that it was better, and that she would be happier, having nothing at all. Early on in the Depression this was convenient evidence to show that a lack of material goods did not necessarily prevent happy families, especially if women could be encouraged to stay at home rather than go to work. Career women films showed how they could be "cured" of their ambition: in *Ann Carver's Profession* (1933) and *Ann Vickers* (1933), high-powered career women, following a traditionally male career track, are eventually convinced to give up their ambition in exchange for being a wife or mother. Likewise, in *Blonde Venus* (1932), Marlene Dietrich finally returns to her small marital home despite having "prostituted" herself in cabaret entertainment, gained vast fame and fortune, and committed adultery with a handsome millionaire played by Cary Grant. In a strangely irresolute ending, she returns to the simplicity and penury of an "honest" life with her "rational" scientist husband and blonde baby.[14] Not only did these stances reflect the gathering momentum of the "back to the hearth" trend at this time, but they justified increased intervention in women's lives, especially in relation to their leisure-time pursuits. It was feared that women, as compulsive consumers, would use their leisure time to indulge in commercial leisure pursuits that damaged family lives and family coffers. At best, aggressive advertising campaigns would expose her to choices that were beyond her means.

Changes in society after World War I provided a catalyst for the flurry of concern about female leisure. Not only was it assumed that women were predisposed to use their leisure to consume wastefully and immorally, but it was also feared that women's leisure had increased more rapidly than men's had.[15] Applying the principles of scientific management, home economists showed women how to make the huge efficiencies in time and energy that had transformed the industrial and business sector. This "Taylorism" in the home had apparently converted domestic work into leisure. Unlike the emasculation that had affected the male producer, technology, it was assumed, had released women from the burdens of household tasks and freed them for more worthwhile pursuits.[16] The sociologist George Lundberg and associates, for example, claimed that housewives had been "largely released from the drudgery of long hours by the changing role of the home, as well as the revolution in the technique of housekeeping."[17] Another observer listed the machines that had prompted this revolution: "The invention of sewing machines, vacuum cleaners, the modern system of water supply in the home, electric irons, dishwashers, washing machines and lights, oil furnaces, and many other devices has also very greatly lightened the work of housewives."[18] Sociologists Martin and Esther Neumayer also observed that women's work had been lessened, leaving them unable to use their time productively: "The Industrial Revolution drove the production of economic goods from the home to the factory, the housewife no longer spins the thread . . . raises vegetables . . . bakes bread and pastry . . . [and the] . . . rapid growth of . . . dining places has taken consumption out of the home. In addition, modern conveniences in the house have lifted the burden of housework.[19]

An advertisement in *Life* magazine in 1936 for an electric "food fixer" argued that "it easily saves over 200 hours of arm-tiring work a year," imploring wives to slip the ad into their husbands pocket in order "to enjoy life more" and telling husbands that "this gift saves your wife 200 hours of hard work a year."[20] Household chores, it was assumed, had lessened because of the new technologies available to women, who, like modern industrial workers, were now "leisured" through machine efficiency.

"What do women do with their leisure?" Neumayer asked. He suggested, "Some, not knowing what to do with it, find the surplus time a bore. Hence the commercial amusements, bridge clubs, beauty parlors, and shopping centers attract their attention."[21] Sociologists concluded that women needed specific education in the new disciplines of domestic science and home economics if all this spare time was to be used productively. As a consequence, women's consumption, especially of modern household machinery, became tied to the notion of female leisure even more fully. Not only did women have time to shop, but they shopped for time.

Although contemporary feminist historians have dismantled the presumption that technology freed women from domestic duties, the assumptions of leisure reformers at the time were strongly reinforced within mass culture.[22] Despite women's decreased spending power during the Depression, observers judged that women, who were already creatures of leisure and consumption, would further fall prey to the temptations of wasteful materialistic purchasing offered by the modern age and—like the woman at the slot machine in Figure 9—spend their reduced incomes in increasingly bizarre and improper ways. Gambling, smoking, or drinking in bars, women were not treated like the heroic Forgotten Man but as selfish mothers who should be spending in a way that was beneficial for her family. These sentiments fueled the presumption that social welfare should serve to curb the jazz age–style spending of out-of-control female consumers before America fell victim to a matriarchy of irrational shoppers.

Building on William Ogburn's theory of "culture lag," many feared that women's free time was being dangerously wasted because they had not been sufficiently educated to adapt to it. Writer and educator Dorothy Fisher saw the new freedom as something frightening for mankind: "A majority of the human beings suddenly flung up by the machine from the ocean of material necessity and stranded on the beach of free choice continue with nervous reflex movements to go on doing . . . what formerly was a condition of survival." Fisher argued that the introduction of the machine into women's lives had left them with free time that they didn't know how to use properly: "The machine makes it possible for a woman to provide her family with good and sufficient food in return for an expenditure of time and effort scarcely a hundredth part of that required from her great-grandmothers."[23]

Sherwood Anderson's view that women were now in control of America because of their relationship to leisure, machinery, and consumption correlated with studies of the consumer made by social scientists. Some, however, saw women's ascendancy in less negative terms. At the start of the Depression, female economist Christine Frederick celebrated

9. Raceland, Louisiana, September 1938. Girl playing a slot machine in a decorated bar. Photo by Russell Lee. Courtesy Library of Congress, Prints and Photographs Division, FSA-OWI Collection [LC-USF34-31411-D].

the new centrality of the female consumer as a potential hope for ending the Depression. As a household engineering expert, Frederick directly addressed the primacy of the female consumer in her 1929 book *Selling Mrs. Consumer*. Writing her profile of the consumer in order to get a better understanding of underlying wider economic trends, she believed that the economy could be better planned to suit purchasing requirements so that "total factory production capacity" could be streamlined with the needs of consumers. Along with many other economists of the Depression, Frederick saw the problem of overproduction and underconsumption as the root cause of economic ills and viewed women's roles as "effective" consumers vital to recovery.

Frederick commented, with much more pleasure than disdain, that "woman has never before attained, in any country, the psychological position that she enjoys in America." Noting that some revulsion had been expressed over this fact, she wrote that visitors from other countries found women's ascendancy so astounding that they often "feel a sharp shock of surprise and revulsion; while even some of our satiric young novelists, like Sinclair Lewis and Louis Bromfield, who spend enough time in Europe to note the contrasts, are convinced that American women autocratically 'rule the roost,' and that men exist and labor largely to pour more spending money into their wives laps."[24]

Frederick claimed that 80 or 90 percent of spending money was in the hands of women and that the female consumer, like the farmer's wife in Figure 10, should be taken into account in national economic planning. Unlike her male contemporaries, Frederick commented that women used their finely tuned sense of commerce to care for and nurture their families in the most sensible way.[25] Despite this, like her male contemporaries, she viewed women as "instinctual" creatures, unable to operate rationally or by theories, despite being finely tuned for successful consumption. To Frederick, the female consumer played a vital role in maintaining quality and demand in a variety of goods by using her feminine ability to purchase "instinctively" well. While she saw this as no bad thing and defended women's role in the marketplace, like other economists she maintained that modern consumption needed to be studied scientifically and demanded that consumer standards be established on a national scale to prevent the whims of the marketplace undermining consumer power and the national economy.

In contrast to Frederick, the perception that America had become a matriarchy of erratic consumers led many others to fear that economic planning would ultimately falter in the face of their whimsical behavior. The nature of the female consumer therefore came under increasing analysis in social science texts during the thirties in an attempt to provide a forecast for the future well-being of the nation. Planning for the market and educating the consumer to consume for the benefit of industrial production was seen as imperative if economic breakdown was to be avoided or reversed. Some economic tracts took this fear to its extreme, implying that sirens of leisure and cosmetics were partly responsible for economic breakdown in the first place.

Corroborating this treatment of the insatiable spendthrift female, Walter Pitkin's extensive tract on modern consumption, *The Consumer: His Nature and His Habits* (1932), included an expansive diatribe against the female consumer. The portion of the book that dealt with the topic was titled "Woman, The Economic Imbecile." Like Anderson, Pitkin saw the mathematical figures of female consumption as evidence of women's ascendancy in modern life. Claiming that women controlled much of the nation's spending money, he feared that in a few decades "we shall have a novel economic matriarchy in which most of the wealth will be received and disbursed by women."[26] Pitkin's book produced extensive psuedo-scientific evidence to prove how disastrous this new matriarchy would be.

Also like Anderson, Pitkin found women's evolutionary adaptation to consumer culture in her organic makeup: "But women, being closer to

10. Durham, N.C., November 1939. Mrs. Evan Wilkins looking in a shop window. She came to town with her husband to sell their tobacco at the tobacco auction and is doing some shopping. Photo by Marion Post Wolcott. Courtesy Library of Congress, Prints and Photographs Division, FSA-OWI Collection [LC-USF33-30731-M5].

our primordial animality, are much more deeply interested in living than in erecting economic systems; more concerned with feeling, sensing, touching, doing, and using than with inventing, organizing, creating, improving, saving, and getting ahead; more absorbed in the here and now than in the long run; more distressed over today's lack than over tomorrow's dangers. In a word, she is the natural consumer, just as man is the natural producer. And we cannot construe the drift of a society like our own unless we understand this fact in all its ramifications."[27]

The ramifications were resounding. Pitkin provided an extended argument on women's physiology to back up his claims that sensory experience was more keenly developed in women and that they reacted more emotionally to stimuli than men. An "enlarged thyroid," responsible for a stimulated nervous system, illustrated that, biologically, women's senses responded to many trivial stimuli, and as a consequence they were "more likely to become hysteric, and to suffer from acquired neurasthenia." Pitkin then quoted from various psychology journals to illustrate that women's poor motor coordination, which he claimed involved them in frequent automobile accidents, enabled them to succeed only in simple tasks such as "sweeping, washing, ironing, and the like." Women's tendency toward "mild invalidism," he claimed, made it virtually impossible for them to achieve in the workplace—and were thus biologically and psychologically unsuitable for industrial production. All types and classes of women were included, as "business and professional women are the world's silliest spenders. They rank with the drunken sailor on shore leave."[28]

Women's imbecility as a consumer appeared strongly connected with her leisure-time interests. Pitkin believed that women had a tendency to boredom and therefore needed constant sensation: "A woman must find fresh impression, lest she go wild. The onward movement of life, for her, involves inexorably an onward movement of stimuli from without. Here is the source of fashion."[29] Women's desire for renewal and attention to surface appearances appeared as their main downfall, both in movies and in Pitkin's text. Women film characters who tended toward prostitution were generally greedy for dresses and trinkets, becoming models, actresses, or showgirls and ending up dissipated and dissatisfied. Evidence of a thriving cosmetic and fashion industry at the height of the Depression illustrated to Pitkin the wastefulness and irrationality of the female, as well as her mental instability: "Even the feeble-minded and the moron females show this same deep fixation on skin looks," he claimed, citing how inmates of insane asylums were shown to be made happier by the application of a bit of rouge. Fashion and cosmetics were strongly related to the emergence of new forms of cinema entertainment—compounding the fear that in their leisure women were learning the "moronic" behavior of actresses and film stars.[30] Being biologically predisposed to consumption, women, it was assumed, had little or no control over their purchasing mania, especially when lacking suitable alternative occupation.

The upshot of Pitkin's tract on the female consumer is that, because of her physiology and psychology and despite, or because of, being "natural consumers," they were a very poor bet indeed:

Now let us sum up the creature's traits, that we may see her as a consumer. She is more sensitive than the man to details of situations as they are taken through eye, ear, nose and skin. This must cause her, as a consumer, to be more uniformly interested in appearances. Secondly, her emotions well up faster and more hotly than man's; therefore, when she considers buying anything, she is much more likely to be swayed by anger, fear, curiosity, and enthusiasm than man. . . . She is much more submissive and compliant than man . . . more easily influenced . . . by the salesman or in the language of an advertisement. . . . Her mathematical incompetence adds a sinister tinge to her ability as a consumer. She dislikes a budget. . . . She finds it hard to refuse a salesman who is deferential and delicately flirtatious.[31]

The matriarchy of shoppers, Pitkin claimed, lowered quality and choice for all consumers: "The imbecile buying habits of young girls and women have been responsible for the flooding of the market with cheap, flimsy, low-grade, and perishable apparel and luxury goods."[32] Worst of all regarding their control over the nation's purses, he claimed, was their lack of ability concerning mathematics that made them unable to budget or spend rationally.[33] Women, he claimed, did not read economic studies and "never would practice their teachings, even if they did read them" and were responsible for the waste, excess, and other failings of the modern commercial market. Having established that women were irrational, were easily influenced by "sex" interests, lacked critical discrimination, were probably insane, had more free time, and had control of 85 percent of the nation's spending money, Pitkin provided fuel to any argument that control over the female spender was an essential part of the nation's economic well-being in the future. To Pitkin, then, economic distress and decline—or in Anderson's terms, the loss of male control and potency—had been caused by the flapper-style spending, or "Jazz Age plunging," of women in the 1920s. The ragtag, unscientific, and female-dominated market had led to an "inevitable trend toward the effeminate, in pace with diffuse prosperity; and . . . the swift dissipation of accumulated wealth."[34]

Such extreme views should not be seen to represent all economic thinking on women and consumption in the thirties. However, the belief that women were more instinctual and sensory was reiterated in other, more academic, economic tracts. Economists Roland Vaile and Helen

Canoyer, for example, stated in 1938 that "women permit the acuteness of their senses to guide their choices even when the particular sensory impression is not directly connected with the use of any other important characteristic of the merchandise."[35] Such assumptions surrounding the irrationality of the female consumer helped establish more fully the need for consumer education programs, and it was in the thirties that consumer education and advocacy groups, as well as scientific market analysis, took a strong hold. Behind this movement lay the premise that along with the free market economy, consumers, who were 80 to 90 percent women, were unpredictable, irrational, and too ill-educated to resist low marketing standards or too whimsical when purchasing leisure or goods. Surveys of the modern consumer in a variety of studies undertaken in the twenties helped to establish the need for rational economic planning based on "proper" consumption.[36]

Studies made by intellectuals such as Robert Lynd and Stuart Chase began to focus on the wasteful and alienating lifestyles of the middle classes, unlike their reform-minded predecessors, who focused on the profligacy of the working classes. Reifying the folk patterns and nonmaterialist lifestyles of ethnic and nonurban working classes, these sociologists argued for an end to materialism as a way of reestablishing family and community cohesion. Believing that irrational and materialistic spenders should learn to live on less, these studies of the modern consumer contained disdain for the emptiness and shallow materialism of what was perceived as middle-class "Babbittry."[37]

Although the roots of these attitudes were based in observations of modern consumption patterns in the 1920s, the Depression appeared to consolidate and confirm many sociologist's fears and findings. At the same time, however, the Depression also appeared to provide an "opportune moment when the failure of the economic system would purge society of its materialistic excesses."[38] Many reformers leapt at this "opportune" moment to pass judgment on the commercial trends in leisure to recommend simpler folk pleasures, traditional amusements, and "back to the hearth" or family-oriented pursuits. In fact, the majority of books, articles, and magazines published during the Depression on this subject saw the lack of spending money as an exciting challenge for individual creativity and imagination. In his book *Americans at Play*, sociologist Jesse Steiner noted that in contrast with the "unusual freedom" with which money had been spent on recreation in the 1920s, he hoped that "perhaps during a period of slower development there may be great success in building up a well-balanced recreational program more carefully planned in the interests of the general welfare."[39] Women's leisure-time activities, as economists had already shown, were central to the success of this new program.

Correct or "proper" consumption was the opposite of the wasteful spending of the twenties and functioned to support family welfare, to purchase legitimate goods, and to support the social structure of the New Deal. Thus, the prominent display of the NRA symbol, a blue eagle, helped to indicate to consumers where they should buy. So it was with great disappointment that sociologists noted that the Depression, in many cases, had done little to change commercial leisure and spending habits developed over the 1920s—and had even spawned new ones. Women were targeted even more fiercely than before by commercial strategies aiming to make them buy more goods. Intensive advertising campaigns that incorporated coupon collecting argued that thrifty housewives could spend, or save through spending, their way out of the Depression, fueling increased consumption. The relationship between leisure and consumption was further consolidated by the introduction of sponsored daytime radio shows that were directed at women. "Soaps" offered women the chance to rest from their domestic tasks as well as the opportunity for manufacturers to increase sales. To many reformers, this increased the need for women to be taught to spend leisure rationally, and at the same time presented the opportunity to create and sustain purchasing trends that would remain into the 1950s. Despite the antimaterialism of many social workers at the start of the Depression, dreams of a leisured future were firmly based on the notion that leisure could be used as a stimulus for consumption and increased production, eventually becoming a new industry itself.

Surveys showed that spending on leisure was still increasing despite the Depression. A study undertaken in 1935–36 of more than a third of a million households illustrated that, for those in employment at least, standards of living had considerably increased. Decreases in food prices had led to increased spending on appearance, cars, and other luxury items.[40] Likewise, entertainment had become cheaper, more commercial, and more widely available; the cost of radios and cars had dropped, with increased possibilities of hire purchase. Widespread use of the car had made commercial leisure more accessible for the suburb dweller, and movie houses had dropped prices and were offering other incentives to increase attendance, such as bingo, double features, air-conditioning, and palatial surroundings. Although soup kitchens and breadlines were a reality for many, the biggest fear for many sociologists of leisure was that, for anyone with spare money, the Depression was potentially an uncontrolled spending bonanza.[41]

These fears over uncontrolled middle-class consumers, however, masked a central concern among economists about the role of the working classes and the behavior of working-class women during the Depression. Criticism of commercial amusements by social scientists was, in many cases, less a moral judgment along the lines of nineteenth-century reformers than a comment on the need for government to regulate all types of industry, especially for the purpose of increasing taxation revenues. The 1935 *Census of Business: Places of Amusement* emphasized the difficulty of providing accurate figures for commercial amusements. For example, only "those establishments charging admission or receiving fees for use of recreational facilities were covered" in the census, and many "seasonal or transient amusement enterprises" could not be canvassed.[42] Because many of the latter failed to declare themselves as taxable businesses, government figures could not be relied upon to present an accurate picture of commercial leisure. Evading financial control, the new leisure needed reclassification and regulation in order to provide much-needed tax revenue.[43]

The informal leisure economy that dominated working-class urban centers had led to "illicit" behavior that undermined white enterprise and economic recovery, threatening both tax revenues and the "planned" economy. As Victoria Wolcott illustrates, working-class responses to racism, sexism, and economic deprivation led to the rise of informal economies that centered on commercial urban recreation. Therefore, while middle-class reformers frowned upon the illicit economy of numbers running, rent parties, prostitution, pool halls, and gambling, in many cases women could achieve authority, status, and cash within working-class communities through these liminal spaces.[44] For African American women, during work shortages these were very often the only types of employment available outside of low-paid, nonunionized domestic work. While an illicit economy expanded in urban centers such as Detroit, to people living in them, these economies were associated with working-class leisure and real opportunities for female employment.

Even without the figures from urban black market economies, economic studies showed that legitimate consumption of recreation and leisure had continued to grow at a steady pace despite the Depression.[45] Among scenes of poverty and desperation, social scientists also saw evidence of a culture of abundance and commercialism—indicated in the frenzied sales of Mickey Mouse watches, cosmetics, refrigerators, and electric shavers during this period. The paradox of abundance during the worst depression Americans had ever known only served to highlight the problems of mass culture as those of waste, lack of organization, poor breeding, and low intellect. Although few leisure surveys actually listed shopping as a leisure activity, a few acknowledged that new labor practices, or work shortages, which gave workers a full- or half-day holiday on a Saturday, meant that "shopping becomes an important ranking activity on Saturday." Leisure surveys showed steady increases in this activity each year, even at the height of the Depression in 1932.[46] Although adolescents and older people were encouraged by the recreation managers to enjoy leisure without spending, the government was actively promoting spending as a way that the country could end the Depression. Sensible purchasing and spending, rather than hoarding, was promoted as a patriotic duty, especially for women. Women were told in 1933, for example, that "the nest egg you have saved can be put into circulation now to good advantage," that "women's greatest weapon against the forces of depression is her buying power," and that "it is not only women's right but their patriotic duty" to spend wisely.[47] Thus, women's "irrational" spending could help to buy society out of the Depression by increasing the flow of products.

As a way of creating new needs and broader markets, it was thought that the consumption of leisure and related goods could help to end the Depression, yet despite the growing "habit" of consumption, consumers were still seen to be irrational "bundles of impulses and habits" in need of guidance.[48] Teaching women to be good consumers both inside and outside of New Deal programs was seen as one way that readjustment to social changes could be made effective. Robert Lynd, for example, saw the combination of private capital and the fallibility of the "emotional" irrational consuming public as a mix that needed planners' intervention in order to determine the course of social change.[49] Roland Vaile, professor of economics and marketing at Minnesota University, and his research associate Helen Canoyer likewise argued in 1938 that this training was closely related to female leisure: "Many women—although by no means all—have spare time that they might use to their own advantage and that of their families in becoming more expert as purchasing agents. To become truly expert in this field would require close attention to the ways in which members of a family want to obtain their satisfactions, on the one hand, and to the want-satisfying qualities of specific goods, on the other. This is no simple task; its proper performance would require continuing adult training of a high order."[50] Vaile and Canoyer argued that women hire, or become, professional experts in order to rationalize the process of consumption and that this should become an extension of her leisure-time activities and domestic duty.

Yet popular views surrounding the central function of the female as consumer belied the fact that as workers they were more vulnerable to lower wages and part-time, exploitative working conditions than ever. Aided by the view of women as "natural" consumers, as well as leisured, the "back to the hearth" trend that followed in the wake of mass unemployment aimed to increase male employment by decreasing married women's participation in the work force. The success of the productive economy, then, relied on keeping women out of the workforce and getting them to work at leisure and consumption. Significantly, the

Depression years contributed to, rather than detracted from, the premise that women were consumers and not producers. Working men may have been unemployed, but all women, it appeared, were innately-even biologically—leisured.[51]

The failure to recognize the productive role of the female worker, or even women as unemployed, extended to the federal government. Work relief legislation prevented more than one family member working in federal employment, and women were only eligible for work relief if they could prove they were the head of the household. The WPA tended to relegate or neglect the position of unemployed women workers in relation to men, and throughout the thirties married women workers came under fearsome assault from the government, unions, and the popular press.[52] Between 1932 and 1937, the New Deal administration introduced legislation that discriminated against married working women. The Federal Economy Act required that one spouse resign if both worked for the federal government, and although it did not specify the sex of the spouse, this tended to be the woman. New Deal policies and WPA discrimination against women meant that women were ignored as workers and limited by the relief measures available.[53] The WPA "did not see working women, even if unemployed, as a notable constituency," and relief programs focused on making women's work an extension of their unpaid, "leisured," domestic role. Women were expected to support government programs through approved consumption that would both benefit the family and help end the Depression—not by working, but by buying.[54]

Economizing in the home and turning it into an efficiently run unit, with the help of new domestic technology and rational purchasing patterns, was seen as a way of turning a wasteful institution into one that would function optimally for both the individual and national economies, without depriving men of work. Thus, leisure-time education for women recommended guidance for health, nutrition, and consumption to help them use their spare time to the benefit of the family. Early in the Depression, experiments with work relief expanded an extensive program of adult education to cover the field of homemaking, offering "training for mothers who were living on home relief." The courses consisted of planning low-cost meals, special diets for children, making and altering clothing, and home nursing.[55]

Work relief programs thereby focused on the establishment of programs for women, which would "occupy destitute women in traditional feminine chores—primarily sewing, housework, mattress making and washing."[56] Over the lifetime of the WPA, of the women who received relief and work assignments, more than half were engaged in "the most traditional of female work—sewing."[57] These programs were intended to direct women into domestic employment; they overlapped with recreation projects that aimed to teach women to use their spare time to the benefit of the family.[58]

Replicating gender and race discrimination in the workplace, many WPA programs trained working-class and nonwhite women for domestic service work in private homes, as seen in Figures 11 and 12. While the programs were generally welcomed, racial stereotyping meant that African Americans were "channeled" back into domestic service work that would enable their female employers to enjoy more leisure.

In Detroit, young African American men were also given training at a "practice house" to become butlers and cooks, placing them "in occupations that they had not held in large numbers since the late nineteenth and early twentieth century."[59] As one National Youth Administration photo starkly depicted, nonwhite domestic servants were trained to serve white women from the recreation division, who were in turn trained to enjoy their increased leisure in such correct activities.[60]

The WPA efforts applied existing stereotypes to work relief programs, aiming to create a stable female population that could sustain the family

11. Pasadena, Los Angeles. National Youth Administration workers preparing to serve the first course of luncheon at the Home Demonstration Project. Courtesy National Archives, Still Picture Branch, RG119-5-5A-16.

through hard times by good housekeeping techniques and improvements in home-based leisure. An example of this was a project created by the Creative Home Planning Division: "The 20 or so artists of the unit built models of apartments with interchangeable walls and furniture with various coverings to demonstrate arrangements and color effects. They

12. Correct serving is practiced on a National Youth Administration Home Demonstration Project in Pasadena, Los Angeles. Courtesy National Archives, Still Picture Branch, RG119-5-5A-5.

13. WPA recreation craft shop in Denver, Colorado. Courtesy National
Archives, Still Picture Branch, RG69N-19958-C.

offered free instruction in choosing and using curtains, furniture, col-
ors, rugs, and lampshades. They gave shopping advice and conducted
shopping tours. . . . Enough housewives were sufficiently convinced that
they filled up classes for making hooked rugs, lampshades, slipcovers,
curtains and quilts."[61]

Most projects, however, tended to encourage traditional leisure pursuits rather than shopping and interior design. Quilting, sewing, and
cooking were seen as appropriate domestic tasks for women to learn, as
shown in Figure 13.

Programs also aimed to make the housewife aware of new scientific
discoveries that would keep her family healthy and, at the same time, to
teach her the proper use of the new leisure that arose from the efficient
use of time and new technologies. By modernizing the image of the
homemaker, consumption was reinforced as the key to traditional family stability.[62] Guided rational consumption by women, it was argued,
could produce more wealth, ensure family happiness, and contribute to
national well-being and stability. Control of women's leisure thus became
tied to control of the consumer and control of the national marketplace.

Although the kind of work relief that engaged women in traditional tasks may seem far from our notion of recreation, recreation and leisure projects consolidated the gendering of women's work by making it both domestic and a form of national leisure. Leisure programs blurred the boundaries between women's nonpaid work in the home and the leisure of the family, teaching what were necessities for many people as an extension of women's leisure obligations. Celebrating this shift back into domesticity and the blurring of boundaries between work and leisure, sociologist Arthur Pack wrote that, because of the Depression, more leisure time had been devoted to "caring for home grounds and gardens, cooking, dress-making and card games," and as a result family relationships had been strengthened. According to Pack:

These new activities . . . were first of all the result of grim necessity. Lacking money to pay a gardener or cook, householders found themselves obliged to do the work themselves, and women who could no longer afford to buy ready-made clothes were forced by circumstances to learn to sew. But, though at the outset these activities were nothing more than inescapable tasks, each one of them entails creative effort, and somewhere between their adoption and the reporting of them as leisure-time activities, the satisfaction that comes from accomplishment had transformed them from mere labor to leisure-time recreation. And it was this very turning back into the home for recreation on the part of those who still possessed some degree of security that constituted the New Leisure.[63]

Social surveys of women workers also collapsed differences between women's work and leisure. Although *The Nonworking Time of Industrial Women Workers* was a study made by female trade unionists under the direction of sociologist Juliet Fisher, it concluded that the shorter working week had given the use of leisure time more importance, despite the fact that four-fifths of women workers had a working week totaling more than forty hours. Despite this, it was in leisure used appropriately, rather than in work, that women would find liberatory potential. Women workers, it suggested, would be wiser to find freedom through leisure than through work in such an economic climate, despite the fact that most of them were in full employment. Fisher argued that the opportunities for self-expression and development were in a worker's leisure time and that the leisure "activities she engages in then affect her health and social relations" and "have a contribution to her role in a democratic society."[64] Despite the fact that most of the women were active union members, this survey of women workers' limited leisure still managed to find more liberatory potential in their educational and philanthropic leisure use than in their union activities or workplace satisfaction.

This conflation of work and leisure as a programmatic return to traditional gender roles also appeared in WPA murals and paintings, where "in the frame of nostalgic leisure, [Treasury Section of Fine Arts]

art eulogized forms of recreation that took place outside the burgeoning arena of consumer culture." In the paintings and murals, gender
oppositions constructed a narrative of harmony: "Men represent labor,
women and children represent domesticity, family and leisure." As women
were not visible as workers, their roles in creating family leisure activities were even more strongly emphasized, and leisure itself was represented in a policy of containment within the art works, through moral
contexts and traditional scenes of rural or family harmony: "By showing
work and leisure together, public art conveyed a view of work as productive but not oppressive, balanced by healthy rest and respite. And at
the same time, such compositions showed respite as the reward of work,
drawing a distinction between such deserved leisure and what might be
called subversive leisure, tainted with implications of idleness or frivolous pleasure."[65] These distinctions between "good" and "bad" leisure
also blurred the boundaries between what was defined as women's work
and their leisure. By constructing domestic work as leisure, official projects sustained a double blindness to the needs of unemployed women
and their domestic hardships.

To some, however, the role of women as workers and producers of
leisure was not so invisible. Stories by working-class and minority writers
consciously tackled this newly inscribed blindness to the role of working
women and those who worked in leisure industries. These stories examined the "problem of leisure" as a problem of class and race privilege
rather than as an economic or cultural crisis. The stories made visible
the labor behind the growth of commercial leisure, a labor that created
and sustained leisure that was very often the labor of a female or nonwhite worker. In this fiction, leisure is not represented as "false consciousness"—as the bourgeoisification of the working class—but directly
as work, as labor itself.

Ramona Lowe's story "The Woman in the Window" depicts the commodification of African American identity for purposes of exhibition,
white leisure, and consumption. The story follows the experiences of
Mrs. Jackson, a black migrant cook in a northern city, as she gets a job
in a restaurant to support her family. The arrival of the new cook gives the
owner a new marketing angle; he decides to sell the restaurant as "southern," moving the cook to the window and dressing her in his vision of a
southern "darkie," an Aunt Jemima. "You'll be displayed just like the
pancakes and the waffles," he tells her. Commenting to his partner, like
a slave owner at a sale, he exclaims, "She'll be a beaut in the window,
Mike, a beaut." Despite her protestations that she "ain' one for a show"
their offer of increased salary leaves her unable to refuse. Despite this,
Mrs. Jackson is unhappy with the plan and critiques their notion of
the South. Not wanting to "look like no circus freak" in the voluminous

purple skirt, white apron, green shawl, and red bandana, she threatens resignation until they increase her wages again. Despite this, her commodification is never complete, and she is unable to smile: "'I spose you think smiles is put on like cloes,' she said. 'I ain' no actress, Mr. Parsons.'" The commodification of her laboring body as a form of marketing and entertainment for whites, as leisure for whites, involves a double labor for the black woman, of which she is acutely aware.[66]

Likewise, Elizabeth Thomas's story "Our House" illustrated how a vacation for the rich, white Burden family involved extra labor for the black servants. While making final preparations to leave, the mistress of the house told the butler Edward, "I've talked everything over with Tilly. She and Dorcus will get the canning finished and clean the house. You're going to help them with the windows and rugs, Edward. Take good care of the house. It will be a vacation for you all."[67] The statement explicitly underlines the power relations of white leisure practices that entail black servitude and labor. Oblivious to the needs of her servants, Mrs. Burden assumes her leisure to be universal—yet even the family name reveals the extent to which the luxuries of rich white lives involve the labor of the people who service them.

Marita Bonner in "The Whipping" likewise illustrated the double discrimination of female workers in both work and work relief. Although Lizabeth would date a man "for just a ten-cent movie and a bottle of pop or a nickel bag of peanuts," it is her exploitative income of "twelve dollars a week scrubbing all night in a theater" rather than her "prostitution" for a trip to the movie, that signified her vulnerability. The daytime leisure of white moviegoers is contrasted with the nighttime labor of the worker who services white leisure. The economic relations she experiences in reality, not as a result of her "false consciousness" sustained by moviegoing, create Lizabeth's degradation. Turned down by the relief agency, and in desperate hunger, she pulls a knife on a relief worker, acutely aware that there are no dreams and no way out for her.[68] Like Richard Wright's protagonist Bigger Thomas in *Native Son* (1940), who becomes chauffeur to a rich white woman he eventually murders, Lizabeth's murderous violence is manufactured by her relationship with, and alienation from, white leisure.

Social scientists, however, remained oblivious to the new gender and race inscriptions that lay beneath the proliferating leisure of mass culture. Fears that the new leisure involved a matriarchy of ascendant women, or subaltern leisure economies, masked the return of traditional hierarchies that conflated domestic work and family leisure, which also placed women and nonwhite workers at the bottom of the economic scale. The reassertion of patriarchy did not go unnoticed, however, as feminist Gertrude Stein commented in *Everybody's Autobiography*.

The return of domesticity was another version of dictatorship: "There is too much fathering going on just now and there's no doubt about it fathers are depressing."[69]

Sherwood Anderson's view that women now controlled American life was triggered by his belief that modern culture had rendered the male impotent. His view on the matriarchy of modernism negotiated a terrain that, by the end of the thirties, was well-trodden ground. Such theories and concerns about women's new role in modern America barely concealed a misogyny that justified increased intervention and control over women's lives. Feminizing some of the causes of the Depression, within the notion of consumer "misspending" and lack of control, gave tacit sanction to federal control over the freewheeling economy, while leisure and training programs focused on controlling women's domestic roles as paid and unpaid service workers or consumers. Through leisure, women could become functional units in the economy without taking jobs from men. However, concerns with the way leisure functioned to aid the rationalization of the economy were only intensified as changing trends in commercial leisure during the thirties presented an ever-increasing challenge for reformers.

Chapter 6
Motion Pictures and Dance Halls

The five-day week, shorter hours, a nominal decrease in unemployment and more leisure time have been NRA features said to benefit the box office.

—Roy Chartier, "Year in Pictures," Variety, January 1, 1935

Idle time is not an asset to any community. Most delinquent and criminal acts are committed during leisure time, and a large percentage of them are performed in order to get the means for the enjoyment of leisure. Prison wardens testify to the desire of young men and young women to do daring things. Many crimes are committed because of a desire to buy pleasures much less satisfying than other forms of recreation which might be provided by the community at little cost.

—George Butler, Introduction to Community Recreation

The combination of woman's perceived weakness as a consumer and her apparent desire to be thrilled and seek new sensations in her leisure appeared, to many observers, to pose a grave threat to the stability of family life and society as a whole. These fears over women's leisure activities, appearing at the same time that crime seemed to be escalating, reinforced perceived dangers of commercial leisure generally, while the moral laxity that appeared to result from these leisure activities seemed to propel spiraling health and welfare costs at a time of reduced tax revenues. These fears emerged in social studies that focused on specific leisure pursuits such as moviegoing and dancing. This chapter examines how these social studies affected the perceptions and practices of leisure in the dance halls and movie palaces, showing how they responded to and fueled social concerns surrounding leisure and its particularly vexed relationship to women throughout the decade.[1]

Movies

The outstanding feature of leisure during the Depression, one that was most noted and commented upon, was the increased popularity of movies despite economic disaster. Writer and movie proponent Gilbert Seldes, for example, highlighted the growth of this leisure activity in his book: "If the entire population of the British Isles went to see a moving picture on Monday and then vanished from the earth, and another population equally great went on Tuesday, and another on Wednesday, Thursday, and Friday, together they would roughly equal the number of people all over the world who actually do see the movies in the course of a week. In eight weeks the moving-picture audiences equal in number the total population of the globe."[2] Despite a brief slump in attendance at the lowest point of the Depression, audience numbers grew at a steady rate over the decade.[3] In 1934, a National Recreation Association survey of the leisure time of five thousand people found that attending the movies was the third most popular leisure activity, only topped by the cheaper pursuits of radio listening and reading newspapers.[4] One educational research committee estimated a weekly attendance of 77 million out of which 36 percent were children or youths.[5] As Farm Security Administration photographs such as Figure 14 show, children went in droves to see the movies.

That moviegoing was one of the most popular commercial leisure pursuits in the 1930s only served to highlight fears that women's predisposed

14. San Augustine, Texas, April 1939. Group of schoolchildren waiting to get into the movies. Photo by Russell Lee. Courtesy Library of Congress, Prints and Photographs Division, FSA-OWI Collection [LC-USF33-12141-M4].

weakness for spending and sensation was fueled and exploited by the movie industry.

These worries were not new. Anxieties over the effect of the movies on women had existed from the very beginning of the medium. Fear of race and class mixing, of women and children's vulnerability, and of exposure to vice are well documented in studies of the early cinema era.[6] Reformers had feared that onscreen immorality, combined with a "low-grade" atmosphere within the movie theater, exposed many women of all classes to demoralization. Yet these fears were increased with the onset of the Depression alongside emergent technological and social changes. The economic crisis caused increased competition for the movie consumers' dollar, and as a result, various survival and marketing techniques erupted in many theaters, which gave the entertainment a more commercial flavor. Overall prices for theater entrance dipped dramatically in the early thirties, not helped by the competition of "shotgun" theaters, charging ten cents admission, in 1931.[7] To the chagrin of those in the movie industry as well as recreation reformers, cheaper entertainment appeared to herald lowered profits and an intensification of the moral problems that had been traditionally associated with the appearance of cinema in the earlier part of the century.

At the same time, the screen industry looked for other ways to increase movie-related revenues outside of box-office receipts. As early as 1930, it was recognized that the success of the industry was also tied to the possible profits of American businesses and potential recovery from the slump. "Motion pictures do exert a profound influence upon the buying habits of mankind," claimed Will Hays in a speech to the National Foreign Trade Council in 1930, creating a "desire for possession" that could stimulate the American economy worldwide.[8] Commercialism in the theaters throughout the thirties aimed to attract the female "shopping" audience with special events and attractions, such as fashion shows, giveaways of domestic items, price reductions, and free child care. Such marketing strategies that were intended to appeal to women as consumers became commonplace, closely connecting women's leisure with mass consumption. Some theaters carefully organized fashion shows, sponsored by local dress shops, that tied in with the fashions exhibited in the featured movie. Others ran short features sponsored by textile manufacturers, combined with lobby displays from local shops that, along with a "fashion film," appeared to increase sales for all parties concerned. When reviewing *This Modern Age* (1931), *Variety* magazine stated that the film was "a shop girl's delight and will do that kind of business . . . which will bore the men . . . and which women will like for the clothes displayed as much as anything else," illustrating that it was commonplace to see films as marketing tools to female customers.[9] Compounding this, screen advertisements were also becoming more common at the time, exposing audiences to increased commercialization that played upon women's assumed vulnerabilities. Sponsored short films started to appear alongside features, apparently eliding art and commerce even further.

In order to attract female consumers, increasingly blatant commercial incentives were offered to women who attended the movies. Cinemas began offering glassware and "bingo" nights to keep the seats full—significantly aiming their offers at women customers. These strategies increased concerns over the type of movies women were being encouraged to see, as the proliferation of "giveaway nights," "dish nights," "double features," and "bank nights," appeared to lure the Depression-hit public into spending their last few dollars on "B" movies in substandard viewing conditions—at cheaper rates than the major first-run theaters in the better parts of town. "Dish Night" started the trend, offering a piece of chinaware free to every woman attending the theater on a given night. Eventually, it was claimed, "women window-shopped the various theaters and finally gave their patronage to the theater having the pattern they liked the best. The picture was a secondary consideration."[10] In March 1937, *The Literary Digest* confirmed this image of the female patron who was lured more by the prospect of gambling and money than seeing a picture: "Mrs Joseph Sebastian Phau, an adult white citizen of the United States, went to a motion picture theater last Monday night. She paid a desperate quarter for an admission ticket, squared her ample shoulders and began the violent task of thrusting her way through 2,000 other citizens fired by a similar zeal. No portentous film was to be screened that night. Indeed, the picture to be shown was of inferior quality. But Mrs Phau didn't mind. It is doubtful that she ever knew what the picture was about, or cared. What brought her there was the 2,000 to 1 chance of going home with $150."[11] To many it appeared that the moviegoing public could be duped into seeing any kind of movie without even knowing what it was they had seen.

Riding on the back of the popularity of premium giveaway nights, theater owners then tried issuing admission tickets with numbers that resulted in the owner of the winning number receiving money. Although this turned out to be a violation of gambling laws, to circumvent them, owners placed a register of names in the lobby with numbers next to them and drew the winning number from a drum in the theater. The prize had to be claimed within a certain length of time (three, five, ten, or fifteen minutes) ensuring that the signer was present in, or near, the cinema.[12] If no one claimed the prize then the money was added to next week's draw.

This idea became copyrighted as "Bank Night" in 1931 and was subsequently "leased out" to cinemas on payment of the appropriate fee.

To circumvent this fee, many imitations proliferated with similar nights such as "Prosperity Night," "Movie Sweepstakes," "Treasury Night," "Cash Award Night," "Buck Night," "Parley Cash Night," "Dividend Night," "Screeno," and "Beano." While saving smaller theaters from bankruptcy, these nights were also accused of creating a lurid atmosphere of criminality and degeneracy—from petty racketeering to gambling and greed—and crass materialism at the cinema. By playing on the desperation of the public, the movie theaters were seen to expose innocent people to crime. *The Literary Digest* wrote, "In the Middle West dismayed police uncovered a new racket, Hoodlums were attending theaters, spotting the winner and hijacking him on the way home."[13] In 1937, *The New Republic* claimed that the night had "made converts of a great many former non-movie goers" and had caused some social and civic groups to change the night of their meetings to avoid conflicting with the immensely popular Bank Night. The article estimated that 60 percent of the movie houses in the country were using the appeal of a giveaway night—in New York City this rose to 90 percent, and in one section of Detroit all ninety theaters were operating a giveaway night from one to four nights each per week. To many, this was equated with introducing the "innocent" viewers, very often women and children, to gambling, poor quality films, and rampant materialism.[14] By 1937, even major chains were running Bank Nights, and numerous lawsuits and police clampdowns were taking place—theater managers were arrested in police raids while the police were "roundly booed by Chicago cinema audiences."[15] Bank night continued to run throughout the thirties despite these attempts to end it. As Figure 15 shows, bank night was still offering instant cash prizes at some theaters even in the late thirties.

These battles between business and the judiciary over the control of movie exhibition standards were not allayed by the invention, in the early thirties, of the drive-in movie theater. While recreation reformers feared that the drive-in theater increased passivity, as patrons no longer had to leave the seats of their cars, others feared that the consequences would be even more serious. The first drive-in theater in Camden, New Jersey, where Sunday pictures were permitted, was situated in close proximity to Philadelphia, where Sunday pictures were banned. As a way of circumventing movie controls and regulations of the urban environment, the drive-ins were potentially lawless, but easily accessible, sites for the voracious movie public. At the drive-in, the backseat of the car replaced the dubious "safety" of the theater seat where peers, or ushers, might censor any action considered immoral or harmful.[16]

Such inventions and changes in technologies were blamed for the changes in female public behavior at this time. Despite being surrounded by poverty and bankruptcy, public taste had "switched to glamorous, shameful ladies, pampered by pent-houses, coddled by limousines, clothed in couturier smartness," claimed *Variety* in 1931, and women who imitated their favorite screen goddess were most at risk from corruption. A spate of "sex" films prior to the 1934 production code enforcement, with the accompanying "sex talk" of young actresses that was imitated by the young women who came to cinema, was enough to send reformers into a flurry of activity.[17] While *Variety* celebrated film's success in instructing women in the latest "modes and manners," where "more important than their clothes, the mannerisms of picture actresses are invaluable text books to audience ladies," other observers saw this new "textbook" as nothing less than demoralizing and dangerous.[18] Consolidating male fears of demanding and voracious sirens emerging from this new behavior, in 1935 Robert and Helen Lynd suggested that the appearance of a nightly parade of grand passions onscreen might result in "new inadequacies" for men.[19]

This imitative behavior triggered fears that traditional forms of behavior previously regulated by parents and other moral guardians were breaking down and leading to emotional and sexual chaos. The sexually charged materialism of the cinema environment led some to fear that women would be induced to perform criminal and murderous acts because of cinema attendance. One writer claimed that it prompted a

15. Farmington, Minnesota, September 1939. This motion picture house advertises "Bank Nite" on Wednesdays and Thursdays, with the winning prize of $220. Photo by Arthur Rothstein. Courtesy Library of Congress, Prints and Photographs Division, FSA-OWI Collection [LC-USF34-28161-D].

"craving for the excitement of the cinema . . . often so great that it will drive children to crime simply to get money to pay for their amusement." Women, however, were doubly in danger because of the craving induced by materialism:

The effect of films on young boys is naturally not the same as on girls. . . . Silk stockings in films have been the cause of many a girl's downfall. Her desire for what she has seen is so strong that she minds little who gives it to her or at what price; the great thing is to get it. The danger to the poor girl is immense and the struggle to resist is a hard one. The love of luxury which is gaining a hold upon the working classes in our towns starts at the pictures. The sensual film, even if not pornographic, poisons the moral sense of young girls. By awakening their sensual instincts it is, as it were, a training-ground for the streets. The seductive power of lovely clothes, high-power motorcars and rich admirers is enormous.[20]

To illustrate her point, the writer described a case where a young servant girl, when refused permission to attend the cinema one evening and left instead in charge of a baby, was so overcome by desire to see the movie that she strangled the child so that she could go the cinema. The story's implications were clear.

By 1933, concerns over the effects of movie culture on the mind and behavior of the viewer had led to a wave of research into the possible dangers of this form of leisure activity. Most notably, research sponsored by the Payne Fund since 1929 began to appear in public debates at the start of the New Deal, underpinning a campaign of movie and leisure reform. Claiming to be the first scientifically based study of the effects of cinema attendance on the minds and morality of the nation's youth, the Payne Fund studies consisted of twelve separate investigations made at the request of the Motion Picture Research Council. These studies were published as a series of reports, including *Motion Pictures and Youth*; *The Emotional Responses of Children to the Motion Picture Situation*; *Children's Sleep*; *Movies and Conduct*; *Movies, Delinquency and Crime*; and *Motion Pictures and the Social Attitudes of Children*. A summary based on the reports was written by freelance journalist Henry Forman in 1933, titled *Our Movie-Made Children*. The hugely popular text, while not entirely representative of the findings of the research, formed the bedrock of mass media and social science observations on the effect of movie attendance throughout the 1930s. The book spawned and informed a debate that helped establish a need for benevolent intervention, regulation, and control. [21]

The new studies used scientific methods of measurement to discover the effect of the cinema experience on the viewer. Doctors monitored heartbeat and blood pressure during the course of the film and for some time afterward. Records of sleep patterns and diaries of cinema attendance were kept so that a relationship between the cause and effect of leisure-time activities could be accurately perceived. The effect of the movies on children's sleep patterns were measured by electrodes connected to their beds, which measured the degree of restlessness (called motility) following certain types of movies. The doctor's conclusions allowed them to have it both ways: increased motility caused fatigue the next day, as did decreased motility—which caused the same type of sleep induced by "soporific drugs." They concluded that the resulting fatigue caused by the loss of quality sleep had serious long-term effects:

"The significant increases of fatigue," [the doctors declare,] "whether induced by sleep impairment following the movies, from overwork, from narcotic drugs or alcohol, or any source of oxygen deprivation, are detrimental to health and growth, not only because of their known physiological consequences, but also because of the fact that the important inhibitions which serve to prevent misconduct are weakened. Frequent indulgence may lead to the formation of the habits of craving further indulgence. The best hygienic regulations for children should therefore include, among other things, only infrequent attendance at selected types of motion picture programs.[22]

These statements reiterated the sentiments concerning the female consumer. As with children, women's indulgence apparently led to cravings for further indulgence, and a cycle, comparable to drug addiction, inevitably followed from too much exposure to modern "stimulations" such as movies.

Although the scientific accuracy of these studies has been called into question, they are heralded as early precursors of contemporary mass communications studies.[23] Despite this, little has been said about how they were built on gendered presumptions that came directly from fears over women's changing role in modernity.[24] The studies automatically assumed that women's responses to mass culture were "naturally" different from men's and often led to different social ills—thus treating women's leisure as a separate issue from that of men. "Not all pictures affect all children alike," stated Forman. "Girls are often affected differently from boys and older children from younger."[25] Most reports observed varying differences in response and reaction to the movie experience between males and females. While the influence of the movies was feared to alter behavior, it appeared to do so not uniformly but in a particularly gendered way. Boys were more typically motivated toward crime and women to consumption and imitation—though both reacted to the movies as a sexual stimulant, often using it as an "aphrodisiac."[26]

From research undertaken in adolescent reform schools, Payne Fund sociologists Herbert Blumer and Philip Hauser noted that "the delinquency of girls and young women is still confined chiefly to sexual misdemeanors" and that the arousal of their sex passion was chiefly due to their exposure to motion pictures. Formerly, a sheltered existence and range of contacts had made women's delinquency rare, the researchers claimed, but the new participation of women in all areas of life had led to an explosion of female delinquency.[27] Young women confessed to the researchers in their diaries that the movies had awakened their passions, leading to their arrest for "sexual delinquency." The diaries showed little regret and strong feelings of passion long after the event, providing somewhat prurient reading for the social reformer and interested reader. In these reports, going to the movies was often the first stage of an evening that ended in dance halls, drinking, roadhouses, and truancy. Alongside this, women's passion for material possession was found to be stimulated by the movies and not unconnected to her sexual delinquency: "Among girls and young women this influence of the movies [in instilling desires for clothes, wealth, and ease] seems even more pronounced [than in men,] for a greater premium seems placed on fine clothes, appearance, and a life of ease in the case of women."[28] As few women found a life of ease through legal means, the researchers noted, "they are receptive, therefore, to easier methods of obtaining these often intensely desired luxuries."[29]

European studies by psychologists, psychiatrists, and criminologists, translated into English and published in America, corroborated the attitudes expressed in the Payne Fund studies. One report by Dr. Fabio Pennacchi of the Perugia Asylum illustrated how the cinema affected the mental health of the viewer, expressing in psycho-scientific terms the same effects noted by the Payne Fund studies, that movie watching induced varying degrees of hysteria. Further, Pennacchi claimed that "the hysterical factor is a contributory cause of most cinema psychoses and neuroses, more especially, of course in women." Cinema psychoses, to which young and "unformed" minds were particularly susceptible, manifested as "nervous disturbances, extending from palpitations of the heart and a hardly perceptible state of nervousness to muscular spasms, tremblings and convulsions; alteration of character and conduct, excessive emotionalism, suggestibility, histrionics; premature awakening of sexual instinct, abuses of all kinds, impulsive tendencies, criminal acts; many and important psycho-sensorial disturbances; serious and polymorphous delirious fancies, states of nervous anxiety, mental confusion and agitation."[30]

The extreme consequences of this emotional hysteria was most notable in reactions to horror movies, according to the Payne Fund research, where a run of Lon Chaney's *The Phantom of the Opera* appeared to lead to "so many faintings and hysterical collapses that the ushers were specially drilled in handling them. Throughout the run there was an average of four faintings a day; on one day eleven people fainted, four of them men. One woman had a miscarriage."[31] Thus, one doctor found that "a picture of extreme emotional content, whether it be tragedy or fear, leaves a physical imprint upon the human being lasting as long as seventy hours."[32] Using recent scientific knowledge obtained from studying World War I soldiers, medical experts claimed that the prolonged and frequent exposure to horror and tense scenes in a movie "have an effect very similar to shell-shock, such as soldiers received in war."

As a threat to social and moral conduct of American youth, reformers blamed the movies for encouraging lifestyles that the young working class especially could not afford and for offering them quick solutions to their restricted circumstances. Heightened fears that increased leisure would lead to criminality grew as Hollywood producers picked up on the popularity of high-profile criminal events and created a spate of gangster and crime films that fueled public belief that crime was increasing as capitalism was collapsing. News stories followed sensational crimes in the early thirties such as the Lindbergh baby kidnapping and the careers of celebrated bank robbers such as John Dillinger (eventually gunned down outside a movie house watching a gangster/Clark Gable film), "Baby Face" Nelson, "Pretty Boy" Floyd, George ("Machine Gun") Kelly, Al Capone, and Bonnie Parker and Clyde Barrow. Gangster movies such as *The Public Enemy* (1931) and *Scarface* (1932) were strongly influenced by events portrayed in the media and were churned out by Hollywood in quick succession. As shown in Figure 16, stars such as James Cagney provided men with a role model that, in the early thirties at least, many feared would tempt young men into a life of crime.

Thus, in a chapter titled "The Path to Delinquency" from *Our Movie-Made Children*, Forman made explicit this relationship between the movies, materialism, and crime:

"As I became older," bluntly admits a lad convicted of robbery, "the luxuries of life showed in the movies partly, made me want to possess them. I could not on the salary I was earning." Another, working off a burglary sentence, is even more explicit: "The ideas that I got from the movies about easy money were from watching pictures where the hero never worked, but seemed always to have lots of money to spend. All the women would be after him . . . I thought it would be great to lead that kind of life. To always have plenty of money and ride around in swell machines, wear good clothes, and grab off a girl whenever you wanted to. I still think it would be a great life."

A great life!—the ideal held up to view in so much of our public entertainment—"lots of money to spend"—"swell machines"—"women"—the cheapest and shoddiest vulgarity even when it is not criminal.[33]

Not only were the movies blamed for showing boys how to become criminals—for as one youth claimed, "Pictures of gangsters enabled me to become one of them"—but, more significantly, they were blamed for

creating an unsustainable desire for luxury and material goods, one that
taught against the work ethic that maximum gain for minimum effort
was possible.

In his 1931 book *Tragic America*, Theodore Dreiser reiterated this
degradation of material ambition, stating that the "madness of material
things . . . makes people run amuck, hooting and snorting to heap up
more and more possessions," and those who don't make enough money
will be encouraged by commercial slogans, telling them to "Take It!"—
to resort to crime. Dreiser linked crime with what he saw as the "sex liberty" of modern culture—where women's materialism had pushed men
to perform crimes in order to win them over. He gave two examples to
illustrate how women's insatiable materialism was behind the increase in
crime, even if not directly the cause. Claiming them to be "quite typical,"

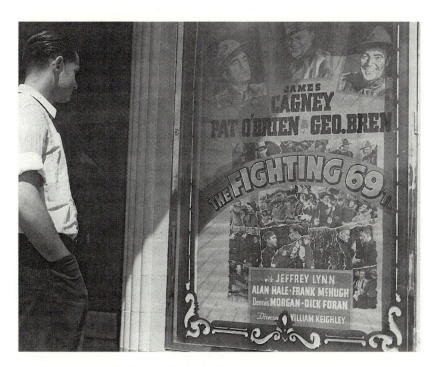

16. San Leandro, California. Hanging around. Twenty years old, his high
school education is over and college was never a part of his plan. His ambition
is to "work into something" in the field of skilled trade. Meanwhile, there are
odd jobs and periods of idleness. Movies provide an escape from his sense of
dislocation in society, and his mind is open to their interpretations of life. The
movie *The Fighting 69th* idealizes war. Courtesy National Archives, Still Picture
Branch, RG119-Cal-190.

Dreiser described one criminal who performed robberies in order to give money to his avaricious girlfriend, and another who attempted a holdup to buy dresses for his sweetheart after her mother told him not to visit her without gifts and dresses. To Dreiser, then, women's materialism, fueled by commercial entertainments such as the cinema, aided and abetted male criminality.[34]

Alongside crimes of material passion, Forman also claimed that the movies encouraged sex crimes by acting as a school for "sex-delinquents":

When forty-three per cent of delinquent girls state that movies gave them the itch to make money easily; when fourteen per cent declare they acquired ideas from the movies for making money by "gold-digging" men; twenty-five per cent, by living with a man and letting him support them; when considerable numbers of young men and boys in penal institutions declare that they used movies as a sexual excitant—then it means a load is added, the burden of which they are unable to bear; that there is probably something wrong, something subversive of the best interests of society in the way a substantial number of movies are made, written and conceived.[35]

Girls were led astray, and boys were induced by the movies to initiate premature sexual advances, often resulting in rape and gang rape. Movies, he claimed, enticed females to prostitution and casual sexual relations by giving them an "education along the left-hand or primrose path of life, to the wreckage of their own lives and to the detriment and cost of society." Hanging around on street corners or outside the movie house, as shown in Figure 17, made casual acquaintance all too easy. While movie attendance was not entirely to blame, Forman's influential book reiterated that the road to delinquency is "heavily dotted with movie addicts" and that movie addiction was a problem almost equal to crime itself.[36]

Fears that moviegoing would expose women to male fantasies and actual physical harm, or at least release their latent sexual desires, were reiterated in popular fictional representations. In 1932, James Farrell, author and trained sociologist, used his knowledge of Chicago youth to construct the *Studs Lonigan* trilogy. While hardly represented as a movie addict, Studs is shown responding to the movies in a way archetypical of the young male delinquents in Forman's book. The weak-willed Studs watches a movie that propels him to desire rape and to hope for violence to occur: "Studs watched, hoping that Arnold would be successful and rape her. . . . Studs could just see him grabbing her, flinging her on the bunk and . . ."[37] Emphasizing the psychical effect of movie watching in a stream-of-consciousness style, Farrell shows how Studs places himself within the movie action, using the narrative of the film to propel his own daydreams: "And under an Alaskan Sunset, Studs Lonigan kissed Gloria and kissed Lucy." Concurring with Forman's study, Farrell writes that "the picture made him want things like that, big dough, travel, broads as gorgeous as Gloria."[38]

Later in the trilogy, Studs returns to the movies to see a gangster picture, and again the young man propels himself into the narrative of the film—merging the gangster with himself as "Joey Studs Lonigan Gallagher." Just as the youth in Forman's study claimed that gangster movies showed him how to become one, Studs wishes to emulate the on-screen gangster/hero:

17. Waiting for the movie house to open at 1 PM Sunday in the small San Joaquin Valley town of Tulare. The boy is an enrolee of the Civilization Conservation Corps. National Archives, Still Picture Branch, RGF119-Cal-93.

"They hijacked. They spoke with crisp hard words, and with barking gats and tattooing machine guns, bumping off friends and foes, letting nothing get in their way. Ah, that was the kind of guy Studs Lonigan wanted to be, really hard and tough, afraid of no goddamn thing in this man's world, giving cold lead as his answer to every rat who stepped in his way."[39]

Paraphrasing the neon sign under which Tony Camonte, in *Scarface* (1932), was shot, "THE WORLD IS YOURS" appears thematically throughout the passage, and Studs apparently falls for this deception as he watches the film. Using a phrase that echoes Dreiser, Lonigan's mental soliloquy merges the materialism of capitalism with the criminality of the gangster: "Studs Lonigan, the world is yours. Take it. Oh, Christ, why hadn't he had an exciting life like Joey Gallagher."[40] Although the trilogy emphasizes the social and environmental factors that influence Studs's entry into petty criminality or degeneracy, and Studs actually visits the movies much less than his contemporaries in reality would have done, Farrell shows how someone with the weakness of character of Studs Lonigan is strongly influenced and manipulated by the movie genre. His fantasies of rape and criminal glory are shown to be a direct result of his movie attendance.

Other fiction writers, influenced by social science research, also depicted commercial leisure as morally corrupting for women. Meridel Le Sueur's reportage essay "Women on the Breadlines," for example, described women that she encountered in an unemployment bureau as victims not only of unemployment but also of the problems associated with commercial leisure. A Polish woman, Berenice, described as easily "taken in," naive, and having a "peasant mind," loved the city as a space of leisure: "It's exciting to her, like a bazaar. She loves to go shopping and get a bargain, hunting out the places where stale bread and cakes can be had for a few cents. She likes walking the streets looking for men to take her to a picture show. Sometimes she goes to five picture shows in one day, or she sits through one the entire day until she knows all the dialogue by heart."[41] Unaware of her own self-deception, Berenice represents the capitalist dupe, so "taken in" by the silver screen that she will casually prostitute herself for a picture show. It seems that her passion for cinema, rather than her unemployment, weakened her resistance to male exploitation.

As an activity that appeared to compromise women sexually and psychologically, cinema attendance was often frowned upon by both liberals and conservatives. To the left, modern leisure was an arena of mass indoctrination whereby workers were transformed into mercenaries for the corporate elite. Tess Slesinger's short story "The Mouse-Trap" illustrated this oppressive connection between the internalized fantasies of

Hollywood and women's sexual and political vulnerability. In the story, Betty Carlisle, a young executive secretary, is proud of her new job in the city, where she fantasizes about her relationship with her boss. Basing her dreams on what she has seen in Hollywood movies, she appears "gracefully conscious of herself, as though she were still at home in Kansas watching a smart New York secretary in the movies floating, brisk and yet charming."[42] With romantic notions sustained by her moviegoing, Betty envisions herself as the future wife of her boss and acts as office "spy" and assistant saboteur of the office rebellion. Once the rebellion and the potential strike against wage cuts is quashed, Betty loses her virginity to her boss in his office in a direct sexual parallel of the exploitation he has sustained over the workers. Bursting the balloon of fantasy at last, the reality of his intentions is made clear when he afterward tells her that he will "see to it [that she has] plenty of nice clothes."[43]

Betty's "prostitution" for Hollywood style fantasies and clothes is shown instantly as another case of false consciousness. Although she then realizes the true nature of her political and economic oppression, the implication remains that Betty's prior naiveté, or distance from reality, has been caused by her moviegoing, and her "awakening" is not a result of her contact with other workers, but because of the comparison of her sexual assault with a Hollywood romance. This view of working women as naive, apolitical, easily influenced by consumer desires, and sexually vulnerable through their contact with the movies appeared in the writing of social workers and fiction writers. Women were seen as especially vulnerable to "brainwashing" during their leisure hours, when they had little resistance to the conservative messages of the films they saw or the sexual advances of the men they saw them with.

Despite concerns, however, there is evidence to show that cinemagoers in the thirties were fully aware of their complicity in the social and sexual fantasies engendered by the cinema. Contemporary oral histories of cinema patrons of the thirties illustrate that, while they certainly copied fashions, hairstyles, dances, and actors' speech, this was as much a development of communal peer culture as it was "brainwashing" on the part of the movies. Many experienced changing social mores within the cinema as liberating and saw the cinema as an arena where traditions could be overturned. For working-class women, whose access to private spaces was often limited and whose homes were small, the cinema provided a warm and cheap mixed-sex environment that was generally safer than all other options.[44]

Similarly, although subject to competitive pricing, not all theaters were low-class dives that appeared threatening to women. Over the twenties and thirties, many theaters upgraded their facilities to cater especially to the female audience and their children, with inducements to women such as "free child care, attended smoking rooms, foyers and lobbies lined with paintings and sculptures, and organ music for those waiting in line." Moreover, the safety of women and children was especially catered for: "In the basement of each [Balaban & Katz] movie palace was a complete playground that included slides, sandboxes, and other objects of fun. For no extra cost children were left in the care of nurses and attendants while families attended the show upstairs. There were afternoon tea shows for women who went shopping with small children and infants. Balaban & Katz advertised that one could come to their movie palace, drop off the children, and enjoy the show. A nurse with complete medical equipment was nearby."[45]

Such improvements, however, did little to allay the fears of the anti-movie lobby, who saw them as further inducements for women to abandon their family role. Although cinemas were offering more supervision, better facilities, and lower prices, Forman found that these facilities merely encouraged women to abandon their children more readily and offered them incentives to be careless mothers. It was with grave misgiving, noted Forman, that "careless mothers, bent upon shopping, bridge-playing, or other errands" used the playroom as "a sort of parking place for children."[46] Women, it seemed, could not even be trusted to use the free child care properly. Forman cited examples provided by nurses left in charge of the playrooms and first aid rooms, stating that "Some mothers, [the nurse] declares, would take extremely young children with them to the motion picture theater. When a child became nervous or tired, the mother would send it to the playroom, where, in extreme cases, it remained for as long as nine hours at a stretch. She recalled cases of children left until one in the morning."[47] Despite this abuse, Forman claimed that they were still better off "than some of the infants compelled by their unintelligent mothers to remain in their seats and watch the unfolding of the screen play." Women, it seemed, when not cruelly abandoning a child, exposed them to damaging horror and fright, "sowing the seeds in the system for future neuroses and psychoses—nervous disorders."[48] If women consumers were already a matriarchy, then they were intent on keeping things this way by emasculating future generations by exposing them to the damaging effects of the cinema.

Forman concluded that the movies emerged as a school for delinquent girls, where, "seventy-two per cent of them admit to having improved their attractiveness by imitating the movies [and] forty per cent admit they were moved to invite men to make love to them after seeing passionate sex-pictures" and moreover that this "movie education" constituted a wreckage of their lives to "the detriment and cost of society."[49] These conclusions angered the original researchers who had worked for years on the Payne Fund studies, who felt that their research had been skewed to fit the publicity aims of the antimovie lobby. In fact, by the time the research was published in Forman's popular book, many of the researchers had reached the conclusion that there was no single or direct link between delinquent behavior and movie watching at all.

The Payne Fund findings, however, had a considerable effect on the output of leisure and recreation research over the thirties. After 1933, few recreation experts failed to mention the results of the Payne Fund studies in their books and articles.[50] Despite this, the Payne Fund researchers found it hard to prove a direct connection between the problems they cited and the leisure participated in. However, as researchers broke the link between movie watching and delinquency, their new conclusions fitted the concerns of recreation reformers even more fully. Thus, sociologist Paul Cressey claimed that delinquency was not the result of moviegoing but of a combination of environmental factors that could be altered only by better neighborhood planning and community organization for youth leisure. Cressey summarized the problems of the urban environment as "the failure to provide collectively for the character-building and recreational facilities for childhood."[51] In line with traditional recreation reform goals, he saw community leisure as a way of cleaning up the streets. These conclusions implied that recreational reform was even more important than movie reform and argued for an increase in supervised "non-material, non-commercial amusements" in order to prevent "social contagion," "criminal infection," and the accumulation of "foreign matter" in interstitial areas of the urban neighborhood.[52]

Appearing at the start of the New Deal, the studies served to increase anxiety over leisure-time activities and promote reform of commercial leisure to ensure that participation in "wholesome" activities would alleviate such "social disease." The Payne Fund studies illustrated the potential influence of the movies as a positive or a negative force over mass consciousness, showing that knowledge could be increased "to a considerable extent by correctly shown information from motion pictures" or decreased by information presented incorrectly.[53] The resulting clean-up campaign from these studies gave impetus to a nationwide movement to promote motion picture appreciation as well as to generate more family-oriented entertainment. Educators attempted to forge a closer bond with Hollywood, seeing film as a potential positive force for improvement, and leisure programs played a significant role in promoting a deeper study of motion picture art, aiming to teach adults and youth to differentiate between good and bad films in the hope that audience demand for "quality" pictures would effect reform.[54]

Even more noticeable were the self-regulating changes made by the movie industry itself. Coming in the wake of the Payne Fund studies, the correction to the motion picture production code was one attempt to clean up this most popular use of leisure time in order to make it safe for women and children. In fact, the code encapsulated the attempts of reformers to turn an "unwise" use of leisure into a "wise" one, by changing the medium into "wholesome" family amusement.

Thus, in 1934, the original code was amended and reinforced to prohibit obscenity, profanity, and vulgarity of word as well as plot. These prohibitions included further indecencies associated with sex delinquency such as sex perversion and miscegenation, or the "sex relationship between the white and black races." The addenda that forbade miscegenation in Hollywood movies underpinned anxieties that "lower" forms of entertainment could seduce females into lower class/race contacts.[55] Underlying such prohibitions was the belief that the intellect was weakened by cinema attendance and that sex crimes and sexual delinquency would lead to further procreation of the feebleminded and criminal.[56]

Dancing

Although moviegoing had become one of the nation's most popular forms of spending leisure, a survey undertaken between 1931 and 1932 of young businesswomen indicated that dancing ranked even higher.[57] Despite being an active form of leisure and having a "greater recreation value than those which do not involve participation," dancing was only of benefit to the individual and community if "it is properly controlled and directed."[58] Sociologists of leisure went to great lengths to differentiate between different types of dancing to illustrate that some were productive, whereas others were destructive. Approved dancing included artistic dancing, folk dancing, and community dances. On the other hand, commercially run-for-profit dances rarely found official approval from the recreation movement. The problems associated with dancing were, in many ways, similar to the problems associated with the movies. The commercialization of the dance hall for profit in a climate of lowered economic possibilities created, to most recreation reformers, leisure that exhausted rather than "revived" the fatigued nation. "The social and esthetic environment [of the commercial dance hall] frequently is unsatisfactory due to late hours, jazz music which has a deadening influence on the higher controls of conduct, the freedom of steps and the close physical contact with the accompanying excessive sex stimulation, promiscuous acquaintances, and the presence of undesirable persons," claimed sociologists.[59] Therefore, although jazz dancing was not the passive amusement designated to many other commercial leisure activities, the problems of dance-hall culture usually warranted special mention in recreation literature of the thirties.

Dancing caused consternation among reformers throughout the first half of the twentieth century, and developments as a result of the Depression exacerbated rather than alleviated these concerns.[60] Four specific developments at this time gave cause for extra worry: the growth of the roadhouse dance venue, which, like the drive-in, could operate cheaply and extralegally in the boundaries between cities, towns, and states (see Figure 18); the proliferation of the taxi dance; the growth of the dance marathon craze, and the repeal of prohibition. Although none of the problems associated with dance culture began solely in the thirties, developments in the way this particular leisure was experienced during the Depression created a wave of backlash reform.

Despite reform during the 1920s, social workers' reports and concerns were testament to the fact that the laws and conventions of public dancing were constantly being flouted. In 1929, for example, social worker Ella Gardner described the difficulties of enforcing regulations in city

18. Williamson County, Illinois, January 1939. A nightclub along the highway patronized by miners and farmers. Photo by Arthur Rothstein. Courtesy Library of Congress, Prints and Photographs Division, FSA-OWI Collection [LC-USF34-26992-D].

dance halls. A result of reform campaigns, regulations and ordinances operated to ensure that dance halls were supervised and that regulations on age, cost, style of dancing, lighting, health, and safety were enforced. While these ordinances were imposed inside the dance hall, police officers and dance-hall managers were also responsible for controlling behavior outside. Their attempts, however, were hampered by evasive techniques that were made possible by the increasing use of automobiles: "Notices were posted in the dressing rooms of some of the Chicago dance halls warning girls not to accept rides after the dances. Several halls had officers stationed at their doors to see that girls were not picked up as they left the hall. Methods of evading this type of protection were reported, such as parking the car a short distance from the hall and taking the girls from the hall to the parking place."[61]

Where reformers like Gardner had had limited success imposing legislation in the city, the roadhouse appeared to circumvent these regulations even further. Gardner stated that "out-of-town dance halls were considered to present the most serious problem in all the cities visited." These roadhouses were outside of city legislation. Easier access to automobiles increased the problem of roadhouse "lawlessness," making "one nighters" and evasions of the law even more common. Women were seen as particularly vulnerable to abuse by accepting lifts to such venues, despite their obvious desire to do so (see Figure 19).

19. Raceland, Louisiana. Dancing in a roadhouse. Photo by Russell Lee. Courtesy Library of Congress, Prints and Photographs Division, FSA-OWI Collection [LC-USF33-11661-M2].

Lack of cooperation from working-class or immigrant parents also appeared to handicap reform, Gardner claimed, as parents were indifferent, ignorant, or believed that "young people must sow their wild oats." To get more control over young people, reform efforts also targeted parents: "The cooperation of parents is . . . so important that public education as to recreation and recreational needs must be increased." Using her conclusion of the report to call for greater provision of community recreation, Gardner stated, "The provision of community recreation and training in recreational activities will not eliminate the commercial dance halls, but they should assist in modifying the character of commercial amusements as well as developing the play interests of the whole population, providing types of amusement not commercially profitable, and developing latent leadership in the provision of a wholesome neighborhood social life."[62]

Such calls for community recreation went hand in hand with sociological surveys of commercial amusements. In 1932, the vice problems associated with dancing came to the fore with the publication of a study undertaken by Paul Cressey before his participation in the Payne Fund research. Cressey's *The Taxi-Dance Hall: A Sociological Study in Commercialized Recreation and City Life* examined the dance hall as a paradigm of commercial amusements and social decline. An introduction by Chicago sociologist Earnest Burgess highlighted the wider concerns that lay behind this research: "This study has a significance that goes far beyond the taxi-dance hall situation. It raises all the main problems of recreation under conditions of modern city life, namely, the insistent human *demand for stimulation*, the growth of *commercial recreation*, the growing *tendency to promiscuity* in the relations of the sexes, and the failure of our ordinary devices of social control to function in a culturally heterogeneous and anonymous society."[63]

Burgess continued by enumerating the trends toward commercialization as "the mounting number of automobiles, the rapid increase in the number of radios, the replacement of the neighborhood saloon with the speakeasy, the expansion of the motion picture with its 20,000 theaters, Miss America beauty pageants, endurance contests including dance marathons, dance palaces, night clubs and the road house." These trends, he claimed, undermined family and neighborhood recreation, which had declined in direct proportion to the growth of "city-wide enterprises intent upon commercializing the human interest in stimulation." "Complicated by the fact of promiscuity," he claimed, the commercialization of amusements detracted considerably from the home and community as centers of personal satisfaction and enjoyment. With fewer commitments to the home, and focusing less on their families, it was feared that women would be attracted to the stimulation offered from commercialized leisure, thereby encouraging them to neglect their children and their husbands and to fall into promiscuous and damaging relationships.[64]

The taxi-dance hall, a place where men paid to dance with a female partner, raised particular ire among reformers. To circumvent prostitution laws, patrons bought a ten-cent ticket that entitled the female "hostess" to a 5-cent beer, from which she kept the change. Nickel hopping, or dime dancing as it was also known, often became a first encounter with drinking or prostitution. Many feared that the hardships caused by the Depression would drive women into taxi dancing as a way of paying the bills, with obvious threats to female morality, the family, and the structure of society.

Beginning as closed halls or dance academies, the taxi dance grew out of immigrant culture in the early part of the century. By 1925, more than eight thousand women in New York worked as taxi dancers, reportedly earning about thirty dollars a week—almost double that of the average white-collar worker. By 1931, Cressey reported that there were more than 100 taxi-dance halls in operation in Manhattan alone.[65] Yet Cressey's "intimate picture of a typical taxi-dance hall with its owner and manager, with its bevy of pretty, vivacious, and often mercenary 'instructresses,' with its motley array of patrons: Orientals, older men, isolated and socially handicapped youth, eager for association with feminine beauty at 'a dime a dance,'"[66] offered a stereotypical picture of "mercenary" women using "disadvantaged" men.

Further, the study illustrated how far women were prepared to flout class and race barriers in their desire to satisfy their craving for sensation and material possession. Natural female weakness of character, it appeared, made them especially susceptible to the thrills and sensations of commercial amusements, a view paralleled in many films of the period where women followed careers such as dancing and modeling, less for financial need than for sensation-hunting pleasure. In the taxi-dance hall, sociologist Paul Cressey noted this addictive quality of the commercial environment, where the dance-hall girls appeared "to be giddy young girls in the first flush of enthusiasm over the thrills, satisfactions, and money" provided by the dance-hall environment.[67]

Burgess likened such dangers of the leisure environment to the appearance of a new kind of "frontier," in which the problems of commercialism were conflated with the problems of urbanization. Just as other social scientists such as Stuart Chase were comparing rural cultural practices with industrial, Burgess compared "wholesome" traditional recreation with modern urban leisure: "In the village of past generations . . . the desire for stimulation and adventure normally found wholesome expression in the varied program of events of village life, or in the pioneering settlement of the West. But with the passing of the frontier, the bright-light areas or 'the jungles' of the city become the locus of excitement and new experience."[68] Sociologists thus saw the urban environment as a new frontier—one that was both racialized and sexualized—to be explored and even tamed.[69]

Controlling the leisure frontier was no simple feat, despite the federally sponsored recreation training and the unprecedented educational and cultural programs of the WPA. In fact, as the first issue of *Life* magazine showed in 1936, the success of some work relief programs appeared to fuel new outposts of the leisure frontier. Examining the growth of shantytowns around a work relief project in Montana, the issue's main feature noted, "Life in Montana's No.1 relief project is one long jamboree slightly joggled by pay day. One of its shanty towns has 16 all night whooperies. The workers are on night shift as well as day with the result that there is always someone yelling for whiskey or calling on the little ladies of Happy Hollow. College boys mingle with bums in the crowds."[70] Illustrated with photographs by Margaret Bourke-White, the feature indicated that the new frontier was not a physical boundary but a frontier between work and leisure, a Wild West where lawlessness and sexual license accompanied work relief prosperity. This was a place where "these taxi-dancers with the chuffed and dusty shoes lope around with their fares in something half way between the old barroom stomp and lackadaisical stroll of the college boys at Roseland. They will lope for a nickel a number. Pay is on the rebate system. The fare buys his lady a five-cent beer for a dime. She drinks the beer and the management refunds the nickel. If she can hold sixty beers she makes three dollars—and frequently she does."[71] Bourke-White's photos in *Life* may have confirmed what Robert Lynd feared, that simple "folk" patterns of community and family leisure, which had emerged as a result of hardship, would be simply thrown down at the first sign of commercial recovery.[72] Both celebrating and mocking, the feature shows New Deal leisure as a frontier where classes (college boys and bums), genders, and even races (in this case American Indian) mixed.

As part of peer culture in the dance halls, alcohol consumption played a significant role in the enjoyment of this particular type of leisure.[73] However, repeal of prohibition at the start of the New Deal increased concerns that women's alcohol consumption in their leisure time would increase, leading to greater loss of control and more promiscuity. The *Life* feature highlighted the way that working-class heterosocial culture casually blended money, drinking, and sex. The photos depicted women and men mingling together at bars, and at least seven of the women in the photos were holding or drinking alcoholic beverages. One waitress was shown at work, sitting her child on the bar while she "kids with the customers." While repeal had ended the gang culture associated with the black market liquor business, it also led to increased concern over women's leisure and behavior, increasing fears that legal alcohol consumption would lead to freer sexual behavior. Observing this on his return to Middletown, Robert Lynd reported that "in June 1935, a beer and dance hall in the center of the business section—dirty, noisy with a general atmosphere of drunken freedom between males and females, and with streetwalkers inside and hanging about outside—was one of the exciting dives in and out of which Middletown's young drifted."[74] Farm Security Administration photographs that parallel Bourke-White's also showed women drinking at bars, smoking, and gambling in heterosocial companionship with men (Figures 20 and 21). Although *Variety* magazine claimed that repeal had been a boon for commercial leisure, public dance halls appeared to introduce women to the taste for drinking in her leisure, most worryingly in the taxi-dance hall environment.

As a "work maker," the Montana relief project was called a "spectacular success," yet the *Life* article concentrated on out-of-work activities almost exclusively. Its depiction of leisure and life in the shanties as "one long jamboree" was equally a product of the conflation of women's leisure

20. Craigsville, Minnesota, September 1937. Saturday night in a saloon. Photo by Russell Lee. Courtesy Library of Congress, Prints and Photographs Division, FSA-OWI Collection [LC-USF34-30584-D].

with work discussed in Chapter 5 and showed working-class women working within the leisure industries of the newly prosperous town. Coded as leisure, however, whether taxi dancing, waitressing, or cleaning, the women in the new "Wild West" were actually at work. Confirming the view of moviemakers and reformers that women *as leisured* worked for pleasure and sensation seeking rather than out of necessity and lack of employment options, women's work servicing male leisure was shown as leisure itself.[75]

The significance of jazz dancing and music as a working-class response to modernity and the Depression was entirely missed by recreation reformers. But not all cultural observers were blind to the significance of dancing as cultural expression. Proletarian writer Lucille Boehm indicated the importance of dance in the lives of poor teenagers in her story "Two-Bit Piece." In it a young girl called Liz keeps the coin she finds despite her family's hunger. Liz withholds the money from her family and then meets up with friends at the local candy store, where they ply the jukebox with coins and dance. Boehm equated the need to dance—a social hunger for pleasure and culture—with the need to eat: "The

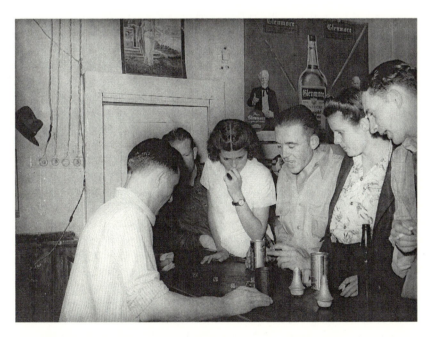

21. Mogollon, New Mexico, June 1940. Shooting for drinks in a gold mining town barroom. Photo by Russell Lee. Courtesy Library of Congress, Prints and Photographs Division, FSA-OWI Collection [LC-USF34-36811-D].

music throbbed out of the lit machine, groaning with the full under-
tone of the running bass. The kids jammed themselves into the little
store and began to dance. Liz was at the hub of the excitement. The
boys took her on in turns, sending her swiftly over the rough boards.
Their dancing was agitated, quick with the restless rhythm of hunger.
One by one nickels plunked into the machine. *Wolverine Blues, Twilight
in Turkey, Doggin' Around.*"[76]

When Liz collapses with hunger the kids still carry on dancing, and
she walks away leaving the "thin shadows of hungry kids and their hungry
dancing." Although concurring with many leisure professionals' suspicions that women would let their families go hungry rather than forsake
certain pleasures ("It would be worth six sacrificed suppers"), Boehm did
not equate misspending on leisure with poverty itself. Liz does not create the poverty by her deceit, but hunger and poverty have become such
an institutionalized part of culture that a craving for enjoyment and
expression through dancing means more to the kids than extra food on
their plates for one evening.[77]

Like the roadhouse and the taxi-dance hall, the dance marathon also
became an increasingly popular form of entertainment in the thirties
that reflected a popular response to changes caused by the Depression.
Although the fad began in the 1920s, the dance marathon took on new
features that reflected the climate of the Depression, much to the consternation of social workers and reformers. Shows took on many formats,
often lasting for weeks, and offered twenty-four-hour live entertainment
based on extreme endurance and suffering. In all formats dancing partners were only allowed to rest for short intervals before continuing to
dance without stopping. Relying on "an audience that was out of work
and on contestants who were willing to work for very little," endurance
contests were a form of theater that "appealed to the sense of loss and
desperation" resulting from the Depression.[78]

Like the commercial atmosphere of the movie house, the dance marathon also appeared to legitimize gambling, as audiences were encouraged to "back" their personal favorites and place bets on prospective
winners. Audiences were also invited to participate in prize-winning
events such as country store night, where a prize draw rewarded some
spectators with a bag of groceries.[79] And like the roadhouse, marathons
were difficult to regulate legally and financially, as they grew into big
money-spinners without achieving true business legitimacy. Transient
businessmen and entertainment troupes would sometimes enter towns
and set up a marathon, leaving before they paid their debts to local businesses or helping to swell local tax budgets.[80] Taxable receipts and revenues were impossible to obtain and standards difficult to enforce, so
that by the midthirties legislation against the competitions was enacted

in all major cities. While fears over morality and health were the main arguments used to legislate against the shows, worries over competition to legitimate businesses and entertainments also underlay reform.[81]

Concerns about marathons by reformers, however, concentrated their efforts on the social, health, and moral implications of the event, charging that easy sexual contact and a materialistic environment corrupted the health and morals of young women during a time of economic vulnerability. Church groups and women's clubs fought to close the marathons, even though many women enjoyed the event and participated freely. Showing that women would dance, sing, and perform for money or just a few minutes of fame, dance marathons laid bare the blatant commercial exchange that was a close correlative of prostitution.[82] Often broadcast live on radio, the cheap twenty-four-hour entertainment reached a very wide audience, overlapping with popular shows such as Amateur Hour and offering commercial tie-ins. Many feared that young women would be tempted to give up honest work or families in order to try and win the often illusory prize money.

Yet, despite fears over the corruption of women's morals, the marathons theatrically illustrated a new female independence. Strong single women were shown winning endurance contests against men, and the female audience, from old ladies with their picnic hampers to the younger evening crowd, appeared to enjoy the theatrical "replaying," or overturning, of traditional heterosexual monogamy.[83] This female dominance was illustrated in the fictional representation of the dance marathon in *Studs Lonigan*, where Studs meekly obeys the wishes of his date who persuades him to watch a marathon against his better judgment or inclination. Once mesmerized, Studs is unable to leave despite several attempts to go, as he is drawn into the drama of the show.[84] Over the course of the story, Studs starts to experience public entertainment spaces as increasingly emasculate, where even the horse races are female dominated: "More women were in the place than he'd imagined. They were certainly taking to the ponies, he thought with persisting surprise. Were they battered down old whores? Most of them seemed like housewives, maybe mothers."[85]

The gender imbalance of commercial recreation was a major concern addressed by sociologists at this time. The mockery of traditional heterosexual relationships in the dance marathon, which usually featured a mock or real wedding between dancers, played up social workers' concerns that marriage was in decline because of depression hardships and modern behavior. One of the main criticisms of commercialized recreation was the fact that it could lead so easily to casual and illicit sexual relationships between men and women, undermining traditional family and marital relations. As an antidote to the dangers of commercial leisure, recreation programs were planned to encourage healthy social interaction between the sexes. This recreation was always supervised, if not by the recreation leader then by a peer group. Guarding against the moral hazards of lax recreation and unorganized leisure, organizers promoted activities that reinforced traditional gender roles and pursuits.

Recreation programs thus developed to counteract the lure of the commercial dance halls and to teach people approved forms of dancing that would lead to "healthier" relationships between men and women. As part of the WPA program, classes were offered in folk and square dancing to communities around the nation. "Artistic" dancing was also sponsored as an extension of the federal theater project.[86] Free dances were a popular part of the FERA amusement program in the summer of 1935 and 1936, noted Lynd in *Middletown in Transition*.[87] Community recreation programs focused on providing healthier alternatives to the commercial variety, often promoting and organizing community barn dances and socials, teaching square dancing, and sponsoring folk dancing.[88] All these were expected to break the lure of the commercial dance hall and provide amusement that would rebuild the family at a time when the traditional family organization was perceived as under duress. Thus, in 1940, recreation expert George Butler commented that "square dances are competing successfully with social dancing for the interest of young people in several cities, and they are better adapted to participation by the entire family than most features in the recreation program."[89]

Recreation experts recommended guidance in corecreational dancing as a way to combat the ills of commercial dancing and to break the unhealthy relationship between dancing, promiscuity, and alcohol. Guidance for women's use of leisure aimed to teach them to use their new role for the benefit of the family, and as an extension of their traditional role as nurturers and unpaid workers in the home. In order to counteract the lure of commercial amusements for young men and women, it was considered necessary to promote healthy and safe mixed sex recreation that would give men and women a chance to socialize without the danger of premarital sex. Recreation leadership was to promote a "healthy heterosexuality" and "normality" in adolescents so that marriages would be fulfilling.[90]

Reformers recommended that activities should remain under the eye of watchful trained adults who would remain in supervision throughout. Unlike the dark cinemas and dance halls that were the bane of reformers lives, supervised activities were brightly lit and all activities subject to the communal gaze of multiple participants (see Figure 22). In a book prepared for the National Recreation Association and the Young Women's Christian Association (YWCA), Mary Breen saw the role of youth leisure as one that would encourage healthy friendships, leading to happier marriages and family lives. Written for young people between the ages of 12 and 30, Breen's book cited the breakdown of traditional communities and leisure forms as one reason why young men and women had difficulties forming healthy friendships. Sympathetic guidance from a specially trained recreation worker could enable boys and girls to develop a "normal, healthy heterosexual relationship during their formative years," without which "they may be emotionally crippled in a very serious and fundamental way." Getting youth to work on a project such as organizing a party or social together, Breen explained, may even be more enjoyable and healthy than the final result of them dancing together. Oblivious to the way that working-class youth culture sought close sexual contact away from the eyes of parents and reformers, Breen saw recreation as a panacea for widespread social improvement.

Modern dancing, Breen claimed, made youths miserable because it created couples and was therefore individualistic and unsocial. Commercialism encouraged sensational "hot" music and dance styles, which led to conduct that is to the "detriment of youth," she added. Using

22. Woodville, California, February 1942. Farm Security Administration farm workers' community. The recreation room. Photo by Russell Lee. Courtesy Library of Congress, Prints and Photographs Division, FSA-OWI Collection [LC-USF34-71757-D].

information on the "evils of modern dancing" from dance-hall reform surveys, Breen saw dancing as an especially dangerous arena that needed to be tackled in order to set youth on the right course in their future relationships. In her book, program directors were instructed to provide dances that were well lit and supervised, with dance floor managers present to discourage "improper dancing." She counseled that dances should be held with other events (such as a basketball game), so that youth may relegate dancing "to its proper place as only one of many recreation activities." "The deadliness of pairing-off and staying paired can be minimized through social games and group dances which are lively and exhilarating," Breen claimed, making dancing more "wholesome" by adopting traditional folk dancing and group participation.[91] Other recreation reformers made similar suggestions, understanding that young people want physical contact with the opposite sex but that this needed regulation in the form of recreation leadership: "Wise leaders introduce many social recreation games which involve pairing off as partners, linking arms, holding hands, standing back to back, running and pulling, turning rapidly, changing places and partners frequently— all including some measure of physical contact but not of an objectionable kind. The old-time square dances which have all these elements, meet this need admirably, as also do the very catchy rhythms and the frequent rapid turns causing dizziness and creating joy."[92]

Mixed-sex recreation was also promoted by Breen as one way of cutting the growing divorce rate in America: an issue that was causing nationwide comment, and something that it was feared had risen alongside unemployment. She explained, that "In the opinion of Mr. Newell Edson, formerly of the American Social Hygiene Association, one of the chief reasons for divorce is that husbands and wives have never learned how to play together. He believes that friction develops when both husband and wife are home, that is, in the after-work hours, and that some of the most frequent divorce complaints—abuse, drink, immorality, evil companions, nagging—show a direct relationship to lack of play. 'If marriage is worth saving,' states Breen, 'boys and girls must be taught how to play together.'"[93]

Not all women of all ages were to be treated the same, however, and leisure manuals instructed that recreation should be tailored to suit the type of individual. In *Recreation for Girls and Women*, Ethel Bowers divided women into distinct social and age groups and divided her book into chapters addressing the needs of each group. Beatrice the Business Girl, for example, should take part in social recreation of a mixed-sex kind, as should Ida the Independent Working Girl, for without organized recreation, "Beatrice may be forced to withdraw from many forms of social recreation for lack of escorts; and Ida may resort to corner or dance hall 'pick-up' acquaintances." "How much better it is," she continued, "for these girls to meet men in dramatic clubs, music groups, inter-club councils, athletic associations, welfare committees, study clubs or at a party or on an outing, at a church, school, community center or some other organization building than at a public dance hall, street corner or on a 'blind date' auto ride!"[94]

"This is the mating age," claimed Bowers, and guidance in the right use of leisure at this point could mean the difference between a successful or a failed marriage. However, Martha the Matron (aged 25 and up and presumably already married), had no need to meet a suitable partner and could use her leisure in single-sex recreation that compensated for the boredom and inadequacy of home life, leaving her refreshed and fulfilled to return happily to her family. Without organized recreation, Martha and so many like her "live under such strains, financial worries, clashing personalities, illnesses and other family problems too numerous to mention that they must find some escape." "Some find temporary relief at a matinee, playing bridge or shopping," but these forms of outlet were only another strain, states Bowers: "Martha usually needs social recreation as a relief from strain, as an outlet for pent-up emotions due to the monotony of married life and household drudgery. Occasionally it happens that Martha has been playing bridge so long and ardently that it has become another strain, *work rather than recreation*, so that social games effect a relief from too much leisure unwisely used" (italics added).[95]

Interestingly, Bowers completed the conflation of women's work and leisure by claiming that modern forms of leisure had become women's work. Despite indicating that the home may not be the ideal environment that reformers so often made it out to be, Bowers saw recreation as something that would enable women to survive the home without leaving it for more attractive pursuits. Physical activities for the matronly Martha were a problem needing special treatment, she claimed, with activities "carefully selected and tactfully presented behind closed doors." Poor old Martha "should not be required to run at any time," Bowers claimed, and should do her exercises lying on the floor. The recreation organizer should make special arrangements for Martha's leisure, being careful to remember that "running is especially dangerous at parties when women in high-heeled shoes attempt to play games on slippery hardwood floors." (See Figure 23.) Instead, married women could be encouraged to play clapping games, "finger plays," and coordination stunts such as "clap clap nose ear."[96]

By the end of the decade, official concern over the leisure problem still illustrated anxiety that modern leisure practices engendered passivity, affected mental or physical health, and was associated with high levels of materialism and low levels of intelligence. Nevertheless, fears that leisure time pursuits would create and sustain high levels of criminal activity in the early thirties gradually shifted by the end of the decade to a central focus on a use of leisure that would support "correct" mating patterns, social welfare, and family health. Commenting on the diseases that were revealed by the selective draft of World War I, Eduard Lindeman argued that "racial health" was another key area in which recreation leaders should be trained.[97]

In a mutation of eugenics goals, the proper use of leisure by women could serve to improve "the race," and a corresponding misuse of leisure would lead to all manner of disintegration. Within this discourse lay the assumption that the women who were genetically responsible for producing "better" progeny were white, were "leisured," and could be "taught" to use that leisure to the benefit of the status quo. Black men and women, conspicuous by their absence from this discourse of leisure, were notable only as servicers of white leisure (e.g., in films), or as a racial threat in subaltern (unregulated) leisure practices such as jazz dancing, taxi dancing, or roadhouses. Similarly, anxieties over dancing and moviegoing revealed barely disguised fears of cross-class and cross-race blending, where pleasure from "lower class" and subaltern forms of entertainment corrupted the purity of the Anglo-Saxon,/blonde female, leading her to release the sublimated animality that was her "true" nature. As a new frontier, commercial leisure needed controlling so that the

23. Butte, Montana. Folk dancing is enjoyed by young and old alike in the WPA recreation program. National Archives, Still Picture Branch, RG69N-18784-C.

"jungle" could be regulated and proper "mating" could be reestablished. As I explain in the final chapter, eugenic principals for improving the population lay beneath this shift, as leisure became the theoretical ground on which social and personal improvement could be enacted. This drive toward health and welfare in the modern state thus served to reinforce a new-style "cult of domesticity" that reinscribed notions of female autonomy and power within the patriarchal discourses of modernity and (male) pleasure.

Chapter 7
Mate Selection

An increasing number of persons believe that the time has come to consider carefully a policy for the future. They believe that population growth should be consciously controlled in the interests of all the people. This will mean an effort to adjust numbers to the means available for their support so that a high standard of living can be maintained. It will also mean careful selection of immigrants, the development of means of preventing the propagation of "the unfit" and in time, perhaps, methods for encouraging the propagation of "the fit" to the end that the quality of stock may be improved.

—*President's Research Committee on Social Trends,* Recent Social
  Trends in the United States

The importance of leisure to many reformers centered around the fact that it was in her leisure that Beatrice the Business Girl, who was crucially at the "mating age," would find her husband and produce America's future progeny. As sociologist George Lundberg wrote in 1932, "The whole sex complex, including courtship, marriage, and the begetting and rearing of children is undoubtedly in large part a recreational pattern of great significance."[1] Correct mating, healthy marriages, and public awareness of "proper" mate selection were seen by many as crucial to the success of modern progress and welfare reforms. The recovery of the nation from the "sickness" of the Depression appeared to rely on the resolution of the problem of leisure as much as on economic recovery: in fact, many saw these economic and the social "cures" as interrelated. Civilization could not progress without better fitness of population, and better fitness, it was assumed, would result from a combination of environmental, social, and genetic improvements throughout the United States. This chapter examines how eugenics in the thirties thus figured not as a separate "scientific" discourse propagated by a few adherents but as a central underlying feature of the newly leisured modern state. Recovery, recreation, and reproductive control were an inseparable triumvirate to planners of the American future.

In 1930 a French film called *Motherhood* was reviewed with the claim that it could help to combat "one of the greatest evils of modern society: voluntary barrenness in marriage." The review argued that this "evil" was caused by the new selfishness that categorized female consumer habits: "In most instances, indeed, such voluntary sterility is due rather to a form of selfishness that regards children as trouble and a spoil-sport than to genuine anxieties of an economic kind. A baby is looked upon as a small tyrant who will keep his mother away from dances, theatres and the cinema and interrupt her reading the latest novel, and whose maintenance and upbringing will curtail her pin-money." The review summarized one aspect of popular eugenic theories of this period, whereby women's (albeit white middle-class) voluntary barrenness led to the "moral and physical decline of the race—to race suicide." As "one of the most burning social questions of our time," the review claimed that the lowered birth rate of the thirties was a product of commercial leisure: "The cinema is one of the many causes responsible for the diffusion of that view of life which makes men decline responsibility for setting up a home and makes women anxious to live their own life and avoid the *impedimenta* of motherhood."[2] Promoting marriage, motherhood, and traditional family values, *Motherhood*, it was argued, could do much to counteract the dysgenic effects of popular leisure-time activities.

Social propaganda films promoting eugenics had circulated throughout the early film period.[3] For the three decades before the Great Depression, the belief that human qualities and characteristics were inherited had dominated social and political reform movements.[4] Changes in immigration and marriage laws in the early part of the century had developed out of the scientific discourse that claimed humans could be improved over a period of several generations by "better breeding." On the converse side of this discourse, it was claimed that if the genetic carriers of weak genes could be encouraged or forced not to reproduce, eventually weakness, disease, and invalidity (both physical and social) could be eradicated. Associated with prison reform movements, the feminist movement, socialism, and medical reform, eugenics filtered into the vast majority of social reform movements, including recreation reform.

Anxieties over emasculation and fears of losing racial dominance as a result of inactive office lifestyles had been present since the early years of the century, when eugenic societies and other reformers condoned exercise routines that would restore manliness and fertility.[5] The appearance of "neurasthenia" (or nerve exhaustion) as a common leisured-class ailment in the late nineteenth century coincided with massive industrialization and immigration. The speeding up of society appeared to have created men whose brains were overworked.[6] Likewise, narratives of white male bodily perfection, personified in the performance art of America's early bodybuilders and physical culturists, were responses to technological and social developments that appeared to threaten white male individualism and identity.[7] Yet the physical health and eugenics movements during the course of the thirties gained increased momentum due to intensified fears of racial decline, male passivity, low levels of intelligence, moral and physical degeneracy, and low fertility, all manifested in public discussions over high divorce rates, lowered marriage and birth rates, low literacy levels, high mental illness rates, and poverty. By the thirties, the concern that hereditary defect caused crime, mental illness, and disease had "resulted in an intensive campaign for custodial care and sterilization of the unfit."[8]

So, while films like *Motherhood* aimed to promote childbearing for "the fit," it was the reproduction of "the unfit" that concerned American eugenicists most of all in the early part of the decade. Although "voluntary barrenness" concerned many, research campaigns had "proved" that "the unfit were particularly fecund . . . and the financial burden for supporting such degenerates was likely to get a lot worse in upcoming years unless the states prevented them from reproducing."[9] Increased belief in the social efficacy of compulsory sterilization came about as social scientists became frustrated with the limitations of immigration and marriage laws, arguing that the "mentally unsound need neither benefit of clergy nor sanction of the law to indulge in sexual intercourse."[10] Sterilization laws, which had been legal in some states from 1907, had "made mandatory the sterilization of confirmed criminals, idiots, imbeciles, and rapists."[11] Yet because of supreme court approval in 1927, as Edward Larson points out, "the 1930s represented the pivotal decade for compulsory eugenic sterilization in the United States," and more legal eugenic sterilizations took place during the 1930s than in any other decade.[12]

The widespread adoption of compulsory sterilization as a method of preventing the "unfit" from reproducing coincided with a decade of economic crisis and reform. Many blamed "cultural lag" for the crash of 1929 and saw it as a manifest result of the "dysgenic" twenties, generated by laissez-faire capitalism and uncontrolled (re)production. To some, the Depression had been caused by the years of dysgenic decline, which had left the modern citizen maladapted to the new modern condition of technological redundancy. Reform eugenicists such as sociologist Frances Oswald saw eugenics as a way of modernizing the nation, claiming in 1931 that "a definite need for some sort of action to limit the number of degenerates has long been acknowledged by all thinking people." To Oswald, only conservative groups such as the church or the ill-informed public hindered greater use of sterilization.[13]

Fears that the weakened "vitality," mental health, and physical strength of the American populace were now emerging as part cause of the nation-wide Depression abounded in the popular press. Reinforcing anxieties over the quality or "vitality" of the nation were statistics that appeared to show that the numbers of "native" whites—or Anglo-Saxons—were diminishing, or at least not increasing as rapidly as other groups. With "the fit" breeding less, and "the unfit" apparently breeding more, many saw the Depression as a eugenic red flag.[14] Images of a weakened and stooped people appeared everywhere, in photographs of malformed bodies and in advertisements for children's health products. In *Recent Social Trends,* population expert Edgar Sydenstricker reported in his chapter "The Vitality of the American People" that many viewed improvements in public welfare as having prolonged the lives of "weaker" children, so that a larger proportion of the population contained weaklings, who were themselves breeding a less "vital" race. The debate over the effects of public health and welfare continued throughout the decade. Increased public welfare appeared to make the problem worse, as many felt that health assistance enabled weaker humans to survive longer, increasing the chance that a distinct race of weaklings would appear with no natural ability to survive.[15]

At the annual meeting of the National Education Association in the summer of 1932, George B. Cutten, a psychologist and the president of Colgate University, summed up the fear that Americans were in danger of degeneracy. While the theory of evolution, he claimed, had made Americans a nation of optimists, believing in the upward thrust of mankind, biologists now showed that degeneracy was a strong possibility, with the prevalent threat of "the abyss from which we climbed and into which we may fall."[16] To some, it may have appeared that the Depression was the abyss. Herbert Agar, economist and historian, for example, warned in 1935 that the nihilism and skepticism resulting from the loss of a belief in progress would lead "nowhere, and man cannot even sustain the will to struggle," with dire results for civilization. Man would be immobilized by disillusion and "stricken with sterility": "In his giant cities he finds himself too bored or too unzestful even to breed normally. . . . Man lies down tired in the midst of his marvels. His numbers dwindle, his cities stand half empty, and once again the beasts of the wilderness prowl among the ruined buildings."[17]

To many, the proper use of leisure signified the prospects of survival for the human race. Cutten summed up the importance that control over leisure was felt to play in the future survival of civilization: "There is no greater responsibility that is put upon us individually or as a race than the proper use of leisure. With the threatened calamity which is ever upon us, and with leisure the only means of escape, the most valuable asset that we have at the present time is our leisure. We cannot afford to squander it or to use it in a way that will be harmful. Above all things we must have intelligent direction if the race is to escape annihilation."[18] Others warned that control over leisure was the only way to prevent the atavism that had resulted in the decline of earlier civilizations. Ralph Aiken claimed that the dangerous "excess of leisure" that the masses now had could lead to united mobs upsetting "the constitutional order of things," resulting in "turbulence in idleness without government assistance" and a chaotic society comparable to ancient Rome: "Like the ancient Romans, the modern idle will be doing what they should not do if they follow their *natural* tendencies. They will seek entertainment and the more drastic its form the better. Of course they will further mock prohibition, if it is possible to mock it further. But they may also remove the deeper prohibitions in decency and clean-living and bring *weakness* openly to the front."[19] Just as eugenicists earlier in the century had argued that Rome declined because of the poorer hereditary quality of its people, many leisure reformers likened the state of national recreation with Rome just before the collapse of the Roman Empire.[20] Others claimed that the economic problems that had beset Europe in the twenties were a direct result of overpopulation, preventable if "the human progenitors had possessed control over themselves equal to that which physical science had given them over the forces of nature."[21] Dire warnings about how ancient civilizations declined were given as ways to prevent similar catastrophes in the United States: "I suppose that while there have been a good many explanations of the fall of ancient civilization, that one of the explanations is unquestionably this, that civilizations up until our own time have never learned how to use their leisure time constructively. Leisure time has been merely a time of indolence, merely a time of laziness, moral flabbiness has come into the social structure because people have been idle. And as a result of that moral flabbiness there has been the progressive decay of civilization itself."[22]

Whether civilization was progressing or in decline appeared to be answered in the way that families were responding to depression. It was with concern, therefore, that Ernest Groves reported in 1935 significant increases in many forms of popular "escape": drinking, movies, and bridge playing. "Idleness has tended to increase gambling," he stated, "thus adding to the economic problems of many households." Crime had increased, along with the prostitution of married women, which had created a "new type of vice problem." The disillusion of youth was contributing to the creation of a "liberal sex code," as well as a shift to radicalism. Sex, he claimed, "has become almost the only recreation for many, naturally leading, particularly in a group that largely lacks adequate contraceptive knowledge or is indifferent to it, to an increase of pregnancies." Despite the fact that the birth rate was in decline, Groves claimed it was highest "where it has been stimulated by the dole." Fears that "the dole" would lead to degenerate leisure, sexual licentiousness, and the propagation of "socially deficient" individuals is encapsulated in his report.[23] The problem of leisure, then, was also a problem of sex, breeding, and class.

Although Groves reported that in some households the depression "has led to a feeling of shame on the part of husbands and rebellion on the part of wives," the shame had a class dimension: "The feeling is widespread that direct relief has been disastrous in its fundamental effects upon the family. There is a unanimous feeling that the relief program has been accepted by a multitude of those on the lower economic level with parasitic responses, while the middle-class group who have suffered most during the depression have had inadequate help, and have been hurt most keenly through loss of self-respect. Direct relief is charged with having demoralized stamina, character and integrity."[24] Groves reiterated the importance of government programs of work relief, indicating how they could function to rebuild the position and dignity of the male in the family, to resurrect class "stamina," and to prevent the "parasitic" response of the laboring classes, who could all too easily get used to receiving money for nothing.

While fears over the collapse of the work ethic underlay these reports, the impoverished southern states provided an even greater example of the "collapse" of civilization and the dire results of "moral flabbiness." Echoing sentiments about the degeneracy of the Roman empire, one Atlanta pediatrician claimed in 1937 that "the South's 'poor white trash,' so aptly named by the Negro, is no doubt the product of the physical and mental unfit, left in the wake of the War between the States" and that all "individuals who are not physically, mentally or emotionally capable of reproducing normal offspring" should be sterilized.[25] Fictionalizing this decline and degeneracy, the novels of Erskine Caldwell confirmed the pediatrician's views on the need to restrict and control the degenerates resulting from this decline. In his novels, the idleness of poverty and unemployment lead naturally, or inevitably, to degeneracy, fecundity, and crime.[26]

In *Tobacco Road* (1932), without work or income, tenant farmer Jeeter Lester has reached the lowest depths of this decline. Although a victim of economic and environmental catastrophe, Jeeter is also the inheritor of poverty and "feeblemindedness." Unable to adapt to changing circumstances and work in the mills, Jeeter is left with depleted land, decaying property, debts, and a ream of "degenerate" and "promiscuous" children, most of whom have deserted the farm. The novel famously opens with the remaining members of the Lester clan scrabbling over a sack of turnips, while Ellie May, Jeeter's harelipped progeny, fornicates with her sister's husband (the owner of the turnips) in the dirt road. Savages and animals by generational decline, the Lesters symbolize the fall of the founding American stock. Emphasizing the importance of inheritance, the beauty and intelligence of Jeeter's youngest daughter, Pearl, are attributed to her illegitimacy: "The truth was, Pearl had far more sense than any of the Lesters; and that, like her hair and eyes, had been inherited from her father. The man who was her father had passed through the country one day, and had never been seen since."[27] With twelve living children out of seventeen, Jeeter only knows the whereabouts of three.

Despite being surrounded by destitution, Sister Bessie cashes her dead husband's insurance to buy a fancy new automobile in order to attract and marry Lester's youngest son of sixteen, Dude Lester. Dude proceeds to drive the car recklessly, without knowledge or understanding of the law—at one point he even drives over his own grandmother without stopping. As pieces of the car break down and fall off over the course of the novel, the automobile comes to parallel the decline and eventual death of the Lester family. Bought, used, and driven in ignorance, the car symbolizes the consequences of cultural lag.

In one of the only contacts with an "official" in the book, the granting of the marriage license for Dude and 39-year-old Sister Bessie illustrates how "ignorance" breeds greed, disease, and poverty in Caldwell's South. Bessie cannot read the license or sign her name, nor does she understand, when asked by the clerk, what venereal disease is. The marriage clerk illustrates official disapproval of such degenerate and mismatched marriages: he emphasizes the difference in Dude's and Bessie's ages but claims he is impotent to prevent it if Jeeter Lester allows it. Jeeter not only allows such mismatching but also seems to thrive on it; for as the clerk notes, Jeeter allowed his twelve-year-old daughter to marry for the price of seven dollars, some quilts, and "nearly a gallon of cylinder oil." With little or no work, the Lester family scrabbles for a living, stealing from each other and wasting what they have, a prime example of Darwinist degeneracy and struggle to survive.[28]

Leisure combined with poverty in the novel creates crime in a casual fashion: Bessie is unwittingly "used" as a prostitute when the "hotel" that she, Dude, and Jeeter stay in turns out to be a brothel; Dude drives lawlessly, killing his grandmother, who is left to die in the road; and the family fight viciously for remaining scraps of food and belongings. In the end, despite Jeeter's death in a fire, the cycle of degeneracy continues when Dude inherits his father's impotent desire to "get me a mule somewhere and some seed-cotton and guano, and grow me a crop of cotton this year." Without meaningful work and community structure, the characters in the novel spend their time trying to satisfy primal urges that precipitate their own destruction. As a parable for Depression-hit Americans, the novel provides dire warnings about the dangers of ignorance and poverty.[29]

Degeneracy also reappeared in Caldwell's next novel, *God's Little Acre* (1933), where Ty Ty Walden digs obsessively for gold on the property he neglects to farm. Symbolic of the "get rich quick" or "gold digging" mentality that had appeared to replace true productivity during the Depression, Ty Ty, like Jeeter, also represents the outcast or Forgotten Man. Kidnapping and lasciviousness are Ty Ty's naive, almost incidental crimes, but the story ends in the murder of one son by another over the affections of his wife. Leading up to this event, Ty Ty visits his wealthy son, Jim Leslie, and offers sympathy for his marriage to an "unfit" wealthy wife: "I sure hate to see you married to a diseased wife, son. Now just look at those two girls, there. Neither of them is diseased. Darling Jill is all right, and so is Griselda. And Rosamond ain't diseased either. They're all nice clean girls son, the three of them. I'd hate to have a girl in my house diseased. . . . It must be pretty hard for you to live with a diseased woman like your wife.

Interbreeding is also treated casually; when Will has sex with one sister-in-law, and later in the novel with another, he claims, "It's all in the family, ain't it? So, what the hell!" Although he disapproved of the term, Caldwell's "poor white trash" live outside of legal perimeters, inhabiting a no-man's land of vice and squalor, a world where the promiscuous Darling Jill fornicates with the kidnapped albino in full view of her family.[30] In these dramas, the central concern is not poverty but the potential catastrophe of sexual degeneracy when combined with lack of meaningful work, especially among those with low intelligence or living in poverty.

The New York Society for the Suppression of Vice attempted to have *God's Little Acre* suppressed as pornography for such scenes of sensuality and degeneracy, yet the action failed because the court found Caldwell's attempt at a realistic portrayal reason to include, with "brutal frankness," intimate details of the lives of "primitive" and impoverished people.[31] Among the many writers and cultural authorities called upon to give evidence in the case was H. L. Mencken, the celebrated southern critic, editor, and columnist who in his own writing used the "sharecropper areas of the South" as prime examples of genetic degeneration. Mencken's extreme views on eugenics were illustrated in an article in *American Mercury* in 1937 titled "Utopia by Sterilization," where he suggested that the inadequacy of the sterilization laws may be compensated for by offering small sums of money to each man volunteering for a vasectomy, taking advantage of the poverty and desperation of "polluters of the race." If the birth rate of "Moronia" continued, he claimed, "there will be a wholesale degeneration of the American stock, and the average of sense and competence in the whole nation will sink to what it is now in the forlorn valleys of Appalachia." He argued for sterilization of the unfit because, even if "all the lunatics in all the asylums of the country were sterilized hereafter, or even electrocuted, the sharecroppers of Mississippi alone would produce enough more in twenty-five years to fill every asylum to bursting." As a method of reducing federal relief expenditure during the Depression, he claimed to have found the solution that would bring "the More Abundant Life to thousands of unhappy and despondent people."[32] Sociologists and reformers confirmed the pathetic state that the southern tenant farm population had reached, albeit with less lasciviousness, saying that "economically they are at bare subsistence levels, mentally and morally they are dependents, without control over their own destinies, with little chance for self-respect or the exercise of individual responsibility."[33]

To many, the New Deal appeared to necessitate further implementation of eugenic goals than before, for the cost of supporting welfare recipients would only increase if they continued their "uncontrolled" breeding. Sterilization of the unfit was seen in many states as one way that welfare costs could be cut, as degenerates could be released into the community without fear that their progeny would return to institutions and swell the welfare budget. Sterilization rates climbed and reached record numbers.[34] In fact, contact with squalid conditions for the first time during the Depression via relief work led many prosperous women to champion eugenics as a way of ending poverty and squalor.[35] Birth control experts like Margaret Sanger warned that "with 4,000,000 families on relief and over 233,000 children born into these homes in the past year, the need for making birth-control information accessible to all classes is obvious."[36]

Family planning became central to the health and welfare policies of New Deal initiatives. The demand for the planned economy was echoed in demands for population planning. Professor Earnest Hooton announced at the annual meeting of the American Association for the Advancement of Science that the United States needed a "biological new deal" to prevent "a progressive deterioration of mankind as a result of the reckless and copious breeding of protected inferiors."[37] To social scientists of the thirties, social welfare meant "the functioning of society so as to produce in each succeeding generation more and more of the 'strong,' the 'normal' and 'good' and less and less of the 'weak,' 'abnormal' and 'bad.'"[38]

In his book *Technics and Civilization*, social critic Lewis Mumford highlighted the new importance that the Darwinist approach held for planners of the New Deal. Theories of social and economic interdependency were established by Darwin's concept of the web of life, he claimed, which taught that balance was vital to the healthy functioning of the total organism. Intelligence and higher forms of living were undermined because Western society was relapsing "at critical points into pre-civilized modes of thought, feeling, and action," he claimed, having "acquiesced too easily in the dehumanization of society through capitalist exploitation." As vital to the rationally planned economy was the rationally planned population, for uncontrolled production was paralleled by equally disastrous uncontrolled reproduction. Creating an "equilibrium" of population via birth control, he claimed, "reduces the number of variables that must be taken account of in planning, and the size of the population in any area can now theoretically be related to the permanent resources for supporting life that it provides."[39]

In a correlation between the problems of overproduction in the factory to overreproduction, or uncontrolled reproduction, of humans, Mumford saw the rational future as a eugenic one: "The first period [of mechanization] was marked by an orgy of uncontrolled production and equally uncontrolled reproduction. In the neo-technic phase the whole emphasis begins to change. Not more births but better births, with greater prospects of survival, with better opportunities for healthy living and healthy parenthood, untainted by ill-health, preventable diseases and poverty. . . . These are the new demands. What rational mind questions their legitimacy? What humane mind would retard their operation?"[40]

While federal policies of planned leisure were being initiated, self-control was also seen as vital to wider social improvement. Equipping people with better libraries, more free time, and bigger sports facilities would be of little use if they continued to "decreate" unintelligently in roadhouses and jazz rooms. A new philosophy of leisure would teach "every human being to acquire an *intelligent control of his own body* as the first step towards intelligent control of anything else, such as the activities of his mind, his passions, the forces of nature, or the fortunes of his fellow citizens, as when he is asked to give his vote at elections."[41]

However, while eugenic ideals filtered into mass culture, the science and social politics of eugenics came under increasing criticism. Even in the early thirties, the President's Committee on Recent Social Trends had described the inherent practical problems of eugenic control: "But what are the practical possibilities of improving a people by conscious selection? The lack of knowledge concerning heredity and the composition of the chromosomes of prospective parents is undoubtedly an obstacle, but breeders of livestock have accomplished results without this information. The obstacles lie rather in obtaining the necessary control, in the lack of agreement as to which combination of traits is desirable . . . the problem is one of research from which in time higher eugenic ideals may emerge."[42]

Likewise, as population specialists Warren Thompson and P. Whelpton noted in 1933, "it seems clear that no population policy can be considered comprehensive which does not take into account the fact that there are native differences between individuals and that as soon as any agreement can be reached about the methods by which 'undesirables' can be selected from the population, they should be prevented from propagating."[43] Despite this, they claimed, eugenics was altogether too unreliable, and vitality should be improved by other measures: "The importance of conserving vitality and promoting enjoyment of life throughout life greatly overshadows, at least at the present, the vague possibilities of lengthening the life span by the scientific breeding of future generations."[44]

The fallibility of the eugenic argument was not of ideals but of practicality. Rather than opposing eugenic ideals per se, social scientists incorporated them into their own methodology, rejecting the biological solutions of the genetic argument out of practicality and replacing them with "environmentalism." So, while many professionals now agreed that there were doubts about the strength of arguments based solely on heredity, they shifted eugenic strategy by combining hereditarian theories with environmentalism and social reform.[45] Haller explains that the theories oddly complement each other, for "improvements in body and mind during one generation could strengthen the body and mind next generation," and securing environmental reforms could be strengthened by hereditarian thought "since such reforms would improve not just the present but also succeeding generations."[46] In an attempt to distance themselves from Nazi policies from 1932 onward social reform eugenicists argued for more popular education and less emphasis on legal restrictions. Others worked to reinvigorate eugenics with democratic principles.[47] For example, sociologist James Woodward indicated in 1936 that fascism could be fought by removing the obstructions to education and eugenics—traditionalism and authoritarianism—"to allow a whole population capable of complex and difficult decisions."[48] American democracy and ascendancy would therefore be defined through its voluntaristic or self-conscious adoption of eugenics as a general principle of self-improvement.

As a result, healthy family policies came to represent the newly modern democratic state. The importance assigned parent craft during this period was illustrated by First Lady Eleanor Roosevelt, who edited a popular magazine called *Babies, Just Babies*, published by physical culture guru and eugenicist Bernarr Macfadden. The magazine offered advice on health, nutrition, child care, and mothering in support of young mothers who might be daunted by their new task. Better breeding and healthy relationships thus became an increasingly important goal of family policy in the thirties. Distancing themselves from increasingly unpopular Nazi eugenic policies, the shift to environmentalism also sig-nified the ascendancy of socialist and reform eugenics within the Amer-ican Eugenics Society at this time. A well-organized leisure policy that developed natural physical and mental superiority through leisure activ-ities appeared to answer both the needs of immediate environmental changes and long-term eugenic possibilities.

More than just a hypothetical link, however, the relationship between leisure and eugenics professionals was compounded in 1937 by a "Con-ference on Recreation and the Use of Leisure Time in Relation to Fam-ily Life," sponsored and arranged by the American Eugenics Society.[49] Chaired by the head of the National Recreation Association, Weaver Pangburn, and with papers by leading recreation experts, the conference aimed to "open up new possibilities for the development of practical eugenic measures" and closed on the agreement that "the recreation group is doing a superb work in conditioning young people to the main-tenance and increase of those standards of family life which are an essential part of the eugenic ideal."[50] Confirming the move toward greater environmentalism, the conference focused on developing "new ways by which environmental improvements can be so directed that they will lead to a corresponding improvement in human inheritance."[51]

The papers focused not on sterilization but on the relationship be-tween recreation and positive eugenics—or the enhancement of breed-ing among "the fit." Pangburn commented that the conference signified a new direction for both eugenics and recreation experts: "Two hitherto strange elements, recreation directors and population experts for the first time were brought together." Common ground between the two movements was stressed, with Pangburn asking, if eugenic and recre-ation ideals are jointly applied, "shall we have large families among the groups most fitted to have them?"[52] The relationship between physical education, balanced personalities, and the "capacity and desire" to bear children, Osborn claimed, made the two goals mutually supporting. In closing, "it was agreed that eugenics revolves around two main problems, economic problems and a changing sense of values" and that eugenicists had much in common with the recreation experts in that they pro-moted simple noncommercial family recreation that aimed toward the same goal of "healthy" family values. The Depression, it seemed, had brought these two groups closer together than ever before; focused on economic hardship, the "decline" in the eugenic quality or health of Americans, and adaptation to rapid industrial change, eugenicists and leisure reformers found much common ground above their traditional differences.

The conference speakers emphasized the way that recreation could prepare youth for family planning, emphasizing how large families needed strong leadership from men who had developed physical strength and leadership qualities in their youth. C. Ward Crampton spoke about the health program of the Boy Scouts of America, describing how the scouts were being encouraged to keep health charts to motivate hygienic living and self-examination, with heredity second on the list of charts kept. Keeping these life records, he claimed, would aid medical guidance, social adjustment, and scientific advancement. The records kept as a continual reminder of their eugenic fitness, it was claimed, would enable the boy to achieve self-control, "to manage his own life, defend his own liberty, and pursue his own happiness in order that the larger individual, the nation, the race may maintain its ancient principles and travel the upward way."[53]

Cheap, family-oriented recreation, it was also claimed, would do much to encourage and entertain those who chose to have larger families. Corecreation received special attention for those who were of the "dating age" (sixteen to twenty years old) and the "mating age" (twenty to thirty years old)—terms directly borrowed from Mary Breen's book discussed in the previous chapter. Frederick Osborn, president of the American Eugenics Society, summarized that corecreation could help to establish "normal relationships between the sexes during the period of adolescence, thus training them for the later relationships of marriage." One eugenic aim of this would be "to provide a wider choice of mates," although he states rather cryptically that "this aim should be kept in the background for many reasons."[54]

Maintaining healthy heterosexuality through leisure activities was essentially a synthesis of traditional reform goals with modern ideas about the scientific role of federal government. Thus, *The Literary Digest* in 1933 asked, "What will the New Deal do for the marriage market?" illustrated with a cartoon of cupid reading a report of marriage statistics, saying, "Gosh, someone better draft a code for marriage recovery!"[55] Although no code was drafted, recreation and eugenics bodies saw the maintenance of family stability and happiness as central to the success of their reform movements. Just months after the leisure and eugenics conference, eugenicist Paul Popenoe wrote "Mate Selection" in the *American Sociological Review*, with suggestions about how to encourage more desirable mate selections, especially among educated women. Popenoe concluded that the best opportunity for an educated person to meet another was in the various recreation organizations offered in the city:

In every city there are almost countless organizations devoted to sport, religion, recreation, philosophy, art, music, literature, science,—everything under the sun. One who wants to make acquaintances should canvass systematically all such groups in whose objects he has, or could acquire, an interest. He (or she) can visit them one at a time, drop them at once if no "worth-while" young people are found, cultivate them further if they promise to be worth their cultivating. . . . Taking two a week, a young person in a large city could visit a hundred groups in a year. It would be surprising if at least one of them did not prove to be repaying![56]

This reformulation of eugenic philosophy was addressed by Frederick Osborn in the *American Sociological Review* in 1937, where he described how the limits of sterilization to only deal with 1 percent of the population necessitated wider measures that disregarded class lines as a basis for selection. "True freedom of parenthood," he claimed, necessitated changes in economic relationships and social attitudes compatible with other social programs of the thirties. Thus, he claimed, the "development of the simpler types of non-commercial recreation should tend to increase the birthrate through improvement in physique and in nervous balance, and by developing healthier attitudes towards family life." By reducing the economic burden of raising a family, he claimed that eugenic family policies were compatible with wider relief. At the same time, he argued, this change in policy necessitated further refinement of methods for measuring "personal qualities" so that a "rating scale for parenthood" could be made effective. Although his article mentioned German marriage loans and Mussolini's efforts to increase the native birth rate, Osborn concluded that "the eugenic philosophy which we have outlined would make eugenic selection a natural and voluntary process. It is thus in full agreement with the concepts of individual liberty and of non-interference by government, which are so closely associated with our form of democracy."[57] By shifting attention away from sterilization to self-improvement, mass leisure, and the family, eugenic ideals became apparently compatible with wider social ideals of the New Deal. In spite of class and race biases expressed in eugenic social studies, self-improvement on a national scale via leisure became a harmonizing goal through which all races and all classes could express their "Americanism."

This philosophy of self- and race-betterment through improvements in the use of leisure time affected social thought within minority communities as well. While struggling to cope with increased poverty and a dearth of basic provisions, African American social workers fought for improvements in recreation provision, arguing that these would help to prevent illegitimate pregnancy and venereal disease. Among complaints about segregated facilities and unfairness in the WPA provision of amenities, the philosophy of recreation reform continued to be seen as one way to end the cycle of poverty. Appealing to their strong belief in the social possibility of recreational improvement, recreation worker Mildred Tucker wrote to Eleanor Roosevelt and Eduard Lindeman, requesting better facilities for Yazoo in the Missisippi Delta. In her letters, she stated that children with no other diversion than the movies spend their idleness in "sexual relations, gambling and other vices." Because there was no physical education teacher, "they learn very little of health and hygiene." Most of the damage was done, she claimed, during vacations when there were no supervised activities at all, "having nothing to do with their leisure time they resort to sex and other vices . . . and as a result little girls hardly reaching their 'teens' become mothers of illegitimate babies. Both boys and girls fall to ruining their young bodies with venereal diseases." "I want to help these children, I want to help our community produce better and stronger young women and men," she argued.[58] Although such rhetoric used eugenic perceptions to improve communities and to redefine racist ideals of beauty and physical fitness, white eugenicists persistently codified the eugenic "other" as "African" or primitive. Nevertheless, such ideals where all races could be equal through social and genetic improvement defined modern America in opposition to the rigid class and ethnic distinctions operating in much of Europe.[59]

The recreation movement over the thirties propagated images of fit and healthy bodies that were used to underpin the message that the proper balance of work and leisure would create the eugenic ideal. WPA murals of workers and families idealized the healthy vital body, where women appeared as earth mothers whose healthy fecundity heralded American-style abundance for the future.[60] The back-to-the-hearth movement was celebrated in these murals as the return of folk culture and "natural" forms of leisure. Artistic expression in the Federal Dance Project also glorified the muscular male body as a returned virility within cultural pluralism. As the body became another way to express "Americanism," new techniques of modern dance explored the way that the physical could express American democracy as an alternative to fascist displays of uniformity.[61]

At the same time, popular culture reflected this new shift toward "mating success" via self-improvement and national athleticism. Ideals of physical beauty that tapped into eugenic principles abounded in mass culture. Choreographer Busby Berkeley filmed production lines of perfectly cloned maidens, women he selected using a composite chart so that even their vital statistics were standardized.[62] And the mass production of females as commodities of amusement appeared in newsreel features of synchronized female swimmers, bathing beauties, and beauty pageants.[63]

Likewise, these eugenic themes were played out in Hollywood films such as *Tarzan, The Ape Man* (1932): as "King of the Jungle," Tarzan reasserts white control over animal, African, pygmy, and dwarf—"a white man with the sexual energies and jungle-wise ways of the black man," but genetically royal, springing from British aristocracy. Reflecting on his meeting his "perfect" mate and genetic equal, advertising copy commented that "modern marriages could learn plenty from this drama of primitive jungle mating!"[64] As a symbol of the perfect athletic model and object of rational recreation, the Report of WPA's Activities of the Golden Gate International Exposition in 1939 (as shown in Figure 24) was illustrated with a photograph of Johnny Weismuller posing for a WPA-employed sculptor. Tarzan appeared in this image as both the ideal mate and model for civilized art.

It was, however, in visions of the American future that the relationship between the new leisure and eugenics became a panacea. Leisure was enshrined in the structure of Granville Hicks's fictional society in *The First to Awaken* (1940), where men and women work only four hours per day and the rest of the time they are free to devote to hobbies, play, or study. The progress of this future is described with the Darwinian metaphor of adaptation: "Today we are beginning to be strong enough to face our limitations. We know that ours is a species just sufficiently adapted

24. Johnny Weismuller at the Golden Gate Exhibition, 1939, modeling for a WPA artist. Photo from Report of WPA Activities of the Golden Gate International Exposition. Courtesy National Archives, Pacific Region, NRHS-69-NCWPA-BOOK.

to the world in which it finds itself to permit survival."[65] Awaking 100 years into the future after being cryogenically stored, Hicks's protagonist discovers that although "there was no attempt to tell people whom they should marry or how many children they should have," several magazines, he noticed, referred to eugenics as an ongoing debate. His spokesman, David, tells him that once environmental differences were eliminated it became scientifically possible to tell what characteristics were due to heredity, so that once all were equal, "natural" weaknesses and strengths became visible. Thus, he states optimistically, "we might do something with eugenics yet."[66]

Other utopian visions of the thirties complemented these views of eugenically improved democratic worlds. In *New Industrial Dawn* (1939), by A. T. Churchill, the protagonist, Fenton—a banker—awakens in the future, after falling into a drunken stupor in 1929, to a eugenically streamlined, perfectly balanced, rational society. Eugenics is emphasized from the start: discovered by a "queenly" Venus—a woman, six feet in height and "perfectly proportioned"—"a feeling of great inferiority came upon him." He is introduced to all aspects of the new society, which is constantly contrasted with his own time; the new world is not a democracy but a "MERITOCRACY DEMOCRATICALLY ADMINISTERED," where rulers take office, not by election but "automatically as they become more efficient politically or industrially." Significantly, race has been eliminated, for there is only one language. The year is divided equally into three periods—the industrial, the vacational, and the scholastic—and is thus "classless," there being no working class. Machines perform most of the work, and the rest is done communally on a rotating basis. The eugenic model is preserved in strict marriage laws involving "mental, physical and parental examination," where couples get assigned "child quotas" according to their eugenic fitness. The vision is a balanced, meritocratically administered, classless, leisured, abundant, and scholastic world of tomorrow, where leisure functions eugenically to promote equality.[67]

Other popular utopias such as James Hilton's *Lost Horizon* (made into a film by Frank Capra in 1937) featured worlds of material plenty, where leisure led to increased knowledge and wisdom. Prestonia Martin, in *Prohibiting Poverty* (1933), a book commended by Eleanor Roosevelt, recommended state organized labor groups in which everyone would serve for a period of eight years, after which all time would be free to pursue civilized leisure and education.[68] These worlds differed little from the futuristic ideals of the technocrats at the start of the New Deal, where population planning dovetailed with other forms of city planning.

Such plans for future organization of society appeared in Buckminster Fuller's *Nine Chains to the Moon* (1938), where a highly planned, organized society featured communities of leisure that housed those unable to work. His book depicted an idealized community where unemployment has been eradicated by moving those unable to get or perform work into worlds/communities of leisure: "Scientific, mobile shelters will be utilized, also, for the constantly moving placement or deployment or city-bogged, nonemployed people to play lands of the world where it would be possible for them to develop in health, strength, and intellectual ability. This might never completely rehabilitate the 'lost' older generation, but would nurture its offspring into harmonious synchronization with and responsible continuance of the emergent age." In this book, Fuller predicted the evolutionary "abolition" of the terms "unemployed" and "on relief"—to be substituted by the terms "social reserve" and "industrial reserve": for "what is called 'unemployment' is the borderline nomenclature for what will be in due course recognized as *socialization of leisure*." To Fuller, the possibility of creating a highly mechanized environment, which sustained a "responsible continuance of the emergent age," involved a godlike reordering of the planned environment along scientific and eugenic principles. "The way is scientific, and heavenly," he claimed.[69]

Technocrat and modern designer Harold Loeb similarly predicted a perfected future based on voluntary genetic engineering to produce "a race of man superior in quality to any now known on earth, a society more exciting, interesting, and variegated than has ever been possible."[70] His vision promoted the use of streamlined leisure, where no time was "wasted" outside of the pursuit of cultural and physical self-improvement. Views that the Depression was a "technological catastrophe," or the byproduct of progress, where man's mechanical abilities had outstripped intellectual ability, were surprisingly in keeping with a technological vision of the future and idealized leisure. Having lost control of machines, the technological future would reharness them for progress and the betterment of society. The leisure resulting from this would be used to further the mastery of the intellect and increase the abilities of the rationalized mind—resulting in a political and cultural renaissance. Yet the image of technology as dystopic was so prevalent that companies were forced to advertise and promote this new vision of the future based on scientific advancement.

A General Electric advertisement of 1938 titled "Test-Tube Babies" encapsulated this attempt to dismantle the notion of technological unemployment and promote a scientific view of the future. Claiming that jobs were the test-tube babies of industry, the advertisement stressed, "Fifteen million American men and women are at work today in jobs that didn't exist in 1900. . . . These jobs are 'test-tube babies,' created in the modern research laboratories of industry."[71] Showing men working inside test tubes, the advertisement depicted the machine-made man in the enviable role of a worker, developed and protected, albeit confined, within the glass wombs of industry. Nurtured by the "maternal" science that produced them, these progeny of technology had no fear of unemployment, and to turn against technological "progress" was self-destructive matricide. Counteracting the view that technology was responsible for the ills of society and unemployment, industry advertised itself as the womb of the future.

Such visions of a future civilization, based on the rational control, or scientific management, of the self through leisure and family and community planning, reached its apotheosis in the New York's World's Fair of 1939. Dubbed "The World of Tomorrow," the fair pandered to and assuaged social anxieties about loss of vitality, energy, control, and power. The narratives and form of the fair gave man optimum control over the new environment, situating him as the omnipotent authority of a hygienically cleansed, deracinated environment. The fair sustained and promoted a vision of modernity, where work and leisure were perfectly complementary within a streamlined, healthy, and ordered environment. The seeds of Lundberg's "dreams with science" came to fruition in this display: the fair showcased the totally planned environment—the mechanized home, the machine servant, and the "Futurama," a streamlined community of the future based on the supreme vision of science as a male womb out of which emerges a new civilization. As the ultimate fantasy of male-controlled production and reproduction, the fair illustrated how the planned future would feature leisure as the mode by which Americans created higher civilization.[72]

Underlying anxieties of cultural lag propelled the vision of the fair, where it was claimed at a founding meeting that "the world is in chaos struggling to master its own inventions. We are in danger of being annihilated by forces which we ourselves set up. The world calls for an answer to this problem of mastering our own inventions and we propose in 1939 to contribute to that answer."[73] Aware that the problem of leisure in the Depression had caused much debate and anxiety, the fair's creators stressed the positive effects of increased leisure as something harmonic with industrial progress. Narrating the history of technology as a transition from work to leisure, the Community Interests exhibit began in a colonial village, where a narrator stressed a life of "work, work, work," and ended in a modern housing project, where the ideal community has liberated man from toil: "Time for interest in government, in community, in the group. Time to plan for our community. At last man is freed . . . freed in time and space."[74] The Food exhibit also stressed such freedom, where, relieved of the necessity of cultivating and growing food, man had been freed to cultivate himself, aided by new scientific nutrition, into a "higher" state of being: "Nutrition is the key to leisure and freedom, to time for science, art, learning and entertainment."[75]

Fair planners predicted that increased leisure and expanded buying power would result in increased time and energy for physical and educational leisure activities, as well as giving rise to a host of new service industries. Human bodies would achieve a perfection parallel to the streamlining of material objects. Modern highways linked communities and enabled families to use their leisure time to explore historical and natural environments, which in turn would enable them to define and comprehend their Americanness. Displays by New Deal agencies at the fair cemented the relationship between leisure and corporate visions of the planned future. The Federal Works Administration (FWA) exhibit claimed that recreational facilities provided an antidote for machine-age tension, and the FAP created photomontage designs depicting geometrically positioned streamlined bodies for the WPA Community and Health Building (see Figures 25 and 26). With time for the arts, hobbies, and politics, physical and mental improvement would make the leisured world of tomorrow the highest form of civilization.[76]

Yet this "highest form" was based on eugenic fantasies that had featured strongly in most expositions throughout the twentieth century. As Robert Rydell has shown, industry, science, and government came together at the fair to promote a streamlined, white, hygienically "engineered" vision of family life in the thirties, most significantly in the "Typical American Family" display—one of the most popular at the fair. With one family winning from each of the forty-eight states, the contestants won a free trip to the fair in a new automobile provided by the Ford Company, where they lived in modern houses built by the Federal Housing Administration. The families chosen were white, native-born Americans with two children, expressing perfectly the eugenically streamlined exclusivity of the world of tomorrow.[77]

As in Fuller's imagined world, the organizers of the World's Fair assigned a place for the anomalies and misfits, the exotic and feminine, in the playlands of the fair—the Amusement Zone.[78] The Amusement Zone, renamed in 1940 as "The Great White Way," was similar to earlier colonial fantasies depicting social-Darwinian ideas of evolution. Juxtaposed with fantasies of a streamlined future and displays of mechanical perfection, this part of the 1939 fair depicts the freakish worlds that the future cannot include, except for amusement:

Here is centered every type of amusement, the romantic and the realistic, the fantastic and the impressive, the unique and the weird. Here are strange people from remote lands which you have read about: pygmies for instance, from the dark forests of central Africa, where mysterious rivers flow in the eternal shadow

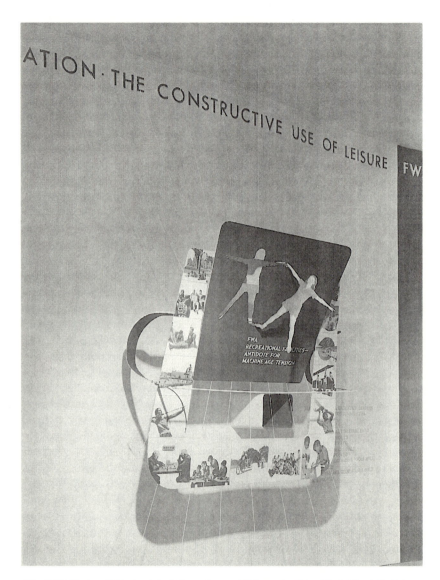

25. WPA Federal Works Administration exhibit at the New York World's Fair. The constructive use of leisure, recreational facilities—antidote for machine-age tension. Courtesy National Archives, Still Picture Branch, RG69-N, folder 863.

26. WPA Federal Art Project, New York World's Fair. Photographic report of work executed by the Federal Art Project of New York City for the WPA Community and Health Building at the World's Fair. Courtesy National Archives, Still Picture Branch, RG69-AN-863-16.

of impenetrable foliage; Ubangi tribesmen from French Equatorial Africa, strange black beings with enormous distended lips; headhunters, too, representatives of the Jivaro and Phantom Indian tribes of Ecuador; fierce savages from Masambo and the Congo; and here you may stare in awe at the giraffe-necked women from Padeung, in the mysterious north of India.[79]

Among the exotic and deformed ("Nature's Mistakes"), the Amusement Zone also featured the idealized (white) female form. The eugenic fetishization of the "perfect" female body appeared in Norman Bel Geddes's "Crystal Lassies," where "a woman's body seemed infinitely replicable like the interchangeable parts on the assembly line."[80] Along with fashion displays, water shows like "Aquacade," and peep shows, the fair encouraged visions of the female form based on the aesthetics of streamlining.[81] These women epitomized the attainment of bodily perfection through a combination of the right breeding (they were always white) with scientific improvements. In these displays, women became objects of erotic fantasies of domination and commodification, central to the leisure of the male observer.[82] Everywhere, not least of all at the New York World's Fair, women were being put on display as the epitome of perfect "human engineering" and as specimens created by a system of mass streamlining. Positioned alongside the Amazon Warriors, the

Midget Auto Race, the Infant Incubator, and the Headless Girl, Geddes's Crystal Palace added to the eugenic message of the Amusement Zone and the fair as a whole by offering a vision of leisure as eugenic fantasy placed among the "threat" of dark "others."

Although the fair promised leisure to both men and women, women's leisure, utilized correctly, would streamline them into perfect mates and commodities for the newly leisured male. Available as leisure commodities, elite white women were expected to provide scientifically managed homes and bodies for the replication of genetically perfect humans. These fantasies reappeared in mass culture outside of the fair. For example, the *New Yorker* advertisement for the Hudnut Success School claimed to manufacture a "slim beauty" out of a "hopelessly fat" girl, enabling her to successfully marry. The school, the advertisement claimed, had done a "complete job of rebuilding—face, figure, personality," illustrated with photos of an exercise regime that looks as if it could have come from a Busby Berkeley musical still.[83] Mass produced and streamlined, women such as the "Slim Beauty," represented the idealized feminine form, based on the merging of eugenic ideals with notions of technological progress. A woman's leisure, then, could be used to rebuild oneself into the kind of mate who would be desirable to a higher grade of male, one who could support a family alone, so that her need to work was greatly diminished. Leisure, in this way, becomes a form of female "work," a manufacturing of oneself in order to produce further leisure.

The image of the leisured future at the New York World's Fair in 1939 illustrated the centrality of leisure to planners' visions. Leisure had come of age as the most significant development in modern culture, as something that could be used to harness the intellectual and creative powers that the machine had apparently laid to waste. The culture of abundance was redeemed through this vision as something that could be controlled and operated to achieve the goals of recreation reformers and city planners of the late nineteenth and early twentieth century, as well as those of midcentury industrialists. The central function of culture in this vision was the "civilizing" process—where intellectual attainment and cultural creativity fueled the rational organization of society to balance production with consumption and reproduction. But this vision of civilized culture was based on the repositioning of the patriarch as a central figure, along with the erasure of problematic social and racial differences.

Dystopian fears about the collapse of civilization and the end of "the race" were swept away with streamlined visions of perfect bodies and homes, where supermen rescued the weak and fought for humanity against the machinations of evil, stronger powers. As wider social reform transformed eugenics, education, personal management, and self-help counseling promised to fit Americans to their new social landscape. Reflecting this at the end of the decade, the eugenically perfect Tarzan was swapped for the superhuman Superman as the hero most able to combat crime and fight for world order. Yet eugenic ideals were never far from the surface. The first issue of the *Superman* comic in 1939 explained not only how Superman came from a planet "whose inhabitants had evolved, after millions of years, to physical perfection," but advised that Earthlings may one day attain this strength too: the front page claimed that "it is not too far fetched to predict that some day our very own planet may be peopled entirely by Supermen!"[84] Unlike Tarzan, he could sublimate his true identity and live in the modern high-rise environment, controlling his personal drives for the sake of the wider community. The epitome of control and self-control, the physical and moral potency of Superman represented the leisure leaders' idealized citizen.

Coda: Forgotten People

Fears over cultural lag and eugenic decline underlay the creation of national leisure facilities. While enjoying popular support, they came at a price. Demand for increased leisure opportunities and "rational" forms of leisure based on the enjoyment of nature led to the creation of the new Shenandoah National Park in 1936. For some rural inhabitants of the Shenandoah in Virginia this meant eviction from their homes during the Great Depression. Unlike earlier parks, the land was not actually a wilderness, and the evictions were forced so that the area could be returned to wilderness for the contemplation of urban and suburban dwellers from the East. Described as "A New Virginia Playground," the park was created to enable the appreciation of nature and the proper use of leisure, a fulfillment of the goals of recreation reform for decades. Yet more than 500 Shenandoah mountain families were displaced by the creation of the park. Some were removed under duress and violence, homes were boarded up, torched, and eventually destroyed "to obliterate the distracting signs of man's presence and to return the land to nature."[85] Many of the mountain people were moved to resettlement areas in the lowlands: planned communities based on the social scientists' notions of the correct way of rural living.

Popular depictions of the families as just more ignorant "white trash" justified their displacement. In 1933, a study made by two sociologists from the University of Chicago lent credence to the myth of white "trash" by describing the families as "a fallen people—not so much malevolent as pathetic—eking out a miserable existence in an arid landscape," ill-educated and hopelessly unmodern.[86] This study was published as *The Hollow Folk* in 1933 and provided the impetus for reform of the

Appalacian community.[87] Further, the park status claimed to save the land "ravaged" by these people and to redeem it for the pleasure of all. Showing them as symbols of "the growth and decline of human culture," the social scientists added credence to the prevalent opinion that cultural renewal could only come about when rationally organized society could impose its will on people living outside of it. At the same time, the re-creation of wilderness was imperative to this modernizing drive— something to offset the modernity and exhaustion of frantic modern life. It is perhaps a fitting irony of the leisure discourse of the thirties that reformers thus modernized a "primitive" people in order to "re-create" a wilderness for the urban masses. Like Henry Ford, who attempted to heal the breaches caused by modernity by re-creating a folk culture among the industrial masses, the reformers imposed an ideal replete with paradox.

The story of the displaced people illustrates how the need for mass leisure, based on the "proper" enjoyment of recreational facilities, undermined the "traditional" culture from which this "folk" leisure was supposed to have come. There was no public transport to the park and the enjoyment ironically involved driving long distances from urban and suburban areas, as well as paying an entrance fee to enjoy the newly salvaged prelapsarian environment. The creation of class-ridden sociological narratives helped to diminish the worth of a group of people who had been living outside of the kind of rationally ordered culture that demanded the construction of such "rational" recreation.

The removal was made for the enjoyment of all and the greater good of the environment, to prevent them from "ravaging" or pillaging the land, and this "sacrifice" of the few for the pleasure of the many has been depicted as little more than "natural" progress. Yet sacrifices for progress were always demanded from the least privileged members of society and necessitated a deference to cultural authority, which were at best misplaced, at worst imbued with class, race, and gender prejudice.

The vision of the world of tomorrow in 1939 did not allow for such "outsiders," for those who were not able to streamline themselves or their lives to fit in with the smooth order of progress. Although these policies bare no comparison to Nazi programs, this vision was based on a support for eugenics from all sides of the political spectrum and entered into the mainstream discourse almost invisibly, via apparently innocuous discussions on leisure. Seeking perfection in society, and within individuals, this vision of a streamlined society alienated people from themselves and each other and ultimately based its "meritocracy" on a perfection that denied the inequalities it was meant to heal.

Conclusion
The Leisured World of Tomorrow, Today

What will be the permanent impression on the work-leisure complex in this culture left by the depression? Has Middletown learned anything permanently from the depression's blow to the prestige of business as a basis for a society's design for living, and from the sudden availability of unprecedented amounts of leisure? Has something of the honorific status traditionally associated with work extended to the new possibilities in the use of leisure? Has the meaning of leisure to the business or working class in any way been altered? Has it become to any less degree an extension of, or an alternative to, working activities in the orbit of getting a living, and acquired a more independent status of its own? Has the depression altered in any way the extent to which leisure is formal, passive, organized, a product shaped by the business and machine age?

—Lynd and Lynd, Middletown in Transition

On their return to Muncie, Indiana, in 1935, after six years of depression, Robert and Helen Lynd found much to be lauded about the changes in leisure wrought by the Depression, changes that gained their approval in comparison to the uninhibited commercialism and the centrality of money of the previous decade. At both ends of the social scale, they claimed, leisure was being practiced that illustrated "a more varied expression of energies." Recreational and civic resources had been expanded, visible in the growth of supervised playgrounds and parks, swimming pools, sports grounds, play centers, public square dances, concerts by unemployed musicians, and open air theatrical performances. "More informality and less expenditure" also characterized changes in behavior, as did the popularity of flower gardening, adult reading, and "inexpensive backyard skills," which illustrated that people had been "finding new leisure-time values in the depression," values "which it may not entirely lose if and when the depression disappears."[1]

Yet the sociologists expressed their approval of these changes with a sting of reproach, warning the citizens and the reader that all the good lessons taught by the Depression could disappear as quickly as they had come: "Like other phases of deliberate social change in Middletown directly traceable to the depression, some of this public provision of leisure facilities, especially of those for adults, is likely to disappear with returning good times." Further on they added:

Here and there, innovations learned under the jarring dislocations of habit in the depression—such, for instance, as the growth of interest in flower gardens—will continue. But the summary balance sheet of Middletown's four years of prosperous growth and six years of depression experience suggests decidedly that the community has not discovered with the help of its "new leisure" new designs for living. In the overwhelming majority of cases, the community has simply in the fat years bought more of the same kinds of leisure, and in the lean years made what curtailments it was forced to make and just marked time pending the return of the time when it could resume the doing of the familiar things.[2]

Arguing that the town of Muncie had ultimately condemned itself to a pecuniary work culture that precluded developing new "fruitful ways of living," the Lynds saw the new leisure as an immense missed opportunity to transform the wasteful and alienating habits of the middle classes.

Despite this, the centrality of leisure to definitions of American democracy remained. By 1940, according to historian Foster Rhea Dulles, it was widely recognized that "what a nation does with its leisure is oftentimes just as significant as how it either maintains itself economically or governs itself." In his book *America Learns to Play*, published in 1940, Dulles charted the growth of leisure-time activities over three centuries as a "thin trickle" to "a riotous torrent, breaking through all barriers as it carved out fresh channels."[3]

Dulles attempted to show how shifts in American society and culture, such as economic depressions or technological inventions, entailed changes in the practice and meanings of leisure—and by reading the meanings of leisure it was possible to better understand broader cultural patterns. Dulles's book not only demonstrated that America had a rich history of popular leisure-time activities, but also it showed how popular amusements had attained significance as cultural and political indicators of the progress of modern American society. Its publication sent a message loud and clear that, by the end of the 1930s, leisure was no longer a trivial subject to be dismissed by historians as unworthy of their interest, but was central to ideas of American civilization. Leisure time, Dulles argued, had crafted the shape of American civilization as much as its antithesis, work, and technological developments had influenced modes of human pleasure as much as they had revolutionized modes of production.

Published at the start of World War II, the book indicated that American democracy was uniquely shaped by how the population had fun. In contrast to the mass leisure of National Socialist Germany or Communist Russia, American-style leisure, it appeared, had evolved organically as an expression of individuality, community, and democratic culture. Rather than seeing the explosion of leisure time and popular amusements as an indicator of degeneration or conflict, Dulles encouraged his reader to see contemporary society as a historical progression from a more primitive and repressed past toward modern liberal democracy.

In many ways, Dulles's book arose from the very conflicts that it attempted to resolve. Written during the most concerted effort ever made by the government to shape the leisure time of the American people, *America Learns to Play* reconciled the rationalized leisure of the industrial masses with a past history of popular nonwork activities, breaching the gap between a folk past and the industrial present. After ten years of economic depression and the rise of European fascism, Dulles's book gave reassurance that American leisure could heal internal social rifts and form the spearhead of a popular front against fascism.

At the start of World War II, *America Learns to Play* functioned to illustrate the difference between totalitarian and democratic leisure. Comparing "Strength Through Joy," Stalin's "Ready for Work and Defense," and Mussolini's "National Agency on After-Work," Dulles wrote, "All the difference in the world, however, lay between the totalitarian and the American approach to this form of recreation." Further, he added, "In the totalitarian countries the trend was very definitely toward the obligatory use of leisure time in the interests of the State; in America it was toward broader opportunities for play as the people might choose to take advantage of them in accord with their own needs and interests."[4] His conclusion argued that no real change to the democratic nature of leisure in America had taken place over the thirties:

Despite the demands made for a greater measure of control over popular amusements, the American people continued in the 1930s to maintain the laissez-faire attitude which was felt to be the essence of democracy. Except in so far as Government undertook to provide the increased opportunities for play that it was now felt the community owed its citizens, there was no legislative interference with recreation. It was not officially ordered to promote industrial efficiency, to bind the people to any political system, or to prepare the country for war. The example of the totalitarian states was not followed. Opportunity, not compulsion, symbolised the American way.[5]

Despite this, the American way of leisure in the thirties was far more a mix of Fordism, nationalism, utopianism, and welfare capitalism than Dulles's statement here indicated, and many changes had taken place in national and public perceptions of the role of leisure. However, his book shows that the proliferation of mass leisure had, by 1940, come to represent the freedom and choice associated with American democracy.

Although this examination of the discourse of leisure reform ends somewhat artificially in 1940, the problem never fully went away. With the start of World War II, when full production and participation in war invalidated the crisis over leisure, the number of publications on the "problem" nose-dived, and other "crises" came to the forefront of mass attention. In the 1950s, the "crisis" of leisure reemerged as a matter for debate among professionals. Yet this time the crisis emerged in a culture of high productivity and employment, showing that the debate is not just a metaphor for unemployment, but also something that can arise at times of rapid change in cultural practices or capitalism. The crisis of leisure, then, is the crisis of culture. In the fifties, the problem of leisure under increasing production displayed similar nuances to Depression-made arguments, when productivity was at an apparent standstill. Experts once again made predictions of the four-day week, the six-month work year, or mass early retirement. Again, how this leisure was to be used became a point of concern:

> These prospects worried the experts. In 1959, the *Harvard Business Review* announced that "boredom, which used to bother only aristocrats, had become a common curse." What would ordinary Americans do with all that extra time? How would housewives cope with having their husbands around the house for three- or four-day weekends? The pending crisis of leisure came in for intensive scrutiny. Foundations funded research projects on it. The American Council of Churches met on the issue of spare time. Institutes and Departments of Leisure Studies cropped up as academia prepared for the onslaught of free time. There were many like Harvard sociologist David Reisman who wrote about "play" in the lonely crowd, and the "abyss" and "stultification" of mass leisure.[6]

Just as in the 1930s, this particular "leisure scare died out as the abyss of free time failed to appear," illustrating how, only twenty years later, little had been remembered from the leisure crisis of the thirties.

Union and reformers' struggles for shorter working hours recovered "leisure" for the workers, only to be lost again some time "between the Depression and the end of the second World War."[7] Perhaps, after prolonged depression, the fight for shorter working hours could engender little support from those who had been faced with such prospects on an apparently permanent basis. Or perhaps the presumption that increased productivity would automatically entail increased leisure had become so ingrained, there seemed little point in demanding the lowered working hours that would "naturally" appear.

From the discourse of leisure we have inherited certain presuppositions and errors that are still apparent in everyday culture: that commercial entertainment is "bad" leisure, that leisure should be used to construct a "whole" and balanced personality, that the "proper" use of leisure can counteract the deficiencies of capitalist culture. More obviously, we still encounter fears over the dangers or passivity of visual entertainment—now computer games, the Internet, as well as television—

which generally call for regulation or intervention from the law. As in the 1930s, these arguments begin with cries over the welfare of young children and gradually transmute into fears over culture and cultural decline as a whole—so that what is regulation for the benefit of minors becomes regulation for all. Although regulation is often an important tool to protect the more vulnerable members of society, it is also important to understand the cultural imperatives of those who control such regulation, as well as the historical context of such anxieties.

Another legacy of the leisure debate is the consistent mislabeling and misrecognition of the work of leisure. Leisure is an industry that employs huge numbers of people whose labor is compromised by the association that leisure has with nonwork (and nonpayment). Frequently nonunion, low grade, temporary, or part-time, those who work in leisure industries are rendered invisible by those they work for and the consumers who buy the products of their labor. The codification of women's domestic labor as "leisure" has effected an inequality for women both in the labor force and in the enjoyment of leisure, which has changed the shape of postwar industrial politics, making the least privileged workers almost invisible. In fact, the enjoyment of leisure is still based on this erasure of labor. Likewise, the work that women do to service family leisure, or that nonwhite workers do to service white leisure—cleaning houses, gardening, and caring for children—is degraded by the association that these jobs have with the leisure of the dominant group they service.[8] Unlike the 1930s utopias such as Hicks's *The First to Awaken,* or Churchill's *New Industrial Dawn*, where all work was valued and paid equally, these workers do not have their work valued equally with more prestigious jobs, and people who work in higher paid jobs rarely undertake the functions of the people servicing their leisure. Rather than a greater equality in the dignity of all labor, as envisioned by some in the thirties, workers who service leisure are very often among the lowest classes economically and socially of all workers.

Changes in the economic structure based on an increased consumption of leisure products has allowed for increased exploitation of those workers whose association with leisure (such as women and part-time workers) has blinded unions, cultural observers, and consumers to the way that utopian visions of leisure erase certain conditions of work. Holding up Greek, medieval, and "primitive" cultures as examples of societies with abundant leisure, even Juliet Schor, author of *The Overworked American*, conveniently forgets the slavery and serfdom upon which those societies depended. Like Stuart Chase, whose *Mexico—A Study of Two Cities* (1931) compared simpler cultures to more advanced industrial worlds, Schor idealizes the past in order to show that the "progress" of capitalism is an illusion—an industrial sleight of hand that deals consumer goods and simultaneously takes leisure away. Although precapitalist civilizations may have had more leisure, it is perhaps naive to believe that this leisure was more "free" than that we experience today. This prelapsarian view denies the forces of social conformity, cultural boundaries and religious, educational, and economic restrictions that may have bounded even the most unsophisticated village dweller in preindustrial times.

Why was it that shorter working hours never happened, despite the fact that nearly everyone saw the future as a leisured one? Why did leisure not increase with the return of full employment and economic prosperity? Why do Americans continue to work longer hours in less family-friendly conditions than ever? The answer to these questions is beyond the scope of this study, but some comparisons between work today and the vision of the past may indicate some possible answers. Rather than the expected decrease of the working week through technological progress, working hours have increased gradually each year—creating a situation of overwork, increased productivity, and increased consumerism whereby "U.S. manufacturing employees currently work 320 more hours—the equivalent of over two months—than their counterparts in West Germany or France."[9] Leisure, rather than indicating prosperity, became victim to it, or perhaps harnessed to it. Contradicting the utopian view of leisured society held by some in the 1930s, which predicted the four-hour workday, the four-month working year, and socialized amusements for all, the "crisis" of leisure today has become the mirror opposite of the 1930s vision. Today's leisure crisis is a crisis of decreasing amounts of leisure time despite, or perhaps because of, increased prosperity and productivity under capitalism.

In many ways, recreation reform of the thirties was a last-ditch attempt to stem the tide of changing social roles and mores associated with increased sexual liberty and social mobility. At the same time, it was also an attempt to create a better society outside of the capitalist work ethic that had dominated life for the past century. Despite this lost turning in American social and political history, it has not been my intention to fuel nostalgia for a new leisured world of tomorrow. The leisure reformers of the 1930s were preoccupied with class, race, and gender while claiming that in leisure they could be transcended, erased, or even "cured." To many, "socialized leisure" became one way that class-bound labor could experience equality without undermining the culture of abundance or existing class structures, which remained at the heart of American dreams. In this very act of utopianism, the fight for equality in employment was relegated to a secondary position whereby the new leisure industries that had begun to proliferate—even at the height of the Depression—were able to exploit their workers even more fully than before. The world of tomorrow in 1939 looked toward a future of leisure based on increased prosperity for all. Yet the narratives of progress presented at the World's Fair structured leisure within a dominant discourse that masked and overwrote social inequities, both within work and leisure. Thus, to present leisure as a panacea for a work-ridden life may only have served to replicate the unequal conditions of labor outside of the working environment, and then to mask them as "ideal" or "equal," fetishizing leisure as a domain free from the inequities of material production.

While we continue to negotiate issues of leisure and consumption in the global marketplace, where the "Americanization" of work (and leisure) reaches beyond national borders, it is perhaps instructive to bear in mind the origins of the debates over leisure and the ideological shifts that have rendered them invisible. As Americans became more leisured—and consumed more leisure commodities—the global economy shifted labor outside of national borders into third-world and developing nations. While those nations look to America for models of leisure, Americans continue to experience leisure as a cultural crisis. Due warning, perhaps, that not all the paths to prosperity lead to more free time or liberty. Likewise, arguments at the height of the Great Depression over the sedentary and passive nature of leisure activities are echoed and enlarged in current concerns over health and fitness, in fears that the easy and abundant life has created an epidemic of obesity and other problems. At the same time, however, the pursuit of idealized images of fitness and beauty has intensified to a degree where body engineering through exercise, surgery, and diet is almost a cultural norm.

From vantage point of the twenty-first century, debates over leisure in the thirties have a relationship to current concerns that has yet to vanish altogether. Much can be gained by revisiting those visions of the universal three-day workweek and four-hour workday, where the march of spare time seemed one route to a better world.

Notes

Introduction

1. President's Research Committee on Social Trends, *Recent Social Trends in the United States: Report of the President's Research Committee on Social Trends*, 2 vols. (New York: McGraw-Hill, 1933). Hereafter, *Recent Social Trends*. For a discussion of *Recent Social Trends* in relation to rational reform of the early twentieth century, see John M. Jordan, *Machine-Age Ideology: Social Engineering and American Liberalism, 1911–1939* (Chapel Hill: University of North Carolina Press, 1994), 179–84.

2. Julius Inberger, "Money Spent for Play: An Index of Opinion," *Public Opinion Quarterly* 2 (April 1938): 257.

3. Steiner, *Recent Social Trends*, vol. 2, 941.

4. Ibid., 956.

5. Warren Susman has shown that while leisure had always existed as "a problem," during the thirties, the debate became charged with new impetus and energy, dramatized by "the enormous growth of literature on the subject": "The leading bibliography lists, roughly, 20 items published in the period 1900–1909. The decade between 1910 and 1919 produced almost 50 new titles; that between 1910 and 1929 about 200. But the period between 1930 and 1939 witnessed the publication of some 450 titles." See *Culture and Commitment, 1929–1945* (New York: Braziller, 1973), 83. Yet Susman's list provides a conservative estimate of the expansion of publications and does not include the enormous number of articles, chapters, and popular commentaries that were also published during this period.

6. Harold Rugg, *An Introduction to the Problems of American Culture* (Boston: Ginn & Company, 1931), 495–513.

7. For studies of thirties popular fads, see Gary Dean Best, *The Nickle and Dime Decade: American Popular Culture During the 1930s* (Westport, Conn.: Praeger, 1993); Harvey Green, *The Uncertainty of Everyday Life, 1915–1945* (New York: Harper Collins, 1992), 187–231; Charles Panati, *Panati's Parade of Fads, Follies and Manias: The Origins of Our Most Cherished Obsessions* (New York: HarperPerennial, 1991), 148–95; and Dixon Wecter, *The Age of the Great Depression, 1929–41* (New York: Macmillan, 1962), 219–71.

8. Rugg, *Introduction to the Problems*, 211.

9. Franklin D. Roosevelt, "The Forgotten Man," April 7, 1932 (Radio Address, Albany, N.Y., April 7, 1932), from The Franklin and Eleanor Roosevelt Institute Web site at http://www.feri.org/archives/speeches/apr0732.cfm.

10. Stuart Chase, *Technocracy: An Interpretation* (New York: The John Day Co., 1933), 11.

11. George Lundberg, Mirra Komarovsky, and Mary McInerney, *Leisure: A Suburban Study* (New York: Columbia University Press, 1934), 6.

12. Ibid., 125.

13. Ibid., 8.

14. Ibid., 18.

15. H. Edmund Bullis, "Play and Keep Mentally Well," *Recreation*, November 1933, 370.

16. John Adams, "The Menace of Leisure," *School and Society* 33 (1931): 656.

17. Lawrence Pearsall Jacks, "Education for Leisure," *Proceedings of the Seventieth Annual Meeting Held at Atlantic City, New Jersey, June 25–July 1, 1932* (Washington, D.C.: National Education Association, 1932), 573. See also Jacks, *Ethical Factors of the Present Crisis* (Baltimore: Williams & Wilkins Co., 1934).

18. Louis Carlisle Walker, *Distributed Leisure: An Approach to the Problem of Overproduction and Underemployment* (New York: Century Co., 1931), 8.

19. Lundberg, Komarovsky, and McInerney, *Leisure*, 3.

20. A selected list of such monographs includes Frank Hobart Cheley, *Investing Leisure Time* (New York: University Society, 1936); George B. Cutten, *Challenge of Leisure* (Columbus, Ohio: American Education Press, 1933); Clifford Cook Furnas, *America's Tomorrow: An Informal Excursion into the Era of the Two-Hour Working Day* (New York: Funk & Wagnalls Co., 1932); Sydney Greenbie, *Leisure for Living* (New York: George Stewart, 1940); Gove Hambridge, *Time to Live: Adventures in the Use of Leisure* (New York: McGraw-Hill, 1933); Mabel C. Hermans and Margaret M. Hannon, *Using Leisure Time* (New York: Harcourt, Brace and Company, 1938); Eduard C. Lindeman, *Leisure—A National Issue: Planning for the Leisure of a Democratic People* (New York: Association Press, 1939); Lundberg, Komarovsky, and McInerney, *Leisure*; Jay B. Nash, *Spectatoritis* (New York: Sears Publishing Co., 1932); Martin H. Neumayer and Esther Neumayer, *Leisure and Recreation: A Study of Leisure and Recreation in Their Sociological Aspects* (New York: A. S. Barnes & Co., 1936); Harry Allen Overstreet, *A Guide to Civilized Loafing* (New York: W. W. Norton & Co., 1934); Arthur Newton Pack, *The Challenge of Leisure* (New York: Macmillan Company, 1934); Weaver Pangburn, *Adventures in Recreation* (New York: A. S. Barnes & Co., 1936); Roger Payne, *Why Work, Or, The Coming "Age of Leisure and Plenty"* (Boston: Meador Publishing Company, 1939); Walter B. Pitkin, *Life Begins at Forty* (New York: McGraw-Hill Book Co, Inc., 1932), and his *Take It Easy: The Art of Relaxation* (New York: Simon and Schuster, 1935); Dorothy Reed, *Leisure Time of Girls in a "Little Italy"* (Portland, Oreg. n.p., 1932); Austen Fox Riggs, *Play: Recreation in a Balanced Life* (New York: Doubleday, Doran & Co., 1935); Russell Sage Foundation, *The New Leisure: Its Significance and Use: A Selected Bibliography* (New York: Russell Sage Foundation, 1933); Fred J. Schmidt, *Leisure Time Bibliography* (Ames: Iowa State College, 1935); Jesse Frederick Steiner, *Americans at Play: Recent Trends in Recreation and Leisure-Time* (New York: McGraw-Hill, 1933); Work Projects Administration (WPA), *Community Recreation Programs: A Study of Recreation Projects* (Washington, D.C.: Government Printing Office, 1940); WPA, *Leisure-Time Leadership* (Washington, D.C.: Government Printing Office, 1938); WPA, *Planning Our Leisure* (Washington, D.C.: WPA, 1938); Federal Works Agency, *Community Recreation Programs: A Study of WPA Recreation Projects* (Washington, D.C.: Work Projects Administration, 1940); Federal Works Agency, Division of Professional and Service Projects, *Adult Recreation* (Washington, DC: Work Projects Administration, 1940); WPA Recreation Division, *Recreation: A Selected Bibliography with Annotations—References*

on *Social and Economic Background, Philosophy of Leisure, Public Administration, Recreation Administration, Periodicals* (Washington, D.C.: Government Printing Office, 1938); Robert B. Weaver, *Amusements and Sports in American Life* (Chicago: University of Chicago Press, 1939); Doris Webster, *How to Spend Your Husband's Leisure* (New York: Leisure League of America, 1934); and Young Women's Christian Associations, *Leisure-Time Interests and Activities of Business Girls: A Research Study Conducted During 1931–33* (New York: Women's Press, 1933).

Chapter 1

1. George D. Butler, *Introduction to Community Recreation* (New York: McGraw-Hill, 1949), 59. See also William Gleason, *The Leisure Ethic: Work and Play in American Literature, 1840–1940* (Stanford: Stanford University Press, 1999), 30–44. Charting the rise of "the leisure ethic," Gleason notes that later play theorists saw the organized team, created through "systematic management," as the highest form of civilization, where the individual self was merged into a "common consciousness," learning the loyalty and civic membership that was so essential to the new industrial order.

2. For histories of the health and fitness movements, see Michael Anton Budd, *The Sculpture Machine: Physical Culture and Body Politics in the Age of Empire* (New York: New York University Press, 1997); Harvey Green, *Fit for America: Health, Fitness, Sport and American Society* (New York: Pantheon Books, 1986); Kathryn Grover, ed., *Fitness in American Culture: Images of Health, Sport and the Body, 1830–1940* (Boston: University of Massachusetts Press, 1989).

3. For a discussion of the application of evolutionary principals to recreation reform, see Lawrence A. Finfer, *Leisure and Social Work in the Urban Community, 1890–1920* (Ann Arbor, Mich.: University Microfilms International, 1981), 1–47. See also Donald J. Mrozek, "The Natural Limits of Unstructured Play, 1880–1914," in *Hard at Play: Leisure in America, 1840–1940*, ed. Katherine Grover (Boston: University of Massachusetts Press, 1992), 210–25.

4. David Nasaw, *Going Out: The Rise and Fall of Public Amusements* (New York: BasicBooks, 1993), 3. See also Claude S. Fischer, "Changes in Leisure Activities, 1890–1940," *Journal of Social History* 27 (spring 1994): 453–75.

5. Cindy S. Aron, *Working at Play: A History of Vacations in the United States* (New York: Oxford University Press, 1999), 237–57.

6. For discussion of anxieties over women's leisure in the early twentieth century, see Lewis A. Erenberg, *Steppin Out: New York Nightlife and the Transformation of American Culture* (Chicago: University of Chicago Press, 1984).

7. For further discussion of regulation, gender, and turn-of-the-century amusements, see Kathy Peiss, *Cheap Amusements: Working Class Women and Leisure in Turn-of-the-Century New York* (Philadelphia: Temple University Press, 1986); Janet Staiger, *Bad Women: Regulating Sexuality in Early American Cinema* (Minneapolis: University of Minnesota Press, 1995).

8. Quoted in Paul Boyer, *Urban Masses and Moral Order in America, 1820–1920,* (Cambridge, Mass.: Harvard University Press, 1995), 226, 227.

9. For the City Beautiful movement, see Boyer, *Urban Masses,* 262–66; William H. Wilson, *The City Beautiful Movement* (Baltimore: Johns Hopkins University Press, 1989). On the playground movement, see Boyer, *Urban Masses,* 180–81, 242–51. See also Roy Rosenzweig, *Eight Hours for What We Will: Workers and Leisure in an Industrial City, 1870–1920* (Cambridge: Cambridge University Press, 1983), 143–53.

10. Boyer, *Urban Masses*, 242.

11. Randy McBee, *Dance-Hall Days: Intimacy and Leisure Among Working-Class Immigrants in the United States* (New York: New York University Press, 2000), 15. See also Butler, *Introduction to Community Recreation*, 60.

12. Butler, *Introduction to Community Recreation*, 61. For a detailed examination of the growth of the recreation movement and the connection between leisure reform and the development of social work, see Finfer, *Leisure and Social Work*, 100–290.

13. Butler, *Introduction to Community Recreation*, 232–51.

14. Ibid., 251.

15. See Gary Cross, *A Social History of Leisure Since 1600* (State College, Pa.: Venture Publishing, 1990), 76–81.

16. See Lizabeth Cohen, *Making a New Deal: Industrial Workers in Chicago, 1919–1939* (Cambridge: Cambridge University Press, 1990), 176–81; Rosenzweig, *Eight Hours for What We Will.*

17. Nikki Mandell, *The Corporation as Family: The Gendering of Corporate Welfare, 1890–1930* (Chapel Hill: University of North Carolina Press, 2002).

18. Stuart D. Brandes, *American Welfare Capitalism, 1880–1940* (Chicago: University of Chicago Press, 1976), 78.

19. Ibid., 79.

20. Company employer quoted in Brandes, *American Welfare Capitalism*, 77.

21. Michael Denning, *The Cultural Front: The Laboring of American Culture in the Twentieth Century* (New York: Verso, 1997), 68.

22. Cohen, *Making a New Deal*, 88–94.

23. For example, the old-world view of parents was seen by social workers as part of the problem of leisure; recreation work intended to breach the divide between old and new worlds and offer youth the chance to become fully American. See, for example, Reed, *Leisure Time of Girls,* 31.

24. Lynn Dumenil, *Modern Temper: American Culture and Society in the 1920s* (New York: Hill and Wang, 1995), 70.

25. Terry Smith, *Making the Modern: Industry, Art, and Design in America* (Chicago: University of Chicago Press, 1993), 48. Smith has pointed out how Ford's "commitment to order" hinted at later developments in welfare capitalism where "the scale of the system was the first concrete manifestation at a significant magnitude" of "the planned society, the government of resources, needs and growth, albeit by private enterprise," and as such was already a specter haunting laissez-faire and competitive individualism. See Smith, *Making the Modern*, 35.

26. Antonio Gramsci, "Americanism and Fordism," in *Selections from the Prison Notebooks*, ed. Quinton Hoare and Geoffry Nowell-Smith (London: Lawrence and Wishart, 1971), 303. For more information on Ford's lesser-known activities, see Ford R. Bryan, *Beyond the Model T: The Other Ventures of Henry Ford* (Detroit: Wayne State University Press, 1997).

27. Dumenil, *Modern Temper*, 77.

28. Dumenil points out that the hours worked were not uniform among workers and were disproportionately distributed between skilled and nonskilled workers, with skilled workers being the main beneficiaries. See Dumenil, *Modern Temper*, 79.

29. In *Bad Women*, a study of silent cinema, Janet Steiger has pointed out that regulation of leisure and popular images takes place in a multitude of ways. In my discussion I have simplified the notion of regulation as one that comes from the "top down." Reform, however, happens in more complex ways than mere pressure of an influential minority on ruling bodies. In a Foucauldian analysis

of regulation, Steiger examines wider social and cultural ideologies governing censorship rather than the influence of one specific body such as the National Board of Censorship. In this argument, censorship becomes something of a negotiation between conflicting middle-class moralities. Likewise for an examination of how popular/working-class leisure practices can effect resistances to reform or influence changes to wider social ideologies from the "bottom up." See Peiss, *Cheap Amusements*.

30. Lundberg, Komarovsky, and McInerney, *Leisure*, 4.

31. For example, Columbia professor and New Deal intellectual Rexford Tugwell and economist Stuart Chase popularized this opinion. For details, see Amy Sue Bix, *Inventing Ourselves out of Jobs: America's Debate Over Technological Unemployment, 1929–1981* (Baltimore: Johns Hopkins University Press, 2000), 31–42.

32. Jesse Fiering Williams, "Health and Physical Education: An Analysis of Trend and Emphasis in Professional Periodicals," *Journal of Higher Education* 10 (December 1939): 491.

33. Martin H. Neumayer, "The New Leisure and Social Objectives," *Sociology and Social Research* 20 (1936): 347.

34. Benjamin Kline Hunnicutt discusses how the onset of the Depression led to the imposition of the six-hour day in the Kellogg's company, influenced by theories of play reform that had emerged from earlier health movements. His book highlights the centrality of the debate over shorter working hours to wider issues about leisure during the thirties. However, Hunnicutt claims that the New Deal government soon abandoned the idea of shorter working hours, although they remained central to Kellogg's corporate policy in this era. As this book shows, the pursuit of leisure that functioned to replace work was, in fact, a central feature of the New Deal. See Benjamin Kline Hunnicutt, *Kellogg's Six-Hour Day* (Philadelphia: Temple University Press, 1996), 4–5.

35. For a thorough examination of the arguments over machine-made unemployment and the penetration of the ideas of technological unemployment within mass culture and the New Deal, see Bix, *Inventing Ourselves out of Jobs*. See also William Akin, *Technocracy and the American Dream: The Technocrat Movement, 1900–1941* (Berkeley: University of California Press, 1977); Jordan, *Machine-Age Ideology*.

36. Stuart Chase, "Play," in *Whither Mankind: A Panorama of Modern Civilization*, ed. Charles Beard (New York: Blue Ribbon Books, 1934), 353.

37. Stuart Chase, *Men and Machines* (New York: Macmillan Company, 1935) 264.

38. Ibid., 264, 258.

39. Riggs, *Play*, 2–3.

40. Neumayer and Neumayer, *Leisure and Recreation*, 36, 37 (see intro., n. 20).

41. Frank Kingdon, "Leisure Time Recreation," *Recreation*, February 1933, 512.

42. Pack, *The Challenge of Leisure*, 240 (see intro., n. 20).

43. Lundberg, Komarovsky, and McInerney, *Leisure*, preface.

44. Ibid., 1.

45. Ibid., 124.

46. As recent scholarship has shown, popular responses to modernity certainly negotiated with the speeding up and mechanization of culture, though not with the detrimental effects that elite social observers anticipated. For example, Joel Dinerstein illustrates how swing music and dance culture were popular responses to modernity and technological change that enabled Americans to respond to the mechanization of culture. See his *Swinging the Machine: Modernity, Technology, and African American Culture Between the Wars* (Boston: University of Massachusetts Press, 2003). Dinerstein discusses these responses as "survival technology"

that expressed new ways of cultural participation in mass culture, constituting "significant social practices of cultural resistance that helped Americans regain a sense of their own individual bodies set against assembly line realities," 19. This chapter confirms Dinerstein's point that the popular and empowering response to the new tempo of life in urban America was generally missed by "white liberal intellectuals and artists of the 1930s," 47.

47. Lundberg, Komarovsky, and McInerney, *Leisure*, 7.

48. Ibid., 4.

49. Nash, *Spectatoritis*, 9–16, 36.

50. Jacks, *Ethical Factors*, 37, 74. His four chapters ("Moral Inertia," "Wasted Human Energies," "Indiscipline," "The Coming Leisure") trace how bad the leisure situation had become before describing how to improve it.

51. Owen Geer, *Adventures in Recreation: A Guide to the Planning of Recreation and to the Christian Use of Leisure for Young People in the Epworth League and Church School* (Chicago: Board of Education of the Methodist Episcopal Church, 1935), 5.

52. Dinerstein, *Swinging the Machine*, 52.

53. Neumayer and Neumayer, *Leisure and Recreation*, 65.

54. Rugg, *Introduction to the Problems*, 494.

55. Ibid., 7.

56. Lundberg, Komarovsky, and McInerney, *Leisure*, 12.

57. Franklin D. Roosevelt, "The First Inaugural Address," March 4, 1933, from The Franklin and Eleanor Roosevelt Institute Web site at http://www.feri.org/archives/speeches/mar0433.cfm

58. Cutten, *Challenge of Leisure*, 6–7.

59. Pitkin, *Take It Easy*, 200. Apart from being indicative of the rise in mental health services available, the statistics that Pitkin uses to "prove" the alarming quantity of mentally ill Americans perhaps illustrates more the expansion of psychotherapeutic industries and the growing professionalization of therapy.

60. Neumayer and Neumayer, *Leisure and Recreation*, 64.

61. Nash, *Spectatoritis*, 16.

62. Popular magazine advertisements also used this rhetoric of fatigue to sell commercial products: carpets needing replacement were described as dull and tired, teeth were dull, bowels were sluggish, and children's diets lacked vitamins for energy. One advertisement for Ethyl gasoline described how the frustration of being passed on the road could be combated without having to buy a new car: "But if you must make your old car do a while longer, give it Ethyl—and feel lost youth and power come back as harmful knock and sluggishness disappear." In Roland Marchand, *Advertising the American Dream: Making Way for Modernity, 1920–1940* (Berkeley: University of California Press, 1985), 327. Fatigue and listlessness were not just a problem but something "harmful," a danger to health, life, and morality.

63. Nash, *Spectatoritis,* 36.

64. Kingdon, "Leisure Time Recreation," 513.

65. Riggs, *Play*, 3.

66. Ibid., 37.

67. Ibid., 73.

68. President's Research Committee, *Recent Social Trends*, vol. 1, xlviii.

69. Lundberg, Komarovsky, and McInerney, *Leisure*, 346.

70. Ibid., 16, 22.

71. Pack, *Challenge of Leisure*, 4.

72. Amy Sue Bix argues that the Roosevelt administration took arguments over technological unemployment seriously enough to fund much new research

into the causes of unemployment. See Bix, *Inventing Ourselves out of Jobs*, 52. Leisure surveys were thereby a correlative of the social scientific discussion of unemployment and paralleled the need to control the economy through centralized planning. For the historical background of the social engineering movement in the early twentieth century, see Jordan, *Machine-Age Ideology*. Jesse Frederick Steiner in his *Research Memorandum on Recreation in the Depression* (New York: Social Science Research Council, 1937) called for more coordinated planning and surveys of leisure. The research memoranda series was sponsored by the Social Science Research Committee, whose chairman, William F. Ogburn, was the author of "cultural lag" theories.

Chapter 2

1. Ralph Aiken, "A Laborer's Leisure," *The North American Review* (September 1931): 268.
2. Steiner, *Recent Social Trends*, vol. 2, 957.
3. Thorstein Veblen was one of the first social theorists to assign leisure central importance in the power struggles of elite groups and to recognize the various ways that this system functioned in a gendered way. In his *The Theory of the Leisure Class* (1899), leisure functioned for the bourgeoisie as a sign of their class status, a sign of their ascendancy and power connoted by the "non-productive consumption of time." In this system, women's leisure functioned as a sign of class status for the powerful man. Thus, while "leisured," the upper-class man continued to "work" at status display. For Veblen, leisure functioned as part of a system of signs through which the dominant classes displayed and sustained their power emblematically. The function of "conspicuous leisure" was likened to his theory of conspicuous consumption, as a way to communicate reputability and class status in a modern or alienated environment. According to Veblen, the ultimate goal of the leisured class was to enhance their power through displays of wealth that emphasized their abstinence from productive employment. Lower down the social scale, displays of leisure mimicked bourgeois forms but had little comparative political or symbolic power. In fact, working-class leisure, and specifically women's leisure, functioned to enhance the power of the leisure-class male vicariously but did not display power for workers or women in their own right. Veblen's theory thus suggested that leisure functioned symbolically only to sustain the status of the wealthiest class and appeared to have little to do with the problems of mass leisure in the thirties—though his ideas on gender and class control through leisure remain valent. See Thorstein Veblen, *The Theory of the Leisure Class* (1899; reprint, New York: Macmillan Company, 1953), 46.
4. For a useful and detailed study of the relationship that progressive and left-wing social scientists and intellectuals had with mass culture in the interwar years, see Paul R. Gorman, *Left Intellectuals and Popular Culture in Twentieth Century America* (Chapel Hill: University of North Carolina Press, 1996), 83–107.
5. Roosevelt, "Forgotten Man."
6. Michael Szalay, *New Deal Modernism: American Literature and the Invention of the Welfare State* (Durham, N.C., & London: Duke University Press, 2000), 56.
7. Overstreet, *Guide to Civilized Loaŵng*, 234.
8. Neumayer, "New Leisure and Social Objectives," 347–51.
9. Cutten, *Challenge of Leisure*, 3.
10. "Thirteen Million Hours to While Away," *The Literary Digest*, August 26, 1933, 18.

11. Ibid.

12. "Faced with an Increasing Freedom from Wage-Earning, the NRA Undertakes the Job of Ameliorating Not Excessive Work But Possibly Excessive Play," *The Literary Digest*, December 2, 1933, 10.

13. Raymond Fosdick, chairman of the hearings, was erstwhile president of the Rockefeller Foundation, which supported the sterilization campaign by the National Committee for Mental Hygiene and sponsored a "new science of man" through "human engineering" and "social control." See Christina Cogdell, "The Futurama Recontextualized: Norman Bel Geddes's Eugenic 'World of Tomorrow,'" *American Quarterly* 52 (2000): 202–4.

14. Quoted in "National Recovery Administration Acts to Teach Workers How to Play: Eight Prominent Men Named by Whalen to Study Proper Use of New Leisure," *Recreation*, December 1933, 403. Whalen reappears later in this book as president of the New York World's Fair.

15. Howard Braucher, "Freedom in Leisure," *Recreation*, December 1933, 401.

16. Ibid.

17. "Satan Still Finds Work," *The Nation*, June 13, 1934, 663–64.

18. *New Yorker*, September 2, 1933, quoted in *Recreation*, December 1933, 406.

19. *Daily Editorial Digest*, quoted in *Recreation*, December 1933, 417.

20. Matthew Woll, "Labor and the New Leisure," *Recreation*, December 1933, 428. Indeed, as Michael Denning has pointed out, worker schools and union cultural activities had sustained the cultural politics of the proletarian avant-garde and labor movement workers that were to form the bedrock of the New Deal arts projects. Denning, *Cultural Front*, 68–83.

21. Denning, *Cultural Front*, 68.

22. Stephen M. Gelber, *Hobbies: Leisure and the Culture of Work in America* (New York: Columbia University Press, 1999), 44. See also his "A Job You Can't Lose: Work and Hobbies in the Great Depression," *Journal of Social History* 24 (1991): 741–66.

23. Pack, *Challenge of Leisure*, 153.

24. For example, see Henry M. Busch, "Contributions of Recreation to the Development of Wholesome Personality," *Recreation*, October 1933, 307; and Bullis, "Play and Keep Mentally Well," 370.

25. John H. Finley, "What Will We Do with Our Time," *Recreation*, December 1933, 366–67.

26. Quoted in John P. Diggins, *Mussolini and Fascism: The View from America* (Princeton, N.J.: Princeton University Press, 1972), 280.

27. Victoria De Grazia, *The Culture of Consent: Mass Organization of Leisure in Fascist Italy*, (New York: Cambridge University Press, 1981), 24.

28. Ibid., 26.

29. Ibid., 33.

30. Ibid., 57–58.

31. Ibid., 38–39.

32. Ibid., 42.

33. Ibid., 164.

34. Ibid., 181–216.

35. *Fortune*, July 1934, 57. See also Diane Ghirado, *Building New Communities: New Deal America and Fascist Italy* (Princeton, N.J.: Princeton University Press, 1989).

36. Benjamin L. Alpers, *Dictators, Democracy and American Public Culture: Envisioning the Totalitarian Enemy, 1920s–1950s* (Chapel Hill: University of North Carolina Press, 2003), 16.

37. Diggins, *Mussolini and Fascism*, 279.

38. This report and other correspondence concerning Roosevelt's interest in

the Kraft durch Freude (KdF) is available from the President's Secretary's File (PSF), German Diplomatic Files: Hugh R. Wilson: March–November 1938, Franklin D. Roosevelt Library Digital Archives, available online at http://www.fdrlibrary.marist.edu

39. Louis Bader, "Germany's New Social Institutions in the Making," *Journal of Educational Sociology* 10 (January 1937): 280.

40. For a description of this history, see Stephen Jones, *Sport, Politics and the Working Class: Organized Labor and Sport in Inter War Britain* (Manchester: Manchester University Press, 1998), 166–67.

41. "Summary of Report on Strength Through Joy" p. 2, PSF, German Diplomatic Files: Hugh R. Wilson: Franklin D. Roosevelt Library Digital Archives, at http://www.fdrlibrary.marist.edu/psf/box32/a301j02.html.

42. "The Organization of Leisure Time," p. 62, PSF, German Diplomatic Files: Hugh R. Wilson: March–November 1938, Franklin D. Roosevelt Library Digital Archives at http://www.fdrlibrary.marist.edu/psf/box32/t301v02.html

43. Ibid.

44. Ibid., p. 66, at http://www.fdrlibrary.marist.edu/psf/box32/a301v06.html

45. Ibid., p. 70, at http://www.fdrlibrary.marist.edu/psf/box32/t301v10.html

46. FDR to Hugh Wilson, September 3, 1938, PSF, German Diplomatic Files: Hugh R. Wilson: March–November 1938, Franklin D. Roosevelt Library Digital Archives at http://www.fdrlibrary.marist.edu/psf/box32/t301ad02.html

47. "Memorandum on Strength Through Joy Report," p. 1, PSF, German Diplomatic Files: Hugh R. Wilson: March–November 1938, Franklin D. Roosevelt Library Digital Archives, at http://www.fdrlibrary.marist.edu/psf/box32/a301ad04.html

48. Ibid., p. 2, at http://www.fdrlibrary.marist.edu/psf/box32/t301ad05.html

49. Cross, *Social History of Leisure*, 165.

50. Physical Culture Day was instituted in 1923. See "Red File Timeline" at the PBS Web site, http://www.pbs.org/redfiles/prop/inv/prop_inv_time.htm

51. Lynne Attwood and Catriona Kelly, "Programs for Identity: The 'New Man' and the 'New Woman,'" in *Constructing Russian Culture in the Age of Revolution: 1881–1940,* ed. Catriona Kelly and David Shepherd (Oxford: Oxford University Press, 1998), 264–65.

52. Arthur A. Ekirch Jr., *Ideologies and Utopias: The Impact of the New Deal on American Thought* (Chicago: Quadrangle Books, 1969), 61–62. On the American response to dictatorship in the 1920s and 1930s, see Alpers, *Dictators, Democracy and American Public Culture.*

53. Denning argues that not all left-wing intellectuals were inspired by communism but that the influence of union organizing and social reform shaped cultural output at this time. However, at the start of the New Deal, many left-wing cultural movements were inspired by communist cultural policies to provide noncapitalist, nonprofit culture and leisure. Denning points out that the central feature of this cultural front was the appearance of "a new generation of plebian artists and intellectuals who had grown up in the immigrant and black working-class neighborhoods of the modernist metropolis" and that not all artists were members of the communist party. See Denning, *Cultural Front*, xv.

54. Stephen Jones, *Workers at Play: A Social and Economic History of Leisure, 1918–1939* (London: Routledge, 1986), 7. Jones's books offer an excellent history of the growth of recreational groups in Britain in the interwar period. *Workers at Play* effectively illustrates the relationship and conflicts between these various groups and ideologies, as well as the relationship between the British Labour Movement and working-class leisure.

55. Edward Wight Bakke, *Citizens Without Work: A Study of the Effects of Unemployment upon the Workers' Social Relations and Practices* (New Haven, Conn.: Yale University Press, 1940), 178.

56. Jones, *Sport, Politics, and the Working Class*, 76, 77–94.

57. Ibid., 115–16.

58. Herbert Elvin, quoted in Jones, *Workers at Play*, 138.

59. Jones, *Workers at Play*, 91.

60. Jones, *Sport, Politics, and the Working Class*, 181

61. Benjamin Alpers also notes how the New Deal was a reassertion of patriarchal authority set against the dictatorial governance of Europe. Responding to the perceived need for male authority figures and strong leaders, he argues, "If dictatorship represented extraordinary authority, then the most feasible alternative was the most ordinary authority imaginable in American society during the 1930s—the patriarchal domination of husband and father within the bounds of the nuclear family." Alpers, *Dictators, Democracy, and American Public Culture*, 17, 42–43. If welfare capitalism provided the model for welfare policies in the thirties, then the model of the patriarchal Victorian family would also apply to the New Deal, extending Mandell's argument from corporate welfare to the New Deal. In Mandell, *Corporation as Family.*

62. Quoted in Arthur Schlesinger, *The Age of Roosevelt: The Politics of Upheaval* (Boston: Houghton Mifflin, 1960), 191.

63. Dorothy Cline, *Training for Recreation: An Account of the In Service Training Program, Division of Recreation, Works Progress Administration, Oct. 1935–Oct. 1937* (Washington, D.C.: Government Printing Office, 1939), 7.

64. Charles Loomis Dana, *Play and Health* (New York: National Recreation Association, 1925), quoted in Butler, *Introduction to Community Recreation*, 18.

65. For example, see Butler's paragraph on "recreation and safety" in his *Introduction to Community Recreation*, 23–24.

66. Pack, *Challenge of Leisure*, 240.

67. William F. Russell, "Leisure and National Security," *Proceedings of the Seventieth Annual Meeting Held at Atlantic City, New Jersey, June 25–July 1, 1932* (Washington, D.C.: National Education Association, 1932), 575–79.

68. Ibid., 115.

69. Steiner, "Recreation and Leisure Time Activities," in *Recent Social Trends*, vol. 2, 956.

70. Steiner, *Research Memorandum*, 112.

Chapter 3

1. For a useful study of WPA work relief projects, see Nancy Rose, *Put to Work: Relief Programs in the Great Depression* (New York: Monthly Review Press, 1994).

2. Steiner, *Research Memorandum*, 19.

3. Work Projects Administration, *Community Recreation Programs.* See also C. Gilbert Wrenn and D. L. Harley, *Time on Their Hands: A Report on Leisure, Recreation and Young People* (Washington, D.C.: American Council on Education, 1941), 224–34.

4. Steiner, *Research Memorandum*, 114.

5. See Cline, *Training for Recreation*, 18.

6. Howard W. Okley, "The Civilian Conservation Corps and the Education of the Negro," *Journal of Negro Education* 7 (July 1938): 380.

7. Ibid.

8. Butler, *Introduction to Community Recreation*, 73.

9. Henry Harap, "Planning the Curriculum for Leisure," *Journal of Educational Sociology* 7 (January 1934): 308–20.

10. Butler, *Introduction to Community Recreation*, 73–74.

11. Neumayer and Neumayer, *Leisure and Recreation*, 6.

12. Katherine Glover, *Leisure for Living* (Washington, D.C.: The Committee on Youth Problems, 1936), 21.

13. Ibid., 8.

14. Cline, *Training for Recreation*, 18.

15. Wrenn and Harley, *Time on Their Hands*, 225.

16. Work Projects Administration, *Leisure-Time Leadership*, 1, 22–23.

17. Letter from P. D. Flanner, WPA administrator, to Robert Bradford, executive assistant of the Recreation Division, April 6, 1938, Correspondence of the Recreation and Recreational Instruction Program, Organization of State and Local Programs 216.96, Works Progress Administration, Record Group 69, National Archives and Records Administration, Maryland.

18. Lindeman speech dated October 9, 1936, p. 5, Correspondence of the Recreation and Recreational Instruction Program, Eduard Lindeman's Speeches 216.911, Works Progress Administration, Record Group 69, National Archives and Records Administration, Maryland.

19. Busch, "Contributions of Recreation," 307.

20. Braucher, "Freedom in Leisure," 401.

21. Neumayer and Neumayer, *Leisure and Recreation*, 105.

22. Eduard C. Lindeman, "National Planning and Objectives," *Report of the Recreation Section, United States, Works Progress Administration, Recreation Section* (Washington, D.C.: Works Progress Administration, 1939). Lindeman constantly emphasized the difference between totalitarian and democratic leisure in his reports of the late thirties.

23. Butler, *Introduction to Community Recreation*, 24.

24. For the development of this philosophy within the playground movement, see Mrozek, "Natural Limits of Unstructured Play."

25. Lindeman, "National Planning and Objectives," In a letter attached to this report, Lindeman wrote, "Distribution is limited to State Administrators and Recreation members of their staffs whom we feel desire to be kept informed on the developing relationships of the WPA Recreation projects to the national problem of leisure."

26. See Tom Collins, "Kern (Arvin) Migratory Camp Report for the Week Ending February 22, 1936," Record Group 96 (FSA), Coded Admin. Camp Files, 1933–45, Box 22, Folder RF-CF-16 918-01, February 1936. National Archives and Records Administration, Pacific Sierra Region, San Bruno, CA. Thanks to Stephen Fender for copies of this report.

27. Dorothea Goodrich to Harry Hopkins, June 6, 1938, in Correspondence of the Recreation and Recreational Instruction Program, Criticisms and Suggestions 216.93, Works Progress Administration, Record Group 69, National Archives and Records Administration, Maryland.

28. W. L. Taylor to Harry Hopkins, April 19, 1938; Lemuel L. Foster to Alfred Smith, July 21, 1938, Correspondence of the Recreation and Recreational Instruction Program, Recreation Program for Negroes 216.51, Works Progress Administration, Record Group 69, National Archives and Records Administration, Maryland.

29. Lindeman, *Leisure*, 18–19.

30. Cline, *Training for Recreation*, 18.

31. Lindeman, *Leisure*, 18.

32. Lindeman, "National Planning and Objectives," 21.

33. See also Jane S. Becker, *Selling Tradition: Appalachia and the Construction of an American Folk* (Chapel Hill and London: University of North Carolina Press, 1998).

34. Denning calls this "pan-ethnic Americanism" the most powerful working-class ideology of the age. *Cultural Front*, 130. Also see Denning on the folk revival and the Left, 133–34 and 284.

35. Lindeman, *Leisure*, 21.

36. Clarence S. Marsh, "The Educational Program in the Civilian Conservation Corps," *Recreation*, January 1935, 476.

37. Work Projects Administration, *Recreation*, 6.

38. Katherine Glover, *Leisure for Living* (Washington, D.C.: Committee on Youth Problems, 1936), 14.

39. Works Progress Administration, *Leisure-Time Leadership*, 3–4.

40. Glover, *Leisure for Living*, 12.

41. Ibid., 19.

42. Gorman examines how the reform goals of the liberal and leftist intellectuals of the interwar years adopted a paternalistic stance, which strongly resembled a Victorian moralism at times. See his *Left Intellectuals*.

43. The development of theme parks and new amusement parks away from public transportation is covered by Judith Adams in *The American Amusement Park Industry: A History of Technology and Thrills* (Boston: Twayne Publishers, 1991).

44. Arno B. Cammerer (Director, National Park Service), "National Government Services Through Recreation," *Recreation*, January 1935, 465.

45. Richard D. McKinzie, *The New Deal for Artists* (Princeton: Princeton University Press, 1973), 135.

46. Gelber, *Hobbies*, 227.

47. National Recreation Association, *The Leisure Hours of 5,000 People: A Report of the Study of Leisure Time Activities and Desires* (New York: Teacher's College, Columbia University, 1939), 20.

48. Ibid., 28.

49. Ibid., 29.

50. Howard Braucher, "Going Spiritually Stale," *Recreation*, October 1933, 305.

51. Work Progress Administration, Federal Works Agency, Division of Professional and Service Projects, *Adult Recreation* (Washington, D.C.: Works Progress Administration, 1940), 21–23.

52. Ibid., 3.

53. Aiken, "A Laborer's Leisure," 268.

54. Furnas, *America's Tomorrow*, 226. For a history of the efficiency movement begun by Frederick Taylor's labor studies, see Samuel Haber, *Efficiency and Uplift: Scientific Management in the Progressive Era, 1890–1920* (Chicago: University of Chicago Press, 1964). For social engineering as part of rational reform in the early twentieth century, see Jordan *Machine-Age Ideology*.

55. Furnas, *America's Tomorrow*, 185.

56. Pitkin, *Take It Easy*, 235. For more details on the development and tropes of the personal management trend, see Stephen Recken, "Fitting In: The Redefinition of Success in the 1930s," *Journal of Popular Culture* 27, no. 3 (1993): 205–22.

57. Lundberg, Komarovsky, and McInerney, *Leisure*, 14. Stuart Chase reiterated this point when he said that "what adults need is adjustment as well as exercise. I mean that it is psychological and social as well as physical and we ought always

to be conscious of that fact." Quoted in Williams, "Health and Physical Education," 493.

58. Rugg, *Introduction to the Problems of American Culture*, 213.

59. Paul T. Frankl, *Machine-Made Leisure* (New York: Harper & Bros., 1932), 29.

60. Walker, *Distributed Leisure*, 152.

61. W. Lou Tandy, *Economics of Leisure* (Urbana: University of Illinois Press, 1934), 5.

62. Ibid., 6.

63. Ibid., 8–10.

64. Cheley, *Investing Leisure Time*, 564.

65. Tandy, *Economics of Leisure*, 10.

66. Hambridge, *Time to Live*, 12.

67. Cheley, *Investing Leisure Time*, 21.

68. Marjorie Latta Greenbie, *The Arts of Leisure* (New York: McGraw-Hill, 1935), 32.

69. Works Progress Administration, Illinois, District 6, "March of Leisure Time," silkscreen poster, *By the People, For the People: Posters from the WPA, 1936–1943* (Library of Congress). This poster is available online at http://memory.loc.gov/ammem/wpaposters/wpahome.html.

70. Cheley, *Investing Leisure Time*, 45.

71. George K. Pratt, *Mental Hygiene Bulletin*, November–December 1932, quoted in *Recreation*, February 1934, 513.

72. Works Progress Administration, *Adult Recreation*, 3.

73. Ibid.

74. Gelber, *Hobbies*, 227.

75. Quoted in ibid., 45.

76. Ibid.

77. Lindeman, *Leisure*, 18.

78. Gelber, *Hobbies*, 42.

79. "Industrious Leisure," 14. *Business Week*, February 23, 1935. Gustave Peck of the NRA Labor Advisory Board noted how the new leisure had increased consumption of material goods related to leisure activities. Gustave Peck, "Leisure as an Economic Phenomenon," *Recreation*, February 1934, 510.

80. Pack, *Challenge of Leisure*, 243.

81. Grace Turner, "The New Leisure of the New Deal," *Catholic World*, November 1933, 168.

82. Works Progress Administration, *Leisure-Time Leadership*, 2.

83. Lindeman, *Leisure*, 11.

Chapter 4

1. William Gleason's exemplary study of the interaction between the leisure discourse and literature from 1840 to 1940, *Leisure Ethic*, pioneers a way of contextualizing fictional narratives, one that examines how the issue of leisure interacts with crucial issues of race, class, and gender within American literary discourse. His study focuses on how writers engaged with a "leisure ethic"—counterposed to the work ethic of the Industrial Revolution—yet he only touches upon 1930s literary engagements with the "leisure ethic," seeing the thirties as a time that "unsettled" the discourses of the play reform movement (348). Studies of work, or labor, and literature have typified how the literature of the 1930s has been examined, yet the "historical inextricability of leisure and

labor" created a literature concerned also with the changing meanings of play and leisure (viii). The only writer to focus on this in thirties literature is William Solomon, who has detailed how writers such as Edward Dahlberg, Henry Miller, John Dos Passos, and Nathanael West engaged with mechanized amusements and mass culture through a poetics of disfigurement and a politics of the carnivalized grotesque. While this study examines attempts to revitalize and reinvigorate the "human" in literature through the relationship of writers with wider leisure reform, the opposite trope depicting the "inhuman" in leisure and the fascination with fragmentation and the feminization of culture is equally true of the literary politics of play during the era. Indeed, like myself, Solomon indicates the centrality of the "politicized interplay between literature and amusement" to cultural productions of the era. See William Solomon, *Literature, Amusement and Technology in the Great Depression* (Cambridge: Cambridge University Press, 2002), 31. For the relationship between amusement, play, and writing in Stephen Crane, see also Bill Brown, *The Material Unconscious: American Amusement, Stephen Crane and the Economies of Play* (Cambridge, Mass.: Harvard University Press, 1996).

2. For a detailed description of the interaction between social science and documentary "fiction," see William Stott, *Documentary Expression and Thirties America* (Chicago: University of Chicago Press, 1986), 152–70.

3. Stott illustrates this direct link with Thomas Mineham's *Boy and Girl Tramps of America.* Mineham, a PhD candidate in sociology, was influenced by the surprise film hit *Wild Boys of the Road* (1933) during his revisions of the book, merging methods and genres wherein "it is hard to distinguish social science that panders to the sentimentality of its subjects from the fictions of mass culture—movies and soap operas." Ibid., 169.

4. Quoted in Daniel Aaron, *Writers on the Left: Episodes in American Literary Communism* (New York: Harcourt, Brace and World, 1961), 161.

5. I do not wish to imply that the "proletarianism" was a monolithic style but use the term loosely to describe the fashion in left-wing fiction writing, which focused on working-class issues and realist representation (albeit at times a modernist "realism") and which influenced the production of many political and nonpolitical texts during this time.

6. Laura Hapke, in *Daughters of the Great Depression: Women, Work and Fiction in the American 1930s* (Athens: University of Georgia Press, 1995), elaborates on the political and cultural erasure of women as workers in fiction as well as in left-wing discourse and popular rhetoric. See also Paula Rabinowitz in *Labor and Desire: Women's Revolutionary Fiction in Depression America* (Chapel Hill: University of North Carolina Press, 1991) for the creation of proletarianism as a masculine aesthetic. Even before the stock market crash, communist writer Michael Gold was demanding a new form of writing, one that reflected the masculine experience, where working-class America was an "undiscovered continent" that could provide the writer "with all the primitive material he needs." See Aaron, *Writers on the Left*, 161.

7. Aaron, *Writers on the Left*, 242.

8. Ibid.

9. Rita Barnard, *The Great Depression and the Culture of Abundance: Kenneth Fearing, Nathanael West, and Mass Culture in the 1930s* (New York: Cambridge University Press, 1995), 33.

10. Dorothea Lange and Paul Schuster Taylor, *An American Exodus: A Record of Human Erosion in the Thirties*, rev. ed. (New Haven, Conn.: Yale University Press, 1969), 33, 39, 64.

11. Dinerstein, *Swinging the Machine*, 151.

12. Riggs, *Play*, 1.

13. John Steinbeck, *The Grapes of Wrath* (London: Pan Books, 1975), 40–41.

14. Sherwood Anderson, *Perhaps Women* (New York: H. Liveright, Inc., 1931), introduction.

15. Sherwood Anderson, *Puzzled America* (New York: Paul P. Appel, 1970), 107.

16. Ibid., 108.

17. Frankl, *Machine-Made Leisure*, 12.

18. Sherwood Anderson, *Puzzled America*, 42.

19. James Burkhart Gilbert, *Writers and Partisans: A History of Literary Radicalism in America* (New York: John Wiley and Sons, 1968), 90.

20. Quoted in Ibid. 93. Jacqueline Ellis also writes that the Depression enabled middle-class intellectuals to reengage with society, offering an opportunity, through the lives and experiences of the working class, "to readjust their political and emotional position in American society" (141). See her *Silent Witnesses: Representations of Working-Class Women in the United States* (Bowling Green, Ohio: Bowling Green State University Popular Press, 1998).

21. Henry Hart, ed., *American Writers' Congress* (International Publishers Co., 1935), 191.

22. Ibid., 62.

23. Nash, *Spectatoritis*, 10.

24. Quoted in Raymond M. Bell, *Television in the Thirties* (Ann Arbor, Mich.: University Microfilms, 1973), 48.

25. "Photolibraries: Microphotography Offers Possibility of Volume Reduction By Camera," *Literary Digest*, January 13, 1937, 19.

26. "The Current Fad for Picture Mags: News-Stands Swamped with Demands for Camera Products," *Literary Digest*, January 30, 1937, 20–22.

27. For example, see Susan Smulyan, *Selling Radio: The Commercialization of American Broadcasting, 1920–1934* (Washington, D.C.: Smithsonian Institution Press, 1994).

28. Panati, *Panati's Parade*, 180.

29. Green, *Uncertainty of Everyday Life*, 188.

30. Alice Ames Winter, "The Thrill of the Movies," *Motion Picture Monthly* 4, no. 12 (1930): 4.

31. Edwin Embree, "The Uses of Leisure," *Recreation*, November 1933, 376. For an interesting essay on the use of book ownership as cultural identity and commodity, see Megan Benton, "'Too Many Books': Book Ownership and Cultural Identity in the 1920s," *American Quarterly* 49, no. 2 (1997): 268–97. See also Douglas Waples, *People and Print: Social Aspects of Reading in the Depression* (New York: Social Science Research Council, 1937).

32. "The New Leisure," *Publisher's Weekly*, September 9, 1933, 747.

33. "Fall in Love with Words," Advertisement for Grenville Kleiser's Mail Course in English, *Literary Digest*, March 6, 1937, back cover.

34. "Big Business in Pulp Thrillers," *Literary Digest*, January 23, 1937, 30–31.

35. "March of Spare Time," Advertisement for International Correspondence Schools, *Time*, February 7, 1938, 35.

36. WPA photo, "Reading to the Family," Orlando, Florida, March 31, 1938. The caption reads "Walter Donaldson is shown by the fireside reading to a portion of his family. Donaldson was taught in a WPA educational class." This image is available online at the New Deal Network Web site, http://newdeal. feri.org.

37. In 1936, Dale Carnegie's *How to Win Friends and InXuence People* (New

York: Simon and Schuster, 1936) hit the best-seller lists by claiming that the right use of words, and public speaking abilities, could turn failure into success. Advertisements claimed that by reading just this one book a miserable failure who could not keep jobs or friends could become a blazing success, liked by everyone, including employers. Still sold as a self-help manual, Carnegie's "personal engineering" book promoted methods of behaving and speaking to enhance the self-control and effectiveness of the individual. Learning to be a leader and to speak effectively, he claimed, enabled the individual to be respected, gain authority, make more profit, and enjoy more leisure.

38. Howard Woolston, "American Intellectuals and Social Reform," *American Sociological Review* 1, no. 3 (1936): 363.

39. Quoted in Hart, *American Writers' Congress*, 191.

40. Barnard, *Great Depression and the Culture of Abundance*, 7. Caren Irr in *The Suburb of Dissent: Cultural Politics in the United States and Canada During the 1930s* (Durham, N.C.: Duke University Press, 1998) also examines the relationship between avant-garde and mass culture, claiming that proletarian fiction was hardly a single entity.

41. Denning, *Cultural Front*, 227.

42. Szalay, *New Deal Modernism*, 28.

43. Szalay provides a most useful insight into how literary aesthetics interacted with government policy toward mass market economics during this period, giving evidence that the government and writers responded to the threat of the capitalist free market through imaginative and creative reinvention. For example, see ibid., 46–47 and 50–52.

44. Ibid., 6.

45. Robert Forsythe, *New Masses*, October 1, 1935, reprinted in Susman, *Culture and Commitment*, 258–60.

46. Lewis Mumford, *Technics and Civilization* (New York: Harcourt, Brace and Company, 1934), 427.

47. Ibid., 425.

48. Quoted in Jerre Mangione, *The Dream and the Deal: The Federal Writers' Project, 1935–1943* (Boston: Little, Brown and Company, 1972), 241. For the history of the FWP, see also Monty Noam Penkower, *The Federal Writers' Project: A Study in Government Patronage of the Arts* (Chicago: University of Illinois Press, 1977).

49. McKinzie, *New Deal for Artists*, 198.

50. Ibid.

51. Ibid., 130.

52. Christine Bold, *The WPA Guides: Mapping America* (Jackson: University Press of Mississippi, 1999), 30. Perceiving the creation of the guide series as a battle of representation and political power, Bold sees the editorial control of the project as the "cusp of the modern bureaucratization of culture" (xiii).

53. Mangione, *Dream and the Deal*, 241.

54. Sinclair Lewis, *It Can't Happen Here* (London: Jonathan Cape Ltd., 1935), 9. Barbara Melosh suggests that *It Can't Happen Here* presents a world in which men are emasculated and infantilized by women. See her *Engendering Culture: Manhood and Womanhood in the New Deal Art and Theater* (Washington, D.C.: Smithsonian Institution Press, 1991), 15–31. See also Alpers, *Dictators, Democracy, and American Public Culture*, 55 for a discussion of Lewis.

55. Newton Baker and Raymond Fosdick, "Our Leisure Thinking," *Recreation*, December 1933, 428.

56. Lewis, *It Can't Happen Here*, 15. These objectives were also in keeping with eugenic principles for racial strength and purity discussed in the final chapter.

57. Ibid., 22.

58. Ibid., 315.

59. William Saroyan, "Myself upon the Earth," *The Daring Young Man on the Flying Trapeze* (New York: Modern Age Books, 1937), 28, 31, 33.

60. William Saroyan, "Seventy Thousand Assyrians," *The Daring Young Man,* (New York: Modern Age Books, 1937), 8.

61. Ibid., 3.

62. Ibid., 6.

63. Ibid., 9–10.

64. Ibid., 60.

65. Upton Sinclair, *The Flivver King: A Story of Ford America* (Chicago: Charles H. Kerr, 1984), 65. In his discussion of dance in the thirties, Joel Dinerstein notes how Ford's reaction to modernity led him to call for folk dance to replace jazz. See his *Swinging the Machine,* 29.

66. Sinclair, *Flivver King,* 65.

67. Ibid., 116–17.

68. Edmund Wilson, *The American Earthquake: A Documentary of the Twenties and Thirties* (London: W. H. Allen, 1958), 454.

69. Ibid., 457–58.

70. Reprinted in Harold Clurman, *Famous American Plays of the 1930s* (New York: Dell, 1970), 389.

71. In *Swinging the Machine,* Dinerstein examines the widespread performance of this trope within popular culture, especially in relation to swing music and dance.

72. Albert Halper, *Good-Bye Union Square: A Writer's Memoir of the Thirties* (Chicago: Quadrangle Books, 1970) 104.

73. Ibid., 105.

Chapter 5

1. Robert Lynd and Alice Hanson, "The People as Consumers," in *Recent Social Trends in the United States,* vol. 2, ed. President's Research Committee on Social Trends (New York: McGraw-Hill, 1933), 866.

2. Harold Rugg, *The Great Technology: Social Chaos and the Public Mind* (New York: John Day Company, 1933), 212.

3. Mirra Komarovsky, *The Unemployed Man and His Family—The Effect of Unemployment on the Status of the Man in Fifty-Nine Families* (New York: Dryden Press, 1940). For other studies on the family see Robert Angell, *The Family Encounters the Depression* (Gloucester, Mass.: Peter Smith, 1965); Ruth Cavan and Katherine Ranck, *The Family and the Depression: A Study of One Hundred Chicago Families* (Chicago: University of Chicago Press, 1938); Winona Morgan, *The Family Meets the Depression: A Study of a Group of Highly Selected Families* (Minneapolis: University of Minnesota Institute of Child Welfare, 1939); Earnest Mowrer, *Family Disorganisation* (Chicago: University of Chicago Press, 1939); Samuel Stouffer and Paul Larzarsfeld, *Research Memorandum on the Family in the Depression* (1937; reprint, New York: Arno, 1972).

4. Anderson, *Perhaps Women,* 42.

5. Ibid., 83.

6. Ibid., 55.

7. Ibid., 56.

8. The discourse of leisure is a multilayered one, and the "problem" of gender is deeply embedded within it. Part of "the problem of leisure" is the fact that

it encompasses two definitions of leisure according to gender. Feminist sociologists of leisure have examined the way that women's leisure is coded differently from men's. Because of their unpaid position as homemakers, most women were not considered as workers by sociologists and as a consequence were automatically "leisured" regardless of their individual circumstances. As one contemporary sociologist has pointed out, women's leisure has been defined differently from men's because sociological theories have tended to assume that leisure is time off from paid work, as opposed to housework; that work is full-time (whereas many women work part-time); that work and leisure are enjoyed in separate locations (whereas women's leisure may be in their place of work—the home); that much of what men regard as leisure represents work for women; that women's range of leisure choices have been circumscribed by men; and that individual freedom is a male construct that applies differently to women than men. See Janet Wilson, *Politics and Leisure* (Boston, Mass.: Unwin Hyman, 1988), 12. According to Betsy Wearing, Marxist theory on leisure has emerged as a masculine discourse because work is seen as paid work, without which there cannot be leisure. Leisure viewed in this way—as a break from work—similarly constructs women *as leisure* and defines the leisure experience as male. See Betsy Wearing, *Leisure and Feminist Theory* (London: SGE Publications, 1998), 27. Women's leisure in fact is even defined differently from men's—their leisure is not time out of work but time away from the family, time in the city, time in the shops or the car. The limits on women's leisure also illustrate how it cannot be defined in the same way as men's: "Women have less time for leisure than men and a more limited range of possibilities; women's housework and child care responsibilities generally render them 'on call'; leisure outside the home is problematic in terms of time, resources, child care and respectable and acceptable femininity; women are generally financially poorer than men; and at home women are financially dependent on their husbands." In Wearing, *Leisure and Feminist Theory*, 33.

9. The notion of gender here is used to describe a discourse on sex roles, not biological makeup. Interpretation of the meanings of leisure through gender serves to highlight the often contradictory meanings of leisure and the instability of the notion of a single "leisure discourse." Control over the meaning of leisure—its very definition—can thereby be seen as a "powerful measure of political control by men over women." In Wearing, *Leisure and Feminist Theory*, 27. At the same time, the "fluidity" of the meanings of leisure can also serve to highlight the weaknesses and gaps in that power that can be occupied by oppositions and contradictions, which threaten to dismantle the presumption of power and control.

10. Robert Lynd and Helen Lynd, *Middletown in Transition: A Study in Cultural ConXicts* (New York: Harcourt, Brace, Jovanovich, 1965), 179.

11. Ellen Wiley Todd, "Art, The 'New Woman,' and Consumer Culture: Kenneth Hayes Miller and Reginald Marsh on Fourteenth Street, 1920–1940," in *Gender and American History Since 1890*, ed. Barbara Melosh (New York: Routledge, 1993), 146.

12. Lynd and Hanson, "People as Consumers," 866.

13. Majorie Rosen, *Popcorn Venus: Women, Movies and the American Dream* (London: Peter Owen Ltd., 1975), 176.

14. For a discussion of narrative ambivalence in this film, see Lea Jacobs, *The Wages of Sin: Censorship and the Fallen Woman Film, 1928–1942* (Berkeley: University of California Press, 1997).

15. Tandy, *Economics of Leisure*, 7.

16. See, for example, Silas Bent, *Slaves by the Billion: The Story of Mechanical Progress in the Home* (New York: Longmans, 1938), and Laurel D. Graham, "Domesticating Efficiency: Lillian Gilbreth's Scientific Management of Homemakers, 1924–1930," *Signs: Journal of Women in Culture and Society* 24, no. 3 (1999): 633–75.

17. Lundberg, Komarovsky, and McInerney, *Leisure,* 4.

18. Pangburn, *Adventures in Recreation,* 9 (see Introduction, n. 28).

19. Neumayer and Neumayer, *Leisure and Recreation,* 57.

20. *Life,* November 23, 1936, 2.

21. Neumayer and Neumayer, *Leisure and Recreation,* 57.

22. Feminist historians Susan Strasser and Ruth Schwartz Cowan have dismantled this notion that technology freed women from domestic duties, undercutting the assumption that modernity created more leisure for women and arguing that domestic efficiency and technology was harnessed to reinforce traditional gender roles. See Ruth Schwartz Cowan, *More Work for Mother: The Ironies of Household Technology from the Open Hearth to the Microwave* (New York: Basic Books, 1983), and Susan Strasser, *Never Done: A History of American Housework* (New York: Pantheon, 1982). In fact, studies of domestic changes have noted that technological innovations tied women more fully to the home: Phyllis Palmer sees the reduction in use of domestic servants by middle-class women (combined with the introduction of technology) as increasing the domestic role of middle-class women in the home during this and the postwar period. See Phyllis Palmer, *Domesticity and Dirt: Housewives and Domestic Servants in the United States, 1920–1945* (Philadelphia: Temple University Press, 1989). According to this research, it seems likely that all women—even middle-class ones—experienced less leisure than before, as more working-class women were taking industrial jobs and leaving affluent housewives managing their own "servantless" homes, a point confirmed by Laurel Graham in "Domesticating Efficiency." Cowan has examined how new ideologies of cleanliness and efficiency were introduced along with new technologies, which actually increased women's domestic workload. Women's labor in the home, it appears, did not decrease in modern times but merely shifted to new roles and tasks. Despite this, advertising and the movies directly related consumption to leisure, arguing that both could be used for the betterment (or to the detriment) of the modern nuclear family.

23. Dorothy Canfield Fisher, "The Bright Perilous Face of Leisure," *Journal of Adult Education* (June 1933): 237.

24. Christine Frederick, *Selling Mrs. Consumer* (New York: Business Bourse, 1929), 11.

25. Laurel Graham also notes that Frederick's earlier book *Household Engineering: Scientific Management in the Home* (1920) was written to "stimulate faith among housewives that they could conquer the drudgery and win more leisure time by embracing scientific management." See her "Domesticating Efficiency," 648.

26. Walter B. Pitkin, *The Consumer: His Nature and His Changing Habits* (New York: McGraw-Hill, 1932), 283. Graham notes that by 1920 it was widely believed "that women were responsible for 80–90 per cent of household spending," adding in a footnote, "Although the origin of the 80–90 per cent figure is unknown, it appears to have attained the status of fact by sheer repetition" (644). See also the cover of a pamphlet from the League of Women Shoppers in the late thirties, which states, "Women do Ninety Percent of the Buying." Available at the New York University Web site, http://www.nyu.edu/library/bobst/research/tam/women/shoppers.jpg.

27. Pitkin, *Consumer,* 312.

28. Ibid., 290–99.

29. Ibid., 291. See also Roland Vaile and Helen G. Canoyer, *Income and Consumption* (New York: Henry Holt and Co., 1938), 326–27, for very similar views on women, fashion, and female impulsiveness.

30. Pitkin, *Consumer*, 308. For a study of the relationship between cinema, fashion, and cosmetics, see Sarah M. Berry, *Screen Style: Fashion and Femininity in 1930s Hollywood* (Minneapolis: University of Minnesota Press, 2000).

31. Pitkin, *Consumer*, 297–98.

32. Ibid., 302.

33. Ibid., 281, 286, 289–90.

34. Ibid., 312.

35. Vaile and Canoyer, *Income and Consumption*, 326.

36. For a discussion of consumer movements and the attempt to rationalize consumption, see Berry, *Screen Style*, 4–5. See also Susman, *Culture and Commitment*, 142–43.

37. These views were expressed by the Lynds in *Middletown in Transition* and Stuart Chase in *Mexico—A Study of Two Americas* (New York: Macmillan, 1931).

38. Daniel Horowitz, *The Morality of Spending: Attitudes Toward the Consumer Society in America, 1875–1940* (Baltimore: Johns Hopkins University Press, 1985), 159.

39. Steiner, *Americans at Play*, 196.

40. Horowitz, *Morality of Spending*, 153.

41. Few writers have examined this aspect of the Depression. An exception, which outlines the abundance available to certain sectors of society and charts the growth of commercial leisure opportunities during the thirties is Kevin Starr's *The Dream Endures: California Enters the 1940s* (New York & London: Oxford University Press, 1997). Cindy Aron notes that abundance of leisure was not just for the rich but that "the 1930s witnessed the possibility of vacationing expanding to new sectors of the population as policies granting paid vacations to industrial workers finally reached the majority of wage earners." See her *Working at Play*. For consumer leisure patterns surveyed via consumption patterns, see U.S. Federal Works Agency, Division of Professional and Service Projects, *Adult Recreation* (Washington, D.C.: Works Progress Administration, 1940).

42. U.S. Bureau of the Census, *Census of American Business: Places of Amusement* (Washington, D.C.: Government Printing Office, 1935).

43. Steiner details the severe difficulties of using census information to analyze the growth of recreation and the lack of adequate scientific and statistical information in *Research Memorandum*, 1–19.

44. Victoria Wolcott, *Remaking Respectability: African-American Women in Interwar Detroit* (Chapel Hill: University of North Carolina Press, 2001), 93–130.

45. See Vaile and Canoyer, *Income and Consumption*, 114–15, 175, 232. Also see Roland S. Vaile, *Research Memorandum on Social Aspects of Consumption in the Depression* (New York: Social Science Research Council, 1937), and Julius Weinberger, "Economic Aspects of Recreation," *Harvard Business Review* (summer, 1937): 457.

46. Young Women's Christian Associations, *Leisure-Time Interests and Activities of Business Girls*, 47.

47. National Recovery Administration, *Handbook for Speakers: The President's Emergency Reemployment Program* (Washington, D.C.: Government Printing Office, 1933), 31–32.

48. Lynd and Hanson, "The People as Consumers," 866.

49. Richard Wightman Fox, "Epitaph for Middletown: Robert S. Lynd and the Analysis of Consumer Culture," in *The Culture of Consumption: Critical Essays in American History, 1880–1980*, ed. Richard Wightman Fox and T. J. Lears (New York: Pantheon, 1983), 137.

50. Vaile and Canoyer, *Income and Consumption*, 328.

51. As Laura Hapke has documented in *Daughters of the Great Depression*, working women were effaced in much literature of the period, which distorted the role of work in women's lives—effectively rendering them as the leisured "other" to the male worker.

52. Alice Kessler-Harris, *Out to Work: A History of Wage-Earning Women in the United States* (New York: Oxford University Press, 1982), 250–72. In a 1936 poll in *Fortune* magazine asking, "Do you believe that married women should have a full time job outside the home?" only 15 percent supported working married women.

53. Lois Scharf, *To Work and to Wed: Female Employment, Feminism, and the Great Depression* (Westport, Conn.: Greenwood Press, 1980), 124.

54. Judith Sealander, *As Minority Becomes Majority: Federal Reaction to the Phenomenon of Women in the Workforce, 1920–1963* (Westport, Conn.: Greenwood Press, 1983), 63. Women were asked to only buy where the NRA eagle displaying the slogan "We Do Our Part" was displayed, as "warriors enlisted in an earnest crusade to save our homes and our economic institutions." See National Recovery Administration, *Handbook for Speakers*, 32.

55. Lewis Wilson, "Enlarged Adult Education Opportunities," *Recreation*, February 1934, 507.

56. Sealander, *As Minority Becomes Majority*, 63.

57. Scharf, *To Work and to Wed*, 124.

58. Benjamin Hunnicutt illustrates how women's leisure through reduced working hours often led to increased domesticity and household work, which they classed as free time. See his *Kellogg's Six-Hour Day*, 60–84.

59. Wolcott, *Remaking Respectability*, 230–33.

60. "Colored girls attending WPA household workers training center (serving a tea given for the Phoenix recreation department)" National Youth Administration: Phoenix, Arizona., 1936, control no. NLR-PHOCO-A–5251(107); photograph from the National Archives and Records Administration digital collection at http://arcweb.archives.gov/arc/arc.

61. McKinzie, *New Deal for Artists*, 132.

62. Analyzing this combination of modernity and womanhood in images of popular art at this time, Ellen Todd writes that while "the overt aims of this back-to-the-home movement were to restabilize the family and reaffirm marriage in ways that recognized the new woman's post-franchise equality, the covert ideology was a homebound conception of womanhood which now made the consumption a central part of her role." See her "Art, The 'New Woman,' and Consumer Culture," 138.

63. Pack, *Challenge of Leisure*, 207.

64. Hudson Shore Labor School, *The Nonworking Time of Industrial Women Workers* (Washington, D.C.: Government Printing Office, 1940), 7.

65. Melosh, *Engendering Culture*, 184–85.

66. Ramona Lowe, "The Woman in the Window," in *Writing Red: An Anthology of American Women Writers, 1930–1940*, ed. Charlotte Nekola and Paula Rabinowitz (New York: Feminist Press, 1987), 79–83.

67. Elizabeth Thomas, "Our House," in *Writing Red: An Anthology of American Women Writers, 1930–1940*, ed. Charlotte Nekola and Paula Rabinowitz (New York: Feminist Press, 1987), 86.

68. Marita Bonner, "The Whipping," in *Writing Red: An Anthology of American Women Writers, 1930–1940*, ed. Charlotte Nekola and Paula Rabinowitz (New York: Feminist Press, 1987), 70–78.

69. Alpers, *Dictators, Democracy and American Public Culture*, 133. For contemporary women's criticism of patriarchy in essays and magazines see 44–57.

Chapter 6

1. That the leisure programs and discourses were replete with metanarratives of power and social control I am certain, yet the impact that this had on everyday experience of them is open to question. While I have focused on the rhetoric of sociologists, economists, politicians, writers, and planners, my aim has not been to imply that their ambitions for a rationally planned culture were successful to the point of eliminating alternative, transgressive, or liberating experiences of mainstream, dominant, or mass culture. Women who left their children at free cinema crèches—in the absence of child care provision or to go to work—or men who used WPA art classes to meet women, show how organized leisure was not always used in the way it was intended by the professionals.

2. Gilbert Seldes, *Movies for the Millions* (New York: Charles Scribner's Sons, 1937), 12.

3. During 1932–33 the movie industry recorded heavy losses. But by April 14, 1934, *The Magazine of Wall Street* reported "Sixty Million Customers Weekly" and noted healthy profits and recovery for the film industry at a rate "faster than almost any commercial enterprise" (662–63).

4. National Recreation Association, *Leisure Hours of 5,000 People*, 10.

5. Harap, "Planning the Curriculum for Leisure," 317.

6. For such discussions see Garth Jowett, *Film: The Democratic Art* (Boston: Little, Brown and Company, 1976); Lary May, *Screening out the Past: The Birth of Mass Culture and the Motion Picture Industry* (Chicago: University of Chicago Press, 1983); Nasaw, *Going Out*; and Staiger, *Bad Women*

7. "Worry About 10c Houses," *Variety*, December 22, 1931, 5.

8. "Do Motion Pictures Influence Trade? Business Men Have a Real Interest in Motion Pictures Aside from Recreational Interest Because Films Help Business," *The Motion Picture* 4, no. 7 (1930): 6.

9. See Richard Louis Testa Jr., "Movie Exhibition Practices and Procedures During the Hollywood Studio Era in Providence, Rhode Island (California)," PhD diss., University of Maryland College Park, 1993. Sarah Berry's *Screen Style* also examines the interrelation between film and fashion during this period— claiming that women's use of fashion represented "an ongoing struggle for visible autonomy in the social sphere" (xiv), a "negotiation of modernity and post-traditional identity" (xii), and was consciously used to destabilize older notions of gender, class, and race.

10. Premium advertisers instructed that *only* women were to be given the free giveaways. See, for example, "Bingo!—Aw! Nuts: Movie Temples Lure Monday, Tuesday Patrons with Prize-Money," *The Literary Digest*, March 6, 1937, 36; "Premium Thriller," *Business Week*, December 8, 1934, 24; and Douglas Gomery, *Shared Pleasures: A History of Movie Presentation in the United States* (Madison: University of Wisconsin Press, 1992), 70–71.

11. "Bingo!—Aw! Nuts"

12. In 1936, *Time* magazine claimed that it was normally three minutes. See "Bank Night," *Time*, February 3, 1936, 44.

13. "Bingo!—Aw! Nuts."

14. "Bank Night," *The New Republic*, May 6, 1936, 363.

15. "Bank Night Bans," *Time*, January 11, 1937, 55.

16. "Camden's Drive-In Theatre," *The Literary Digest*, July 22, 1933, 19; "Drive-in Movie Holds Four Hundred," *Popular Mechanics*, September 1933, 326.

17. Thomas Doherty, *Pre-Code Hollywood: Sex, Immorality, and Insurrection in American Cinema, 1930–1934* (New York: Columbia University Press, 1999), 105–36, 171–87, 320–46.

18. "Sinful Girls Lead in 1931," *Variety*, December 29, 1931, 5.

19. Lynd and Lynd, *Middletown in Transition*, 177–78. See also Jowett, *Film*, 263.

20. Mariana Hoffman, "Children and the Cinema," *International Review of Educational Cinematography* (September 1930): 1073.

21. The history and controversies surrounding these studies are well examined in *Children and the Movies: Media Influence and the Payne Fund Controversy*, edited by Garth Jowett, Ian Jarvie, and Katherine Fuller (New York: Cambridge University Press, 1996). As Jowett explains, Forman's book was a popularization of the negative aspects of moviegoing and was written by the freelance journalist to promote antimovie sentiments. Although not representing the research fairly, the book was the most common way that the Payne Fund studies were disseminated. Thus, while the social scientists themselves were not antimovie per se, and during the course of the research they came to believe less and less in the power of the movies to influence behavior, their work ultimately functioned to further negative perceptions surrounding moviegoing.

22. Henry James Forman, *Our Movie-Made Children* (New York: Macmillan Company, 1933), 88.

23. For example, see Jowett, Jarvie, and Fuller, *Children and the Movies*.

24. Similarly, the Payne Fund studies are replete with an underlying class bias.

25. Forman, *Our Movie-Made Children*, 80.

26. Ibid., 231.

27. Herbert Blumer and Philip Hauser, *Movies, Delinquency and Crime* (New York: Macmillan Company, 1933), 95.

28. Ibid., 95–96.

29. Ibid., 98–99.

30. Fabio Pennacchi, "The Cinema and Adolescence with Special Reference to Nervous and Mental Diseases," *International Review of Educational Cinematography* (September 1930): 1062.

31. Arthur Kellogg, "Minds Made by the Movies," *Survey Graphic* 22, no. 5 (May 1933): 249. See also Forman, *Our Movie-Made Children*, 91.

32. Herbert Blumer, *Movies and Conduct* (New York: Macmillan Company, 1933), 103.

33. Forman, *Our Movie-Made Children*, 185–86.

34. Theodore Dreiser, *Tragic America* (New York: Horace Liveright, Inc., 1931), 302.

35. Forman, *Our Movie-Made Children*, 232.

36. Ibid., 231–32.

37. James T. Farrell, *Studs Lonigan* (London: Picador Classics, 1988), 264–65.

38. Ibid., 266.

39. Ibid., 509.

40. Ibid., 513.

41. Meridel Le Sueur, "Women on the Breadlines," in *Ripening: Selected Work*, ed. Elaine Hedges (New York: Feminist Press, 1990), 138.

42. Tess Slesinger, "The Mouse-Trap," in *Writing Red: An Anthology of American Women Writers, 1930–1940*, ed. Charlotte Nekola and Paula Rabinowitz (New York: Feminist Press, 1987), 106.

43. Ibid., 123.

44. See Annette Kuhn, *Dreaming of Fred and Ginger: Cinema and Cultural Memory* (New York: New York University Press, 2002). Although this study is based on interviews of British cinemagoers in the thirties, the responses illustrate the key social role that the movies played in the lives of women at that time.

45. Gomery, *Shared Pleasures*, 49.

46. Forman, *Our Movie-Made Children*, 90.

47. Ibid., 90.

48. Ibid., 104.

49. Ibid., 232.

50. See, for example, Neumayer and Neumayer, *Leisure and Recreation*, 226–33.

51. Paul Cressey, "The Community—A Social Setting for the Motion Picture," in *Children and the Movies: Media InXuence and the Payne Fund Controversy*, ed. Garth Jowett, Ian Jarvey, and Katherine Fuller (New York: Cambridge University Press, 1996), 137.

52. Ibid., 150–60.

53. W. W. Charters, *Motion Pictures and Youth: A Summary* (New York: Macmillan, 1933), 77.

54. Fred Eastman, for example, used much of the Payne Fund findings in his book to argue for public education in motion picture appreciation. See Fred Eastman and Edward Ouellette, *Better Motion Pictures: Learning for Life* (Boston: Pilgrim Press, 1936); Wrenn and Hartley, *Time on Their Hands*, 25–32; Harap, "Planning the Curriculum for Leisure," 317; and Jowett, *Film*, 274–75.

55. Some motion picture reformers had seen the emergence of cinema as a racially "degenerate" force for some time. Fred Eastman, reformer and Christian commentator, wrote, "The movies were born in the slums," where small Jewish cloak and suit merchants would rent a store "to catch the pennies of the recreation starved immigrant workforce" and had been "educating in bad manners, bad morals, and bad philosophy." With Jewish control of "90 per cent" of the industry that specialized in "making money out of muck," Eastman claimed that "it is time for the people to call a halt." See Fred Eastman, "Who Controls the Movies?" *The Christian Century*, February 5, 1930, 173–75.

56. Production Code, quoted in Doherty, *Pre-Code Hollywood*, 348 and 363.

57. Young Women's Christian Associations, *Leisure-Time Interests and Activities of Business Girls*.

58. Neumayer and Neumayer, *Leisure and Recreation*, 233.

59. Ibid., 239.

60. See, for example, Erenberg, *Steppin Out*; Nasaw, *Going Out*; Peiss, *Cheap Amusements*. For a full study of the role and practices of dance-hall culture in working-class life, see McBee, *Dance-Hall Days*. Robert and Helen Lynd noted in *Middletown in Transition* that "the depression stimulated an increase in the number of small, informal dance halls" (269).

61. Ella Gardner, *Public Dance Halls: Their Regulation and Place in the Recreation of Adolescents* (Washington, D.C.: U.S. Department of Labor, Children's Bureau, 1929), 48. See also McBee, *Dance-Hall Days*, for an examination of the way working-class dance culture flouted censors.

62. Gardener, *Public Dance Halls*, 52.

63. Paul G. Cressey, *The Taxi-Dance Hall: A Sociological Study in Commercialized Recreation and City Life* (Chicago: University of Chicago Press, 1932), xi.

64. Ibid., xiv.

65. See McBee, *Dance-Hall Days*, 56–64.

66. Cressey, *Taxi-Dance Hall*, xi.

67. Ibid., 6.

68. Ibid., xiii.

69. Paul Cressey later used this simile of the "urban frontier" in an unpublished Payne Fund study on the effects of moviegoing, called "The Community—A Social Setting for the Motion Picture."

70. "10,000 Relief Workers Make Whoopee on Saturday Night," *Life*, November 23, 1936, 15.

71. Ibid., 9.

72. Lynd and Lynd, *Middletown in Transition*, 293.

73. That repeal would help to boost the commercial leisure business, however, was apparent to those in the business:

Repeal of prohibition is conceded to be another [better condition]. That arrived just before the past year began, when speculation was rife as to just what legal grog would mean at the ticket windows. Consensus of theater operating opinion is that repeal, for no other reason, has assisted by serving as an instrument which helps draw people out of the home. In many cities there had been no downtown life to speak of for the 13 years of the Great Mistake, whereas repeal had the effect of immediately bringing life to hotels, restaurants and other places in such downtown zones where theaters are located. Repeal also provided employment and increased manufacture in certain lines, besides greatly stirring the circulation of money and, in the opinion of most showmen, having the effect of liberating a public mind which had gotten used to denying itself amusements other than radio and bridge." Roy Chartier, "Year in Pictures," *Variety*, January 1, 1935, 3.

74. Lynd and Lynd, *Middletown in Transition*, 278. Drinking in dance halls was a significant part of working-class leisure. See McBee, *Dance-Hall Days,* 4–5, 74–75, 77–78, 181–82.

75. See images in *Life*, "10,000 Relief Workers Make Whoopee on Saturday Night," 9, 13, 14, and 17.

76. Lucille Boehm, "Two-Bit Piece," in *Writing Red: An Anthology of American Women Writers, 1930–1940,* ed. Charlotte Nekola and Paula Rabinowitz (New York: Feminist Press, 1987), 69.

77. This story confirms Dinerstein's argument that dance, especially popular dances like the Lindy-Hop, were not only expressions of fun but ways of dealing with the emotional trauma of the Depression and mechanized working conditions. Dinerstein shows how dances like the Lindy-Hop became new cultural expressions that were liberating to the traditionally disenfranchised. See Dinerstein, *Swinging the Machine,* 253–64.

78. Carol Martin argues that marathons were a mockery of social Darwinism, turning "the struggle for survival into something performed," yet "this mimicry resembled a con game that was unique to American culture." See Carol Martin, *Dance Marathons: Performing American Culture in the 1920s and 1930s* (Jackson: University Press of Mississippi, 1994), 43.

79. Ibid., 57.

80. Ibid., 45.

81. Ibid., 133.

82. Ibid., 69–86.

83. Ibid. For an excellent study of the way that women shaped social spaces in working-class dance halls, see McBee, *Dance-Hall Days,* 82–114.

84. Farrell, *Studs Lonigan,* 679–94.

85. Ibid., 632.

86. Julia L. Foulkes, *Modern Bodies: Dance and American Modernism from Martha Graham to Alvin Ailey* (Chapel Hill: University of North Carolina Press, 2002), 123.

87. Lynd and Lynd, *Middletown in Transition*, 269.

88. Butler, *Introduction to Community Recreation,* 384–86.

89. Ibid., 384.

90. Mary Breen, *Partners in Play: Recreation for Young Men and Young Women Together* (New York: A. S. Barnes & Co., 1936), 3–4.

91. Ibid., 2, 33, 35, 34.

92. Ethel Bowers, *Recreation for Girls and Women* (New York: A. S. Barnes & Co., 1934), 174.

93. Breen, *Partners in Play,* 5–6. Not only was divorce a problem, but the marriage rate had dropped to an all-time low in 1932.

94. Bowers, *Recreation for Girls and Women,* 172.

95. Ibid., 194.

96. Ibid., 181.

97. Lindeman, "National Planning and Objectives," 11, 21.

Chapter 7

1. Lundberg, Komarovsky, and McInerney, *Leisure,* 170.

2. "Social Propaganda Films: 'Motherhood,'" *International Review of Educational Cinematography* (March 1930): 275.

3. Martin Pernick, *The Black Stork: Eugenics and the Death of "Defective" Babies in American Medicine and Motion Pictures Since 1915* (New York: Oxford University Press, 1996), 129–43.

4. There are a number of excellent books on the history of eugenics in American culture. For example, Christina Cogdell, *Eugenic Design: Streamlining America in the 1930s* (Philadelphia: University of Pennsylvania Press, 2004); Ian Robert Dowbiggin, *Keeping America Sane: Psychiatry and Eugenics in the United States and Canada, 1880–1940* (Ithaca, N.Y.: Cornell University Press, 1997); Nicole Hahn Rafter, ed., *White Trash: The Eugenic Family Studies, 1877–1919* (Boston: Northeastern University Press, 1988); Mark H. Haller, *Eugenics: Hereditarian Attitudes in American Thought* (New Brunswick, N.J.: Rutgers University Press, 1963); Daniel J. Kevles, "Eugenics in North America," in *Essays in the History of Eugenics,* ed. Robert A. Peel (London: Galton Institute, 1998), 208–25, also his *In the Name of Eugenics* (Cambridge, Mass.: Harvard University Press, 1985); Wendy Kline, *Building a Better Race: Gender, Sexuality, and Eugenics from the Turn of the Century to the Baby Boom* (Berkeley: University of California Press, 2001); Edward J. Larson, *Sex, Race and Science: Eugenics in the Deep South* (Baltimore: Johns Hopkins University Press, 1995); Nancy Ordover, *American Eugenics: Race, Queer Anatomy, and the Science of Nationalism* (Minneapolis: University of Minnesota Press, 2003); Diane Paul, *Controlling Human Heredity, 1865 to the Present* (Atlantic Highlands, N.J.: Humanities Press, 1995); Pernick, *Black Stork;* Mark Pittenger, *American Socialists and Evolutionary Thought, 1870–1920* (Madison: University of Wisconsin Press, 1993); Robert Rydell, *World of Fairs: The Century-of-Progress Expositions* (Chicago: University of Chicago Press, 1993); Steven Selden, *Inheriting Shame: The Story of Eugenics & Racism in America* (New York: Teacher's College Press, 1999). In her article "The Futurama Recontextualized," Christina Cogdell notes that "eugenics experienced a resurgence during the 1930s in the realm of popular culture" (202), and that "eugenic thinking in the U.S. and abroad underwrote key legislation, hotly debated social issues, basic high school education, and various facets of popular culture" (205).

5. See Cogdell, "Futurama Recontextualized," 207.

6. Green, *Fit for America,* 137–40. Green notes how neurasthenia in men was taken as a sign of their eugenic superiority, but for women, it was taken as a sign that they "had fallen behind in the evolutionary development of the human

race" and that immigrant and working-class women were more "vigorous." Thus the discourse of "nervousness" in response to urban or mechanized environments was implicitly eugenic and contained gendered connotations (140).

7. John Kasson, *Houdini, Tarzan and the Perfect Man: The White Male Body and the Challenge of Modernity in America* (New York: Hill and Wang, 2001), 10–11.

8. Haller, *Eugenics*, 92.

9. Dowbiggin, *Keeping America Sane*, 75.

10. Frances Oswald, "Eugenical Sterilization in the United States," *The American Journal of Sociology* 36, no. 1 (1930): 70–71.

11. Dowbiggin, *Keeping America Sane*, 77.

12. Larson, *Sex, Race and Science*, 119.

13. Oswald, "Eugenical Sterilization in the United States," 70.

14. George B. Cutten used this expression in his talk at the 1932 annual meeting of the National Education Association—stating that "cases like these are waving a red flag to us, and we wonder sometimes if we are not running past our signals!" See "The Saving Power of Leisure," *Proceedings of the Seventieth Annual Meeting—June 25–July 1, 1932*. National Education Association of the United States, vol. 70, 583.

15. This argument was made by Alexis Carrel in his *Man the Unknown* (New York: Harper and Brothers, 1935). The argument was refuted by others as unsubstantiated science. See, for example, T. Swann Harding, "Are We Breeding Weaklings?" *American Journal of Sociology* 42, no. 5 (1937): 672–81.

16. Cutten, "Saving Power of Leisure," 579–84.

17. Herbert Agar, "Culture Versus Colonialism in America," *The Southern Review*, July 1935, 1–19, reprinted in Susman, *Culture and Commitment*, 36.

18. Cutten, *Challenge of Leisure*, 583.

19. Aiken, "Laborer's Leisure," 268.

20. Haller, *Eugenics*, 78.

21. Jacks, *Ethical Factors*, 27.

22. Kingdon, "Leisure Time Recreation," 512.

23. Ernest Groves, "Adaptations of Family Life," *The American Journal of Sociology* 40, no. 6 (1935): 774.

24. Ibid., 777.

25. Quoted in Larson, *Sex, Race and Science*, 1.

26. In 1935, Caldwell in fact called sterilization a "superficial" solution. See *Some American People* (New York: R. M. McBride & Co., 1935), 236. For the relationship between his novel writing and eugenics, see Karen Keeley, "Poverty, Sterilization, and Eugenics in Erskine Caldwell's *Tobacco Road*," *Journal of American Studies* 36, no. 1 (2002): 23–42.

27. Erskine Caldwell, *Tobacco Road* (1932; reprint, New York: Modern Library, 1940), 40.

28. Ibid., 32.

29. Ibid., 195, 241.

30. Erskine Caldwell, *God's Little Acre* (New York: Modern Library, 1934), 169. In the foreword to *God's Little Acre*, Caldwell wrote that this "Negro expression" (i.e., "white trash") can only be explained by the observation that "the Negro has yet to sink as low, economically and morally, as the white man. He holds much the same position to the white man as the male of the human race does to the female. No man reached the depths to which a woman can sink; and I doubt very much if the Negro will ever fall to the lowest depths of the white race" (xi).

31. Appendix to Caldwell, *God's Little Acre.*

32. H. L. Mencken, "Utopia by Sterilization," *The American Mercury* 41 (1937): 400.

33. Edwin Embree, "Southern Farm Tenancy: The Way out of Its Evils," *Survey Graphic* 25, no. 3 (1936): 149.

34. Larson, *Sex, Race and Science*, 120; Kevles, "Eugenics in North America," 220.

35. Larson, *Sex, Race and Science*, 132.

36. Norman Himes, "Memorandum," *Eugenics Review* 27, no. 1 (1935): 22.

37. Ibid., 21.

38. Howard Odum, "Public Welfare Activities," *Recent Social Trends*, vol. 2, 1227.

39. Mumford, *Technics and Civilization*, 256, 303, 262–63, 262.

40. Ibid., 263.

41. Jacks, *Ethical Factors*, 42.

42. President's Research Committee on Social Trends, *Recent Social Trends*, vol. 1, xxiii.

43. Warren S. Thompson and Pascal Whelpton, "The Population of the Nation," *Recent Social Trends*, vol. 1, 55. Both Thompson and Whelpton were eugenicists and members of the Population Association of America.

44. Edgar Sydenstricker, "The Vitality of the American People," *Recent Social Trends*, vol. 1, 659.

45. See Kline, *Building a Better Race*, 130. Stefan Kühl, *The Nazi Connection: Eugenics, American Racism, and German National Socialism* (New York: Oxford University Press), 82–83. On socialism and eugenics, see Diane Paul, "Eugenics and the Left," *Journal of the History of Ideas* 45, no. 4 (1984): 567–90.

46. Haller, *Eugenics*, 23–24. For the relationship between heredity and environmentalism, see Donald A. MacKenzie, *Statistics in Britain, 1865–1930: The Social Construction of Scientific Knowledge* (Edinburgh, U.K.: Edinburgh University Press, 1981).

47. Paul Popenoe, "Mate Selection," *American Sociological Review* 2, no. 5 (1937): 736.

48. James W. Woodward, "A New Classification of Culture and a Restatement of the Culture Lag Theory," *American Sociological Review* 1, no. 1 (1936): 100.

49. I am grateful to Christina Cogdell for alerting me to this conference, and to Robert Cox and the library staff at the American Philosophical Society for sending me copies of the papers and proceedings. See also Kline, *Building a Better Race*, 131.

50. Frederick Osborn, "Summary of the Proceedings of the Conference on Recreation and the Use of Leisure Time in Relation to Family Life," January 22, 1937, Conferences file, American Eugenic Society (AES) Papers, 1–4.

51. E. Dana Caulkins, "Home and Family Recreation," Conference on Recreation and the Use of Leisure Time in Relation to Family Life, January 22, 1937, Conferences file, AES Papers, 1.

52. Weaver Pangburn, "Recreation and Eugenics," Conference on Recreation and the Use of Leisure Time in Relation to Family Life, January 22, 1937, Conferences file, AES Papers, 3.

53. C. Ward Crampton, "Health Program of the Boy Scouts of America," Conference on Recreation and the Use of Leisure Time in Relation to Family Life, January 22, 1937, Conferences file, AES Papers, 4.

54. Osborn, "Summary of the Proceedings," 3.

55. "The Falling off of the Marriage Market," *The Literary Digest*, July 22, 1933, 7.

56. Popenoe, "Mate Selection," 741. On how eugenicists such as Popenoe promoted family values in the 1930–60 period, see Kline, *Building a Better Race*, 124–57.

57. Frederick Osborn, "Development of a Eugenic Philosophy," *American Sociological Review* 2, no. 3 (1937): 392, 397, 395.

58. Mildred Tucker to Eleanor Roosevelt, February 18, 1938; To Katherine Lennox, Dept. of Labor, February 6, 1938; and to Eduard Lindeman, received March 21, 1938, Correspondence of the Recreation and Recreational Instruction Program, Recreation Program for Negroes, 216.51, Works Progress Administration, Record Group 69, National Archives and Records Administration, Maryland.

59. The relationship between African American intellectuals and eugenics—as a form of racial uplift and improvement during the interwar period—has been examined by some scholars. See Jamie Hart, "Who Should Have the Children? Discussions of Birth Control Among African-American Intellectuals, 1920–1939," *Journal of Negro History* 79, no. 1 (1994): 71–84. The development of discourses of "race consciousness" among whites and blacks was an ideology of social and self-improvement, where white racial purity was paralleled by black seperationists arguing for an ideal "blackness."

60. See Melosh, *Engendering Culture.*

61. For a study of modern dance as a celebration of cultural pluralism in the WPA Federal Dance Project, see Foulkes, *Modern Bodies.* For a discussion of the fetishization of virile male bodies, see 94–95.

62. Ann Lloyd, ed., *Movies of the Thirties* (London: Book Club Associates, 1984), 75. Such a chart appears a direct descendant of Francis Galton's own attempts to measure and quantify beauty. See Stephen Jay Gould, *The Mismeasure of Man* (London: Penguin, 1981), 75–76. For a discussion of Berkeley's choreography as a response to modernism, see Dinerstein, *Swinging the Machine,* 202–20.

63. For the relationship between machines, modernity and mass production, see Peter Wollen, "Cinema/Americanism/the Robot," in *Modernity and Mass Culture,* ed. James Naremore and Patrick Brantlinger (Bloomington: Indiana University Press, 1991), 42–69.

64. Doherty, *Pre-Code Hollywood,* 257, 262.

65. Quoted in Vernon L. Parrington, *American Dreams: A Study of American Utopias* (New York: Russell & Russell, 1964), 213.

66. Granville Hicks and Richard Bennett, *The First to Awaken* (New York: Modern Age Books, 1940), 212.

67. A. T. Churchill, *New Industrial Dawn* (Seattle, Wash.: Lowman and Hanford Company, 1939), 10, 36, 64.

68. Parrington, *American Dreams,* 204. Prestonia Martin, *Prohibiting Poverty: Suggestions for a Method of Obtaining Economic Security* (New York: Farrar, 1933).

69. Buckminster Fuller, *Nine Chains to the Moon* (New York: J. B. Lippincott Co., 1938), 272, 333, 334.

70. Harold Loeb, *Life in a Technocracy,* 1933, quoted in Howard P. Segal, *Technological Utopianism in American Culture* (Chicago: University of Chicago Press, 1985), 144.

71. "Test-Tube Babies," General Electric Advertisement, *Survey Graphic,* March 1938. This image is available online at the New Deal Network Site, http://newdeal.feri.org.

72. See Cogdell, "Futurama Recontextualized," in which she describes how at the World's Fair the male gaze was used as a controlling force over both women and the built environment. Cogdell shows how Geddes created Crystal Lassies using the male gaze as an erotic penetration and impregnation of the female space he created (224), leaving the woman inside the polygon without agency, bound by the imaginary world of the white male. Like the worker inside the test tubes of industry, Geddes's display shows how male science constructed itself as life giver to those placed within the structures it built. Along these lines, Cogdell sees the Futurama exhibit as a chance for males "to unconsciously satisfy their

desire for copulation and progeny through the tour" (225), which presented a small-scale model as the embryonic world waiting to be born out of a "womb like" building (227). Whereas in the Crystal Lassies "the feminine was the passive vehicle used to give birth to the male vision of the world," the Futurama depicted a vision of male creation that depended on complete control over every process of the planned environment, from birth to death.

73. Joseph P. Cusker, "The World of Tomorrow: Science Culture and Community at the New York World's Fair," *Dawn of a New Day: The New York World's Fair*, ed. Helen A. Harrison (New York: New York University Press, 1980), 6.

74. Ibid., 8.

75. Ibid.

76. Ibid., 13–14.

77. The connection between the World Fair, the eugenic movement, and elite eugenic sensibilities is ably documented by Rydell in *World of Fairs*. By 1939, he states, it was quite standard for race-betterment ideals to have "spilled over" into the exposition, where planners "shared presuppositions about the primacy of racial categories in determining citizenship in the world of tomorrow," where world fairs were established as one of the most effective vehicles for transmitting ideas of scientific racism from intellectual elites to millions of ordinary Americans (39).

78. As Rydell notes, this part of the fair was integral to the narrative of progress and imperial domination and was an important part of the fair. During colonist expansions in the nineteenth century, signifying the "progress" from "savagery" to "civilization," "and in a world alive with social-Darwinian ideas of evolution, displays of material and natural abundance became an outward sign of inward racial 'fitness' and 'culture'" (19).

79. *Building the World of Tomorrow: Official Guide Book, New York World's Fair, 1939* (New York: Exposition Publications, 1939), 6.

80. Rydell, *World of Fairs*, 139.

81. Ibid., 144.

82. Norman Bel Geddes's display at the 1939 New York World's Fair—The Crystal Lassies—epitomized the ideal, placing a dancing white woman in the center of a polygonal glass structure that reflected her thousands of times from every possible angle, using mirrors. See Cogdell, "Futurama Recontextualized." Both Rydell and Cogdell examine the gender implications of exhibits such as Bel Geddes's highly acclaimed "Futurama" and his more lascivious "Crystal Lassies." To Rydell, the "Crystal Lassies" peep show, where a nude blonde woman danced in a polygonally shaped dome of mirrors, "revealed just how much the 'pursuit of happiness' in the future perfect world . . . depended upon eroticized fantasies of male power" See *World of Fairs,* 135.

83. "Slim Beauty," advertisement for the Hudnut Success School, *New Yorker,* November 18, 1939, image online at the Duke University Digital Scriptorium, AdAccess Collection, http://scriptorium.lib.duke.edu:80/dynaweb/adaccess/beauty/cosmetics1930s.

84. Les Daniels, *Superman* (San Francisco: Chronicle Books, 1998), 42.

85. Eddie Dean, "Appalachian Trail of Tears," *Washington City Paper,* February 28, 1997, 18. A narrative of the evictions is also available at "The Ground Beneath Our Feet—Shenandoah National Park" Web site at http://www.vahistory.org/shenandoah.html

86. Dean, "Appalachian Trail of Tears," 22.

87. Mandel Sherman and Thomas R. Henry, *The Hollow Folk* (New York: Thomas V. Crowell, 1933).

Conclusion

1. Lynd and Lynd, *Middletown in Transition*, 251.

2. Ibid., 293.

3. Foster Rhea Dulles, *America Learns to Play: A History of Popular Recreation, 1607–1940* (Gloucester, Mass.: Peter Smith, 1963), ix.

4. Ibid., 350.

5. Ibid., 373.

6. Juliet Schor, *The Overworked American: The Unexpected Decline of Leisure* (New York: Basic Books, 1991), 4.

7. Ibid., 7.

8. Barbarah Ehrenreich shows how middle-class women have used poorer women's labor to enable them to break through the "glass-ceiling" of discrimination—essentially enabling them to work. But the low pay and status of this work is a result of the lack of recognition that all women have received for unpaid domestic work in the home. It is this low-status, frequently unseen, labor that gives wealthier women the choice to work or not. See Barbarah Ehrenreich and Arlie Russell Hochschild, eds., *Global Woman: Nannies, Maids, and Sex Workers in the New Economy* (New York: Metropolitan Books, 2003).

9. Schor, *Overworked American*, 2. Schor dates the "decline" of leisure from the thirties.

Index

Dillinger, John, 134
Dinerstein, Joel, 24, 195–96 n.46, 207
   n.65, 215 n.77
"dish night" at movies, 128
displacement: of farm families, 78; of
   mountain families, 181–82
*Distributed Leisure: An Approach to the Problem
   of Overproduction and Underemployment*
   (Walker), 7
"Dividend Night" at movies, 129
divorce, cause of, 154
documentary fiction. *See* literature and
   leisure
Documentary Fiction and Thirties America
   (Stott), 76
Doggin' Around (song), 150
"Domesticating Efficiency" (Graham), 209
   n.22
*Domesticity and Dirt: Housewives and Domestic
   Servants in the United States, 1920–1945*
   (Palmer), 209 n.22
domestic service, 118, 123, 156, 209 n.22,
   221 n.8
domestic technology, 106–7, 117, 120, 209
   nn. 22, 25
Dormouse, 92
Dos Passos, John, 88, 203–4 n.1
Dreiser, Theodore, 135–36, 138
drive-in theaters, 129
drudgery, freedom from, 106–7, 117, 209
   nn. 22, 25
Dulles, Foster Rhea, 184–85
"dumbing down," 84
Dumenil, Lynn, 17
dystopias, 9, 180. *See also* utopias

Easiest Way, The (movie), 105
economy, 3, 5–6, 29, 68, 90, 187, 206 n.43;
   capitalism, 5, 27, 49, 77, 88, 167, 188;
   economic revival and leisure, 2–3, 5;
   laissez-faire industrial economics, 29;
   and women, 108–10, 112
editorial control of FWP, 92
Edson, Newell, 154
education: adult education, 117; consumer
   education programs, 113; "dumbing-
   down" effect of movies, 84; and
   employment, 85; and leisure, 7, 52, 96;
   and movies, 141, 214 n.54; physical
   education, 172; and planned society, 6;
   in traditional skills and crafts, 64–65;
   universal schooling, 4; work relief and

learning new skills, 72; Works Progress
   Administration programs, 147
Ehrenreich, Barbarah, 221 n.8
Ellis, Jacqueline, 205 n.20
emasculation, 105, 159; of culture, 77; by
   technology, 106; by unemployment, 32,
   78, 103. *See also* impotency
Embree, Edwin, 85
emotional hysteria and movies, 133
*Emotional Responses of Children to the Motion
   Picture Situation, The* (Motion Picture
   Research Council), 131
employment, 11, 85; of recreation workers,
   48–49, 53. *See also* unemployment
endurance contests. *See* dance halls
entertainment, twenty-four-hour, 151
ethics: leisure ethic, 193 n.1, 203–4 n.1;
   work ethic, 5, 163, 188, 203–4 n.1
eugenics, 11, 156, 158–82, 206 n.56,
   216–17 n.6, 219 n.59, 220 n.77; positive,
   169. *See also* sterilization laws
European leisure models, 8, 11, 38–47, 54,
   184–85, 200 n.61; differences with US
   programs, 55–56
Everybody's Autobiography (Stein), 123–24
excesses of leisure, 162
exercise. *See* physical fitness
exploitation of leisure workers, 187
Extension Service of the Department of
   Agriculture. *See* Department of
   Agriculture, Extension Service

"Fall in Love with Words and You, too,
   May Climb the Ladder of Fame"
   (advertisement), 85
families and leisure, 66, 73
FAP. *See* Federal Art Project
Farm Security Administration, 70, 126,
   148
Farrell, James Thomas, 77, 136–38
fascism, 47, 50, 54, 55, 168
Fascist Sunday (Italy), 39
fashions and movies, 212 n.9
fatherly approach. *See* patriarchy
fatigue, 26, 132, 196 n.62; and passive
   leisure activities, 23
Federal Art Project, 64, 91; exhibit, 177
Federal Dance Project, 172
Federal Economy Act, 117
Federal Emergency Relief Administration,
   49, 51, 152
Federal Theater Project, 52

Acknowledgments

This book would not have been possible without the excellent library collections and helpful staff at the McKeldin Library, University of Maryland, College Park; George Washington University Library; the National Archives and Records Administration; the Library of Congress; the British Library; the American Philosophical Society library; and libraries at the Universities of Sussex and Nottingham. For financial and institutional support, I thank the American studies department at the University of Maryland, College Park; the Fulbright Commission in London; the Humanities Research Board of The British Academy; the Marcus Cunliffe Centre at Sussex University; the American studies department at George Washington University; the Leverhulme Foundation; and the School of American and Canadian Studies at Nottingham University.

For commenting on various drafts, and for their professional support of this book, along with their friendship, I thank friends and colleagues at Sussex University (especially Stephen Fender, Vivien Hart, Maria Lauret, Peter Nicholls, and Nerys Williams) and friends and colleagues at the University of Nottingham (especially Eithne Quinn, Paul Grainge, Peter Messent, Anna Notaro, Celeste-Marie Bernier, Mark Jancovich, Douglas Tallack, and David Murray). An extended thanks to all others at these institutions and academic conferences who responded with insightful comments and suggestions. Thanks to Bob Lockhart for encouragement as well as patient editing. Thanks also to editors and readers at the University of Pennsylvania Press. A special thanks to Min Kim for intellectual and material support from a wonderful friend. I also owe thanks to my parents, Frank and Pauline, who have encouraged me to keep writing, while helping to take care of my children so that I might do so. Similarly, to Roger and Maureen Pleece, who have unstintingly given time to look after my family while I've worked on this book or traveled away from home. A special thanks to Louise Currell for child care when it mattered. My biggest thanks is to Warren Pleece, who has been my fellow traveler through this entire journey. I dedicate this to you and our children, Frank and Georgy.